Personal Insurance

Portfolio Management

Cheryl L. Ferguson, CPCU, API, AU
Senior Director of Curriculum
American Institute for CPCU/Insurance Institute of America

Pamela A. Lyons, BA, AIIC, FIIC
President
Pamela Lyons and Associates

First Edition

American Institute for Chartered Property Casualty Underwriters/
Insurance Institute of America
720 Providence Road, Malvern, Pennsylvania 19355

Unless otherwise indicated, all examples used in this text are based on hypothetical situations and are for purposes of illustration only. Any names included in these examples are fictional and are not intended to represent any true-to-life person, place, product, or organization.

First Edition • Seventh Printing • May 2006

Library of Congress Catalog Number: 00-132432
ISBN 978-0-89462-141-3

Foreword

The American Institute for Chartered Property Casualty Underwriters and the Insurance Institute of America (the Institutes) are independent, not-for-profit organizations committed to expanding the knowledge of professionals in risk management, insurance, financial services, and related fields through education and research.

In accordance with our belief that professionalism is grounded in education, experience, and ethical behavior, the Institutes provide a wide range of educational programs designed to meet the needs of individuals working in property-casualty insurance and risk management. The American Institute offers the Chartered Property Casualty Underwriter (CPCU®) professional designation. You select a specialization in the CPCU program with either a commercial or a personal risk management and insurance focus, depending on your professional needs. In addition to this specialization, the CPCU program gives you a broad understanding of the property-casualty insurance industry.

The Insurance Institute of America (IIA) offers designations and certificate programs in a wide range of disciplines, including the following:

- Claims
- Commercial underwriting
- Fidelity and surety bonding
- General insurance
- Insurance accounting and finance
- Insurance information technology
- Insurance production and agency management
- Insurance regulation and compliance
- Management
- Marine insurance
- Personal insurance
- Premium auditing
- Quality insurance services
- Reinsurance
- Risk management
- Surplus lines

No matter which Institute program you choose, you will gain practical knowledge and skills that will help you to grow personally and professionally.

The American Institute for CPCU was founded in 1942 through a collaborative effort between industry professionals and academics, led by the faculty members at The Wharton School of the University of Pennsylvania. In 1953, the American Institute for CPCU merged with the IIA, which was founded in 1909 and which remains the oldest continuously functioning national organization offering educational programs for the property-casualty insurance business. The Institutes continuously strive to maximize the value of your education and qualifications in the expanding insurance market. In 2005, the Institutes extended their global reach by forming the CPCU Institute of Greater China (CPCUIGC). In addition, many CPCU and IIA courses now qualify for credits towards certain associate's, bachelor's, and master's degrees at several prestigious colleges and universities, and all CPCU and IIA courses carry college credit recommendations from the American Council on Education (ACE).

The Insurance Research Council (IRC), founded in 1977, helps the Institutes fulfill the research aspect of their mission. The IRC is a division of the Institutes and is supported by industry members. The IRC is a not-for-profit research organization that examines public policy issues of interest to property-casualty insurers, insurance customers, and the general public. IRC research reports are distributed widely to insurance-related organizations, public policy authorities, and the media.

Our textbooks are an essential component of the education we provide. Each book is specifically designed both to provide you with the practical knowledge and skills you need to enhance your job performance and career and also to deliver that knowledge in a clear manner. The content is developed by the Institutes in collaboration with insurance and risk management professionals and members of the academic community. We welcome comments from our students and course leaders because your feedback helps us to continuously improve the quality of our study materials. Through our combined efforts, we will truly be *succeeding together*.

Peter L. Miller
Interim and Acting President and CEO
American Institute for CPCU
Insurance Institute of America

Preface

Personal Insurance: Portfolio Management is a text developed for the Insurance Institute of America's API 29 course. API 29 is one of four courses leading to the Associate in Personal Insurance (API) designation awarded by the Institute.

Several combinations of courses can lead to the API designation. Frequently, students choose the following combination and sequence of courses:

- INS 21—Property and Liability Insurance Principles creates a foundation for understanding the property and liability insurance business.
- INS 22—Personal Insurance examines personal insurance contracts and the coverages they afford.
- API 28—Personal Insurance: Underwriting and Marketing Practices provides a practical approach to personal risk management and risk selection from an individual account perspective.
- API 29—Personal Insurance: Portfolio Management places insurance within the larger context of the insurance industry. API 29 examines the management of a portfolio of policies with the overall objective of achieving profitability and other goals of an insurance company.

Personal insurance as a major product line is the focal point of this text. The forces that influence personal insurance are dynamic. Understanding the forces and their influence can help an insurance professional recognize elements in the insurance environment that can be the catalyst of change. This same understanding can help an insurance professional predict possible outcomes of the change and prepare to deal with the change effectively.

The underwriting of personal insurance policies is changing. Many insurance companies have shifted the emphasis on activity from individual application or account underwriting to management of an entire portfolio of insurance policies. Insurers need new strategies to compare results to goals and to achieve an insurance organization's financial and strategic objectives. This text addresses the product changes, goals, pricing strategies, reunderwriting, and underwriting expense control required of a portfolio manager.

Portfolio management is a new text topic. Whenever such new topics are placed in print, the role of the reviewers in comparing statements to real-world practices is crucial to develop a reliable account of industry practices.

Members of the API Advisory Committee and their associates served as subject matter experts and reviewers:

L. Vaughan Cooper, CPCU, AU, API

Theresa Dalton

Jeffrey J. DeTurris, CPCU

Mary E. Del Cueto, SPHR

James E. Dooley

Marsha D. Egan, CPCU, CPIW, API

Susan A. Erney-Skelton

Edward J. Glinski, Jr., AU, CIC, CTM

Eric J. Holden

Carla "Jean" Kutz, CPCU, API

Margaret McCullough, CPCU, CIC

William C. Riedley, CPCU, CLU, ChFC

Patricia C. Sturm, CPCU, CLU, ChFC

Christine A. Sullivan, CPCU, AIM

Bruce W. Thomas, CPCU

For more information about the Institutes' programs, please call our Customer Service department at (800) 644-2101, e-mail us at cserv@cpcuiia.org, or visit our Web site at www.aicpcu.org.

Cheryl Ferguson

Contents

Forces That Define Personal Insurance Products

Chapter 1

Educational Objectives

1. Describe personal insurers' goals for maintaining profitability, providing service, and meeting stakeholders' needs; and explain the following: (pp. 1-4 to 1-10)
   a. What actions do insurers take to meet these goals?
   b. Why do insurers have difficulty achieving these goals?
2. Explain how personal insurers' goals affect personal lines insurance products. (pp. 1-10 to 1-11)
3. Given a case study, illustrate how insurers can meet customer expectations. (pp. 1-11 to 1-20)

   In order to meet this objective, you should be able to:
   a. Describe customers' expectations for personal insurance products and services.
   b. Describe insurers' difficulties in meeting their customers' expectations.
4. Explain how personal insurance is affected by each of the following: (pp. 1-21 to 1-25)
   a. Social pressures
   b. Legislation
   c. Insurance regulation
   d. Judicial decisions
5. Explain how reinsurance affects the personal insurance products available from primary insurers and the price of these products. (p. 1-25)
6. Given a case study, explain how insurers', customers', regulators', and reinsurers' actions can change personal insurance products. (pp. 1-26 to 1-31)

Outline

I. Personal Insurers' Goals
   A. Profitability goals
   B. Service goals
   C. Goals to meet stakeholders' needs
   D. How personal insurers' goals affect personal lines insurance products

II. Customers' Expectations for Personal Insurance
   A. Affordability
   B. Availability
   C. Service
   D. Fair treatment

III. Insurers' Difficulties in Meeting Customer Expectations
   A. The customer's definition of service
   B. Role of the media in influencing customer expectations

IV. Social Issues, Legislation, Regulation, and Judicial Decisions
   A. Social issues
   B. Legislation
   C. Regulation and insurer compliance
   D. Judicial decisions and case law

V. Reinsurance in Personal Lines

VI. Case Study: Forces Affecting Personal Insurance Products
   A. Hurricane Andrew: August 24, 1992
   B. Aftermath of Hurricane Andrew
   C. Changes to the insurance product as a result of Hurricane Andrew

VII. Summary

Chapter 1

Forces That Define Personal Insurance Products

Jargon Alert!

Personal insurance consists of insurance coverage designed to transfer the financial consequences of personal losses from individuals and families to an insurer. Within the insurance industry, personal insurance is also referred to as *personal lines* or *personal lines insurance*. A *line* is a reference to a line of business as it appears in an insurer's annual statement to a state insurance department. Thus, an insurance company can be referred to as a personal lines insurer or a personal insurance company. Similarly, a reference might be made to the personal lines market or the personal insurance market. This text uses the terms *personal insurance*, *personal lines*, and *personal lines insurance* interchangeably.

An understanding of personal lines insurance requires a view from many different perspectives. INS 21 begins with a foundation of insurance principles. INS 22 examines personal insurance contracts and coverages. API 28 provides a view of personal insurance from the perspective of the underwriting decisions made on individual policies and lines of coverage. API 29 provides insights into personal insurance as a product line. Together these courses explain the dynamic environment of personal lines insurance.

The first three chapters of this text address the following issues regarding personal lines insurance:

1. *Forces that define personal insurance products*. This chapter addresses the interests of insurers, customers, regulators, and reinsurers, and how the forces created by these interests determine personal insurance products.
2. *The personal insurance market*. Insurance cycles, technology, strategic alliances formed by insurance providers, and fraud in the market influence the personal insurance environment. These and other factors shape the market in which the personal insurance products are sold.
3. *Competing in the personal insurance market*. While developing insurance products, insurers select strategies for competing.

By understanding the forces shaping personal insurance products, the personal insurance market, and competition, you, as a student of insurance, can better understand how individual decisions made by insurers fit into larger issues affecting insurance companies and the industry in general. This can be a new perspective for work in personal lines. For example, underwriters are often selected and rewarded based on their ability to focus on the details surrounding individual accounts. By understanding the larger issues, underwriters can make more informed decisions that support the strategies of their organizations. In addition, underwriters are often given responsibility for territory or portfolio management; this responsibility increases the need for underwriters to understand and respond to their organizations' strategies as well as to the issues driving personal insurance as a market. Consequently, some insurance companies are requiring additional professional competencies for underwriters, such as the ability to analyze competitors in order to better respond to market competition.

The major forces defining personal insurance products sold by insurers are generated by insurers' goals, reinsurers' and customers' needs, and social issues surrounding customers' needs. Exhibit 1-1 illustrates those major forces.

Exhibit 1-1
Major Forces That Define Personal Insurance Products

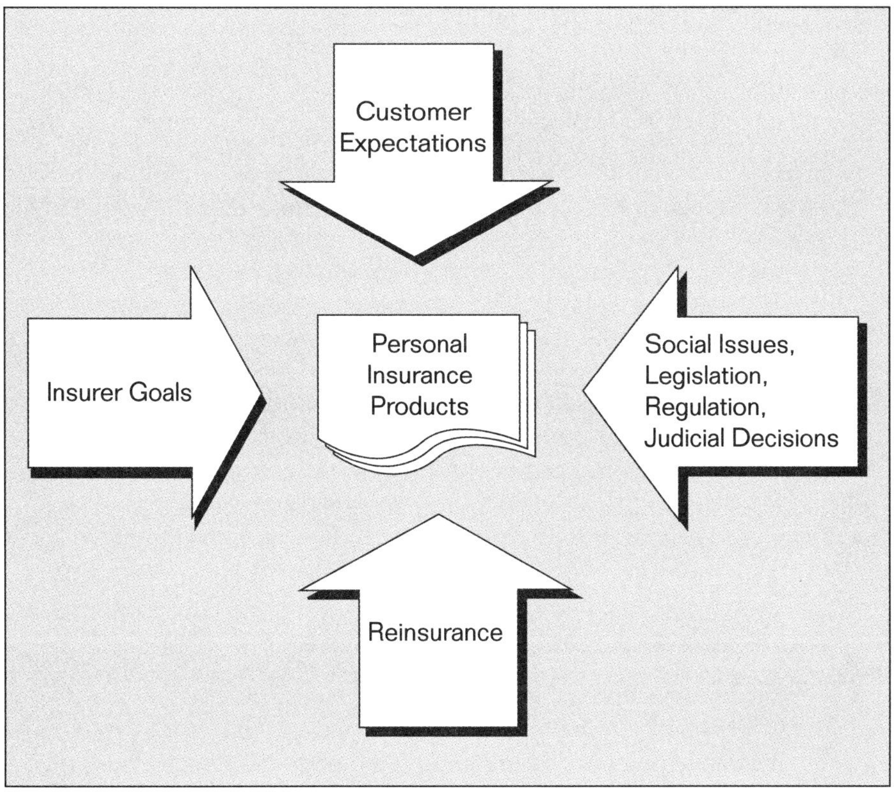

Educational Objective 1

Describe personal insurers' goals for maintaining profitability, providing service, and meeting stakeholders' needs; and explain the following:

a. What actions do insurers take to meet these goals?
b. Why do insurers have difficulty achieving these goals?

Personal Insurers' Goals

The personal insurance product is more than the insurance policy and the coverage it provides. The policy is only the legal contract that defines the relationships between the insurer and the policyholder. The insurance product consists of all of the services delivered to the customers as well as the coverages in the policy contract. An insurer considers these facets of the personal insurance product and balances them with their associated costs in meeting profitability goals. In addition, personal lines insurers address the needs of other stakeholders associated with their companies who count on the insurers to remain viable and profitable organizations. In other words, insurers must find equilibrium among profitability goals and address service, coverage, and stakeholders' needs to attain stability.

Profitability Goals

Underwriting income is the difference between the premium income and the losses and expenses for a specific time period.

Investment income is interest, dividends, and net realized capital gains received by the insurer from the financial assets it owns, minus investment expenses.

Every insurer has goals involving profit if it is a stock company, or additions to surplus if it is a mutually owned company. (For simplicity, this text will refer to both profit and additions to surplus as profit.) Because personal lines insurers are profit-making organizations, they establish goals to pay for expected claims, to meet expenses, and to generate a profit.

Insurers have two primary sources of income: **underwriting income** and **investment income.** From the underwriting income and investment income, insurers must pay losses and expenses. As shown in Exhibit 1-2, what remains, if anything, is operating profit.

Exhibit 1-2
Formula for Determining Operating Profit and Examples

Formula for Profit:	Example A	Example B
Investment income or loss (from investments)	$1,100,000	$1,100,000
+ Underwriting income or loss (earned premiums minus losses and expenses)	+ ($1,000,000)*	+ ($1,200,000)
= Operating profit or loss	= $ 100,000	= ($ 100,000)

* Parentheses indicate negative numbers, or losses.

Although underwriting income is a potential source of revenue for an insurer, insurers usually experience extremely low or nonexistent underwriting income because personal lines insurance policies are priced very close to insurers' expenses, with narrow profit margins. During years without underwriting income, the losses and expenses exceed the premiums earned, causing insurers to have negative underwriting income or an underwriting loss. However, insurers might still have an overall operating profit because their underwriting losses have been offset by their investment income. This scenario is shown in Example A of Exhibit 1-2. However, if investment income does not offset underwriting losses, an insurer must dip into surplus to offset an operating loss. This scenario is shown in Example B of Exhibit 1-2.

Unlike other industries that offer products, the insurance industry does not necessarily increase profit by generating more insurance sales. Although an insurer can gain some **economy of scale** in policy processing by writing more policies, a significant portion of insurance premium is used to pay claims and expenses. Claims and expenses (other than those benefits gained by economies of scale) grow with an insurer's written premium.

Economy of scale is a reduction in the average cost of a product or a process as the size of a company increases.

As an example to illustrate results that can be considered typical since 1980, Exhibit 1-3 displays the premium components and dollar allocations for the property and liability insurance industry in 1995.

Exhibit 1-3
Premium Components and Dollar Allocations for
1995 Property-Liability Insurance (Excludes Investment Results)

Components	Allocations
Claims	78.3 cents
Operating Expenses	23.7 cents
Taxes (excluding federal and foreign income and real estate taxes)	2.7 cents
Dividends	1.1 cents
Total	$1.06 (rounded)

A.M. Best Co., Inc., as published in *The Fact Book, 1998: Property/Casualty Insurance Facts* (New York: Insurance Information Institute, 1997), p. 16.

In the sample year displayed in Exhibit 1-3, insurers spent $1.06 for every $1.00 of premium income, which resulted in an underwriting loss. Any profit insurers made would have come from an investment income in excess of the 6 percent underwriting loss.

Factors Affecting Profitability of Personal Lines Insurance

Just as organizations in other industries, insurers face competition, increasing prices for labor, and increasing prices for goods purchased. But insurers must also face the uncertainties of the risks they insure. These uncertainties make it difficult for an insurer to properly price its products and generate a profit. Some of the factors that affect profitability of personal lines insurance are addressed in the following section.

Underwriting guidelines specify the characteristics of those customers who are likely to file the numbers and types of claims for which the insurer's products and rates were designed.

For insurance purposes, the Property Claims Services Division of American Insurance Services Group defines a **catastrophe** as an event that results in insured losses exceeding a threshold of $25 million and that affects a significant number of policyholders and insurance companies. The dollar threshold used to define a catastrophe occurring before January 1, 1997, was $5 million.

Extracontractual liability is an insurer's obligation that goes beyond the terms of a contract.

Catastrophe modeling involves using computerized simulations to identify the potential extent of damage from a single catastrophic event such as a hurricane or an earthquake.

Jargon Alert!

Claims consciousness refers to public awareness about the possibilities of receiving compensation for a personal misfortune. Claims consciousness can increase the frequency of claims.

The Changing Nature of Claims

Claims are not a static expense allocation that an insurer can calculate with absolute accuracy each year. An insurer, when establishing goals for the year, can establish prices and **underwriting guidelines** that will help to control the frequency of loss for policies written and the premium on those policies. The insurer can also predict with some accuracy the costs it will incur to distribute, market, and process the policies. However, the cost of claims is the largest variable in writing insurance. Historical data can help to predict the number of claims and the losses the insurer will incur over a long period of time, but factors such as the occurrence of a **catastrophe** make it difficult to predict the dollar amount of losses with accuracy. Policyholders' increased *claims consciousness* can lead to the filing of more claims, which can increase the number of losses an insurer incurs without any other change in risk or coverage occurring. In addition, **extracontractual liability** can create loss payments that were not anticipated when the rates were established for coverage provided by insurance contracts.

Catastrophes

Hurricanes, tornadoes, earthquakes, and winter storms can result in catastrophes that can cause devastating losses for personal lines insurers. Insurers attempt to predict possible losses resulting from catastrophes through **catastrophe modeling**. Insurers also spread their policy writing geographically so that all of their insured property is not likely to be damaged by one event and purchase reinsurance to reduce the effect of catastrophes. However, since 1989, catastrophic events have exceeded insurers' predictions and resulted in losses that have reduced the profitability of personal lines property insurers. Many smaller insurers have become insolvent or have been acquired by larger insurers as a result of these incurred losses.

To reduce the financial effects of future catastrophic losses, insurers have taken the following actions:

- Increased catastrophe reinsurance coverage
- Increased overall geographic spread of risk
- Increased premiums charged for property policies with catastrophe exposures
- Decreased or terminated policy writing in geographic areas with catastrophic exposures
- Increased allowances in annual budgets as contingencies for catastrophic losses
- Increased policy writing in product lines that are unaffected by catastrophic losses, such as personal auto liability insurance
- Decreased windstorm exposure by eliminating coverage for that peril on residential policies in areas offering insureds windstorm coverage through a state pool

Claims Consciousness

Overall, policyholders and members of the public are more aware of claims and claim reporting now than they were in the 1960s or 1970s. This awareness has positive and negative effects on insurers. The positive effect is that policyholders know more about the coverage provided by their personal insurance policies, and they are more willing to make claims for the losses that those policies cover. Policyholders are also more responsible about seeking insurance coverages that protect them from financial loss. The negative effect is the tendency of some members of the public to make unnecessary or fraudulent property and liability claims or to sue for large damages even if the actual losses are minor.

Extracontractual Liability

Extracontractual liability can create unanticipated claims. Extracontractual liability generally occurs in personal lines insurance when a claim is submitted for a loss for which the policyholder believes he or she should have insurance under an insurance contract. If the claim is denied because, in the insurer's opinion, coverage is not provided under the contract, the policyholder might sue for a resolution of the disagreement. If enough policyholders have a similar type of loss, the plaintiff's attorneys might try a test case or initiate a class action suit to obtain coverage for all policyholders involved. If the suit is successful and the court orders payment of the claim, the result could be losses—which the insurer would be obligated to pay—that are beyond the scope of what the insurer thought was contained in the contract. As a result, the insurer might have inadequate premium for the coverage it is required to provide. For example, this type of extracontractual liability occurred in South Carolina following Hurricane Hugo. Insurers denied claims for the loss of freezer contents under a homeowners policy when policyholders lost electrical power because the homeowners policy excludes losses for power failures that occur as a result of damage occurring away from the premises. In a test case, the judge ruled that a policyholder should *expect* that this type of loss would be covered regardless of the insurance contact language; therefore, all insurers were then obligated to reimburse policyholders in that state for this type of loss as a result of the precedent set by the case. Insurers have the option of appealing such a case; however, the insurers must weigh the cost of an appeal and the potentially negative publicity against the cost of paying the claims.

Service Goals

Insurance companies balance customer demands for services with the expenses to provide those services. For example, customers would like to be able to contact their insurers twenty-four hours a day. Insurers must balance the costs of that service (which entail costs for additional staff, telephone networking, and possible outsourcing) with the customer demand and the possible consequences, such as loss of policyholders and loss of premium, if the demand is not met.

Service and responsiveness are not free, but they are not strictly expenses. Service creates operational costs, but it is the factor that gains and retains customers. Systems that allow insurers to respond quickly to a customer's needs cost money to develop but gain insurers a positive reputation that attracts new policyholders. Consequently, insurance companies must factor the cost of service expense components into their overall costs of doing business.

Insurance companies react to current customer-driven needs, but they also try to anticipate future service needs. Technology is available to address customer needs, but it is difficult to know how to apply that technology without a clear need expressed by the customers. Insurers expend energy and development dollars attempting to anticipate their customers' needs to meet those needs before other insurers surpass them.

Relationship building is a method for delivering services that approaches the customer as an associate rather than as a source for sales.

Some insurers seek **relationship building** as a service goal. A relationship-building system is a tool used in insurance service that requires technology and is relatively expensive to build. A relationship-building system is assisted by an extensive database containing detailed information about a customer that could help an insurer identify the customer's loss exposures, coverage needs, or related service needs. Ultimately, technology supporting a relationship-building database could identify the loss exposures, notify the insurer about the exposures, and provide advice to help the client avoid an unanticipated retained loss.

Event marketing is activity aimed at filling a customer's needs at the time of a triggering event.

Insurers who develop relationship-building databases will be able to engage in **event marketing**. With a customer profile, which includes information about home, property, family members, recreation, and activities, an insurer can identify events occurring that can create loss exposures that can be addressed by insurance, or a need that can be addressed by other services. For example, a child nearing college age could signal the need for additional finances for tuition, an additional automobile in the household, and property in a dormitory room. Life insurance agents have used customer profiles for years to suggest additional coverage limits or to specifically tailor life insurance products to address financial exposures. Property and liability insurance companies are beginning to use customer profiles to identify events that create additional property and liability loss exposures for customers. The intent of event marketing is not just the sale of additional coverage; the intent is to build a relationship with the customer by providing advice and service when the customer needs them. Exhibit 1-4 provides an example of relationship building and event marketing.

This view of service is distinctly different from the individual policy management of the past. As might be expected, the cost to build this technology and complete this type of database is substantial, but some companies are making that investment in the 1990s. However, the positive return for the insurer is better service to customers and ultimately better customer acquisition and retention.

Exhibit 1-4
Example: Relationship Building and Event Marketing

> Single events can create many service needs for a customer. Suppose an insured has a total loss of his automobile in an accident. In addition to having to make the claim payment for the automobile, the insured might require a new vehicle and a loan to help pay for it. A **virtual team** can help the customer meet all of his or her needs resulting from the event. All team members have access to the same customer's profile in a database to better help address his or her needs. Team member activity might include the following:
>
> - Team members identify the type of automobile that was totaled and refer the customer to local car dealerships selling similar vehicles. This could be especially useful to a customer who is new to an area. If needed, the insurance company representative can even provide directions to the car sales lots.
> - A team member refers the customer to a loan officer at a bank who can help the customer finance the new vehicle. The loan officer has access to the same database as the team member has and is able to access the customer's history to expedite the loan.
> - A team member identifies the customer's car rental needs while the customer is making a decision on a replacement vehicle. The adjuster authorizes the car rental with the appropriate rental agency. The service representative at the rental agency has access to the same database as the team member has, draws the required information from the database regarding insurance coverage and drivers in the household, and expedites the agreement.
> - After the customer selects a new vehicle, an insurance company representative contacts the policyholder to provide advice and verify the coverage that the customer would like to have on the new vehicle. The representative obtains the vehicle information and lienholder information through the database.
>
> Consider how this technology might be used as a relationship-building tool if the customer's daughter is going to college or if the customer's son is getting married. All of the associated insurance exposures, financing, housing, and related needs could be addressed by accessing a single database.

A **virtual team** is a group of insurance company employees or employees of associated organizations. The team members might not work at the same location, but they share information through a database and converse through electronic media.

Goals To Meet Stakeholders' Needs

Stakeholders are individuals and organizations having an interest in an insurer's success. In addition to service provided to customers, insurers must also meet other stakeholders' needs. Stock insurance companies attempt to increase stock values and create returns on investment for stockholders. Mutual insurance companies and reciprocal exchanges attempt to create returns in the form of dividends to policyholders as well as increases in surplus. The expectation of a return is a force that works to define an insurer's goals and resulting activity. An insurer that does not respond to stockholders' and policyholders' demands can lose stock value or policyholders.

Employees are also stakeholders in insurance companies. Employees attempt to fulfill their personal goals through their affiliation with an employer. Personal goals might include income, career advancement, educational opportunities, professional contacts, or social affiliations. Insurers, as employers, seek to retain those employees by helping employees achieve their personal goals. An insurer that does not respond to employees to help them meet personal goals can lose valuable employees to competitors and ultimately spend more money in acquiring new employees, training, and lost productivity.

In addition, insurance producers are another group of stakeholders for an insurer; however, insurance producers and insurers do not always agree about the product that should be offered. While insurers seek to balance income and services in defining what they can offer as a product, insurance producers have their own goals for income and services. An independent insurance agency offers an example of a producer's goals and the way they define the personal insurance product. Assume that an independent agency has targeted affluent, professional, personal insurance customers as clientele. It has determined that these customers generate substantial annual premiums. The independent agency offers the services that these clients demand in order to retain them as customers. The independent agency will balance the commission generated from these customers with the services the agency must provide, such as videotaping the customers' inventories of furniture and fine arts or personal property inspections. However, the agency will also make demands on the insurers it represents to offer the coverages that the affluent clientele require. The independent agency will expect the insurer to work with it to help it to meet its goals, or the agency will seek a contract with another insurer that can offer the needed product.

When establishing goals, personal lines insurers balance expenses—such as those for dividends and returns to stockholders, employee benefits, and the products and service producers seek—with the returns the insurers expect to receive as a result. Of course, not all expenses are calculated on the basis of a monetary return. For example, many human resource expenses are invested to achieve the goals of developing and retaining qualified employees. However, insurers are increasingly seeking ways to measure even the investment return on human resource-related expenses.

Educational Objective 2

Explain how personal insurers' goals affect personal lines insurance products.

How Personal Insurers' Goals Affect Personal Lines Insurance Products

Insurers attempt to balance the products provided to customers, stakeholders' requirements, and profits. An insurer cannot offer limitless coverages or services without charging an associated price, or the insurer would be bankrupt. Similarly, an insurer cannot offer coverage that is so restricted that it is valueless to the customer, or the insurer would not be able to sell any policies. Furthermore, an insurer cannot reduce compensation and benefits below those of competitors, or it will lose valuable employees and incur additional costs to obtain and train new employees.

While balancing service goals with their associated costs, insurers must also be responsive to customers' needs, or else the customers will seek other, more responsive insurers. Insurers have worked to learn more about what customers want, and they have found innovative ways to meet those needs. As a result, customers receive service that is faster and more responsive.

Innovation in insurance products and service is also affected by an insurer's profitability goals. Insurers determine whether they are in a position to afford capital investments and innovations that have a good chance to improve future profitability, to withhold innovations and investments until they are in a position to make the investment, or to wait until the benefit created by the investment seems more certain. Some companies find themselves in a position of having to make investments just to stay even with the competition in offering prices and services that sell policies.

Educational Objective 3

Given a case study, illustrate how insurers can meet customer expectations.

In order to meet this objective, you should be able to:

a. Describe customers' expectations for personal insurance products and services.
b. Describe insurers' difficulties in meeting their customers' expectations.

Customers' Expectations for Personal Insurance

Personal insurance customers have some universal expectations about insurance affordability, availability, service, and fair treatment. If their expectations are not fulfilled, then their image of the insurer is negative. The following section describes universal customer expectations and some of the problems insurers have in meeting those expectations.

Affordability

Although customers expect personal insurance to be affordable, many think that it costs more than they can afford to pay. In 1995, insurance expenditures constituted 6.8 percent of total household spending. Insurance expenditures, which include automobile, home, health, life, and other personal insurance, exceeded expenditures for noninsurance health care (2.7 percent), entertainment (5.0 percent), and clothing

(5.3 percent). Personal automobile insurance alone amounted to 2.2 percent of total household spending.[1] This helps to explain why customers think the cost of insurance is too high and at times unaffordable. Consider that a family's refrigerator will probably last for twenty years. The annual premium for a family's automobile insurance could be more than the cost of a refrigerator. Insurance is a major household expense, perhaps ranking third behind mortgage and car payments.

Among insurance customers surveyed in a study conducted by the Insurance Research Council, 19 percent said that paying for automobile insurance represented a major problem for their household budgets. Another 39 percent said that paying for automobile insurance was somewhat of a problem. With the cost of automobile insurance averaging $665.52 per year per vehicle, customers recognize that insurance is a major and sometime prohibitive expense.[2]

Dissatisfaction arises when the following occur:

- *The value of the promise is not apparent.* Customers might not believe that the product is worth the price. Customers pay for the promise of protection should a loss occur; however, comparatively few people actually experience claims and the resulting benefits of having a claim paid.
- *The value of the security is not apparent.* Security is a primary benefit of insurance; however, customers might not perceive the value of that security. The peace of mind that insurance provides is a benefit that customers tend to take for granted because insurance is usually available for most major loss exposures. In addition, insurance customers often overlook the fact that insurance premiums are a reasonable expense when compared to the thousands of dollars that might be payable in the event of a loss.

Because the value of the promise and the security might not be readily apparent, customers perceive the cost of insurance as too high. In actuality, customers usually are paying fair premiums for their coverages. However, customers do not realize how costly claim settlements are. The claim costs following automobile accidents for medical treatment, replacement of lost income, damaged property, and legal expenses consume most of the money paid for automobile insurance premiums. As claim costs rise, insurance premiums must also rise.

Availability

Closely linked to insurance affordability is the issue of insurance availability. Personal insurance coverage is usually available from many sources for most major personal loss exposures. However, under unusual circumstances, personal insurance coverage for what customers believe is an affordable price is unavailable from any source. In personal lines this has occurred in some states for high-risk drivers and certain residential property owners. The following are examples:

- *High-risk drivers*. High-risk drivers pay a substantially higher premium than other drivers because of the increased chance that they will have losses in the future. **Residual markets** are often the only option available for high-risk drivers to obtain automobile insurance. Although the higher rates charged in residual markets are justified, many policyholders in these markets think that the premiums are unaffordable.

- *Property owners in urban areas*. Many urban property owners have difficulty obtaining insurance because they live in areas that have increased exposures to loss; some insurers are unwilling to offer coverage based on the increased exposures. Homeowners insurance is particularly difficult to obtain in congested urban centers. Often, urban homeowners cannot obtain insurance because of conditions over which they have no control, such as a nearby vacant building that increases the exposure to fire loss. Fair Access to Insurance Requirements (FAIR) plans, similar to the residual market in automobile insurance, make property insurance available to such homeowners. In addition, FAIR plans make property insurance available to homeowners with residences exposed to wildfires, mudslides, and other high-risk loss exposures. However, the extent of this coverage might not be what a homeowner would like to have or might not be offered at a price that a homeowner believes is affordable.
- *Property owners in coastal areas*. Because of catastrophic losses in coastal areas, property owners in such locations experience difficulty in obtaining homeowners insurance or renewing it. Some states have established residual markets for property insurance by arranging special risk pooling to provide windstorm coverage for coastal property. In such states, homeowners policies that are available from the voluntary market exclude coverage for major windstorms because customers can buy that coverage from the residual market. In other situations, insurers in the voluntary market accept property policies only on a quota basis. In other words, they will write only a specific number of property policies per month for property exposed in windstorm areas.

The **residual market** (also called the involuntary market, shared market, or automobile insurance plan) makes automobile insurance available to most drivers who cannot obtain insurance in the voluntary market. The voluntary market includes those coverages that insurers willingly provide at a standard price to applicants who meet their underwriting guidelines.

Service

Customer expectations about insurance service are influenced by the service they receive from other industries. Automatic teller machines provide round-the-clock banking services. Investment firms offer toll-free numbers with twenty-four-hour access. Banks provide a twenty-four-hour turnaround on loan applications. Customers see the increasing responsiveness in other service industries, and they expect similar service from insurance organizations.

Insurers therefore have reexamined their responsiveness to customers. Through the 1980s, an insurer evaluated its service by how quickly it delivered its policies to customers compared to other insurers. During that period, the acceptable time required to process a homeowners application and send a completed policy to the applicant was thirty days. Today, even fifteen days is a relatively slow delivery time for policy processing. Customers are concerned that slow policy delivery time might characterize an insurer's general responsiveness to customers and be typical of the insurer's claim service; a fifteen-day delay in receiving a claim payment would be unacceptable to a customer.

Service is particularly important to the insurance customer because insurance is an intangible product. A large part of what people see as the insurance product is the insurer's service. Thus, one guiding principle is that customers expect fast, reliable service that meets their specific needs and that is provided at a time convenient to them. Another guiding principle is that customers tend to think that businesses that cannot get the little things right are also unlikely to get the big things right.

Research conducted by Berry, Parasuraman, and Zeithaml identified ten dimensions of service applicable to all service industries. Insurers can use these dimensions to evaluate the service they provide to customers and their interaction with customers.[3] Those ten dimensions are listed below:

1. *Access*. Being able to easily contact the insurer
2. *Communication*. Using clear language that both the customers and the insurer understand
3. *Competence*. Demonstrating the knowledge and skills needed to perform a particular job
4. *Courtesy*. Exhibiting the traits of people who are polite, friendly, patient, and respectful
5. *Credibility*. Conveying believability, trustworthiness, and technical competence
6. *Reliability*. Consistently providing expected levels of service
7. *Responsiveness*. Contacting and responding in a timely manner and with an attitude of helpfulness
8. *Security*. Making the customer aware of the insurer's financial security and the financial security provided by the insurance contract
9. *Tangibles*. Presenting professional physical surroundings and physical representations in offices, applications, and policies
10. *Understanding the customer*. Making a sincere effort to address customer needs

Fair Treatment

Customers expect to be treated fairly, which means that they want coverage availability, policy renewals, and price to be based on understandable and consistently applied factors. In addition, they expect to be paid promptly and fairly for claims.

The underwriting process attempts to discriminate fairly among risks according to the risks' characteristics. The claim handling process is guided by procedures and deadlines for action. Following are the problems that can occur in these processes and the actions to address these problems:

- *A customer thinks that the underwriting process is unfairly discriminatory*. Unfair discrimination occurs when risks with similar characteristics are not similarly underwritten. The underwriting process, however, ensures that customers with similar characteristics are treated equally. Communication with the applicant or policyholder and communication regarding the criteria used in underwriting can help to explain the insurer's actions; however, the decision still might not be acceptable to a customer. For example, a house might have an increased chance of a fire loss because of trash accumulation in a vacant lot next to the property. This could make the homeowners application unacceptable to the insurer, but the hazard is beyond the applicant's control, and the decision seems unfair.
- *A customer believes that a nonrenewal or cancellation is unfair.* Insurance customers rarely accept the discontinuation of a policy cheerfully; however, knowing in advance the rules that govern the process can help to reduce the unpleasant surprise. The cancellation and nonrenewal conditions are established in every personal insurance policy to ensure that insurers comply with the rules.
- *A customer thinks that he or she is not treated fairly in the claim process*. Customers expect claims to be handled promptly and paid fairly. They also expect those involved in the claim process to be open, honest, responsive, understanding, caring, and knowledgeable. Almost all states have enacted legislation prohibiting unfair and deceptive claim settlement practices. Most unfair claim practices involve delaying the settlement of claims, failing to communicate with the policyholder, and denying claims improperly. Some states specify the time period within which an insurer must respond to, pay, or deny a claim after proof of loss has been received.

Customers are generally skeptical of insurance company actions. Insurers compete for credibility in the market. The customer confidence needed for long-term loyalty can be earned only by companies that establish an image of fairness. Fairness is especially important for insurance companies, whose product is intangible and difficult to evaluate, forcing customers to rely on trust. Exhibit 1-5 identifies specific types of incidents and service practices that trigger judgments of unfair behavior.[4]

Insurers' Difficulties in Meeting Customer Expectations

In the previous section, universal customer expectations were presented; these expectations are common to almost any personal insurance customer. However, customers' requirements for service to meet their expectations vary. While some customers seek extensive contact and support from insurers, other customers want low prices, fast access to information, and little unsolicited insurer contact. The following

Exhibit 1-5
Types of Unfair Practices

Exploitation
- Deception (missing, misleading, or unclear information)
- Misrepresentation
- Invasion of privacy
- Hidden agenda

Lack of Accountability
- Negligent service operations
- Wasting customers' time
- Denying responsibility
- Nonenforcement of regulations
- Hiding behind unreasonable policies

Discrimination
- Targeted bias (discrimination based on race, religion, or other groups)
- Selective manipulation (inferior service to vulnerable groups)

Based on a table adapted by Kathleen Seiders and Leonard L. Berry, "Service Fairness: What it is and Why it Matters," *The Academy of Management Executives*, May 1998, p. 11.

are some of the factors that drive customers' expectations regarding services they require from an insurer:

- *Age and life phase*. Young adults attending school and still living with their parents have insurance coverage and service needs that are different from those of other people in different life phases or different ages, such as new families buying their first homes or retirees.
- *Economic circumstances*. Individuals with few financial resources and few possessions will seek services that differ from those of individuals who have large homes, substantial possessions, significant liability exposures, and many assets that require protection. The price of insurance is the major concern of individuals with few financial resources. For individuals with many assets, service becomes a more important concern.
- *Comfort with technology*. Individuals who have experience with Internet access will have a greater level of comfort with that technology than those individuals who have had limited access to computer systems. Individuals who have comfort with technology might be more willing to purchase insurance through Internet access.
- *Comfort with risk*. Individuals who have a high comfort level with risk are more willing to retain exposures and assume responsibility for determining their own coverage needs. Individuals who have a low comfort level with risk will be less willing to retain exposures and are more likely to seek advice regarding their loss exposures and insurance needs.

All of these factors represent needs driven by individual characteristics. These characteristics can be grouped to form **demographic profiles** of market segments within a population. For example, individuals who are comfortable with technology and have a computer in their home with an Internet connection constitute the demographic profile of one type of specific market.

Demographic profiles are the common characteristics of a group of people. Demographic profiles can be used to identify market segments.

Customers shift among demographic groups as their needs change. Many customers follow a shift in needs as their life situation changes. Exhibit 1-6 demonstrates a possible sequence of changing insurance needs in relation to changing life situations.

Exhibit 1-6
Example: Sequence of Insurance Need Changes Relating to Changing Life Situations

Age	Life Situation	Insurance Needs
20-25	Individual establishes a household in a rented apartment with minimal contents and purchases a used vehicle.	Property exposures are minimal. Liability insurance purchase decisions might follow those made by the individual's parents.
25-35	Individual starts a family and purchases the first house. Finances are strained as income is stretched to include a mortgage and the expenses associated with child rearing.	Property exposures are increased, and liability exposures become more of a concern. Life insurance and medical insurance are purchased as new policies or at increased limits. Economical insurance premiums and ease of doing business are key factors in insurance selection.
35-55	The family matures, and the children graduate high school and attend college.	Property and liability exposures become more complex as the children purchase automobiles and establish their own residences. The family has increasing needs for advice and responsiveness of service. The level of expectation regarding services provided by an insurer increases.
55 through retirement	Income sources become fixed through retirement, and the individual loses the ability to rebuild assets that have been accumulated throughout a lifetime.	Security becomes a primary issue, and individuals are more willing to expend the money required to protect that security. Advice regarding risk protection through changing life arrangements becomes more important. Trust in insurance products becomes a crucial issue.

No set answers exist regarding the service and price that insurers should offer to meet customers' demands; the answers vary according to the customers' needs. Expectations vary according to each customer's definition of service and each customer's interest, time, and mood.

The Customer's Definition of Service

Customer demands are powerful forces in shaping insurance products. Insurers are sensitive to customers' needs in pricing insurance products and developing services. If they fail to meet customer demands, insurers might find that they have a package of products and services without a buyer.

Satisfactory service is the value that an individual customer seeks from a provider. The definition of satisfactory service varies by customer and situation.

Customers expect **satisfactory service**. The perspective of satisfactory service demanded by a customer is situational. The customer's expectations of satisfactory service will change dramatically depending on the event occurring. For example, a customer's expectations of satisfactory service at the time of a claim vary significantly from that same customer's expectations when nothing of significance is occurring. The following are examples of satisfactory service perspectives:

- A *significant claim*. During a significant claim, a customer realizes the importance of insurance coverage and services associated with claim payments. An insured attempting to settle a claim with an insurer that is available only during office hours five days a week might decide that claim response that is available twenty-four hours a day and seven days a week is a valuable service that he or she will seek in the future.
- A *life change*. During a life change, such as a child leaving for college, or the purchase of a new automobile, a customer seeks professional advice regarding appropriate coverage for the new exposures. That advice should be timely, accurate, and complete.
- A *period of inactivity*. When no changes are occurring in a customer's life, the customer wants little contact from the insurance company. The customer could view unnecessary contact as an intrusion into his or her life at a time when the customer is not in need of information or service.

The wide range of demands from customers makes it difficult for insurers to provide blanket services that fit everyone's needs. Insurers cannot lump all customers into categories; they must provide immediate and complete responses when the customers demand them, and they must be prepared to provide the level of service demanded. A customer with one set of expectations today might have a completely different set of expectations tomorrow.

Customers have a wide variety of expectations regarding the insurance product. Some customers seek the type of service that is available through relationship building and event marketing. These customers seek a full range of services from an insurer. They depend on insurers and producers to advise them regarding their exposures to loss and the most appropriate techniques for addressing those exposures. Other customers view insurance as a commodity; the insurance coverage and services are fairly interchangeable, and price is the key factor in their selection of an insurer. Customers who shop on the Internet or use rating services to compare prices for comparable coverage limits are a driving force shaping the commodity image of the insurance product.

Interest, Time, and Mood

Any effective service depends on the customer's interest, time, and mood at the time of contact. Event-controlled marketing increases the opportunity for positive interaction because the contact is made at a time when a customer has immediate interest in the subject. Mood can also be a factor of timing in customer contact and the relationship developed between the insurer and customer.

Interest, time, and mood are the keys to understanding the level of service demanded by a customer at a point in time. The following are examples illustrating how a customer's interest, time, and mood can vary:

- A customer who travels frequently has just noticed a dent in the bumper of his car. This might have occurred while it was parked in the garage at the airport. He is not in a hurry to settle the loss.
- A customer has had a significant fire in her home and is temporarily staying in a hotel with her three children. She is extremely eager to begin repairs.
- A surgeon has called from the hospital; he will go into surgery in twenty minutes. He needs a premium quotation on a necklace he is giving as a gift tomorrow.
- A customer has called from the car dealership where she is buying a new car. She needs to know how much her insurance premium will increase depending on the type of car she selects.
- A policyholder is moving her parent's furniture into her basement next month. The furniture will be stored there for the next year. She wants to know if the furniture is covered by her homeowners policy.
- A retiree is contemplating selling his car and moving to an assisted-living facility. He is uncertain about the change in his lifestyle, and he wants to talk about his options.
- A customer has just renewed all of her insurance policies and is satisfied with the coverage and price.

Each customer illustrated will have a different level of interest in talking with an insurance representative, different time expectations for response, different time expectations for the length of conversation, and different moods regarding the situation. The insurance professional providing service to these customers must assess the customer's individual needs and respond appropriately. The quality of service perceived by each customer will depend on the individual customer's interest, time, and mood.

No Surprises

Even though a customer's measurement of the quality of service is situational, customers share one expectation: Communication from an insurer should contain no surprises. This expectation is particularly true in billing and in claim service. Anticipating customers' needs and acting to address them in advance to minimize surprises is another insurance company challenge that defines products and services. Proactive measures insurers can take to prevent customers' unpleasant surprises include the following:

- Communicate billing cycles and the timing of expected increases caused by changes in the policy.
- Write policies in easy-to-understand language.
- Thoroughly explain policy coverages, exclusions, conditions, and limits.
- Provide abbreviated lists and guides that help to more thoroughly communicate the policy contents.
- Explain the claim system and ways for contacting the insurer in the event of a claim.
- Communicate the time required to complete applications, receive policies, or receive claim payments.

Role of the Media in Influencing Customer Expectations

The media work to drive customers' insurance expectations as well as to inform customers about insurance issues. The media have had a role in changing customers' perceptions regarding the fairness of the treatment they are receiving from insurers. For example, the availability of replacement cost coverage on homes located in inner cities is an issue of fairness in insurance that has captured media attention. Whether the availability is judged to be fair by individual customers can be a factor of the media's reporting of the issues.

The media also play a large role in customers' perceptions of their fair treatment during a claim. Customers who are frustrated by their own desire to settle a claim quickly, their uncertainty regarding the value of their loss, and possible delays in an insurer's response can easily believe the legal advertisements reinforcing their frustrations and uncertainties. Insurers can dispel these emotions by communicating claim processes before a loss occurs and creating systems that provide prompt and appropriate responses after a loss occurs.

An additional role of the media is encouraging insurance customers to compare premiums among insurance companies. For example, Consumers Union, the publisher of *Consumer Reports*, provides personal auto insurance price quote services in several states via a toll-free telephone number. Insurance customers who are price conscious will use this service to more extensively price shop. However, the media can be a source of confusion as well as a source of information to insurance customers. Individuals in the media do not always understand insurance issues or report all sides of issues. Insurance customers can be especially confused when the media recommend coverages or coverage limits that do not necessarily meet their individual needs.

Educational Objective 4
Explain how personal insurance is affected by each of the following:
a. Social pressures
b. Legislation
c. Insurance regulation
d. Judicial decisions

Social Issues, Legislation, Regulation, and Judicial Decisions

A number of forces affect insurance company operations, decisions, and ultimately personal insurance products. These forces, depicted in Exhibit 1-7, can work independently, or they can involve the sequence of events that is shown. The following section describes how these forces act independently or in sequence.

Exhibit 1-7
Forces That Affect Personal Insurance Products

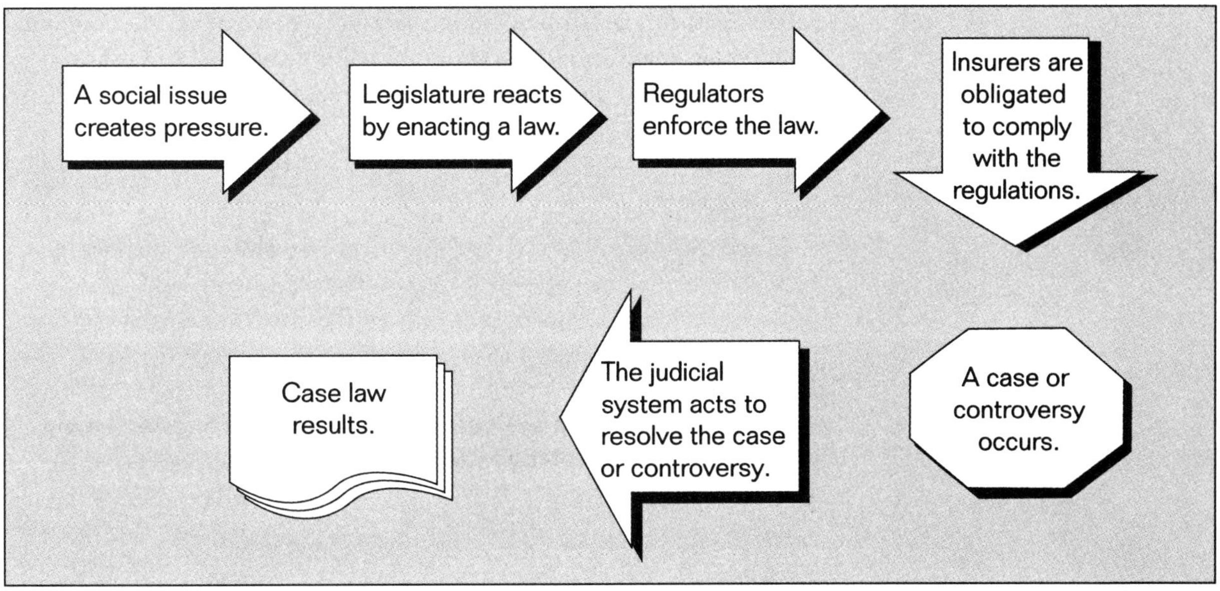

Social Issues

In most states, insurance is a requirement to obtain a mortgage on a residence or to own and operate an automobile. When insurance is not available or affordable, individuals are unable to conduct some of the activities they would like to engage in. For example, an individual's freedom to purchase a home in an inner city might be restricted if the individual cannot find affordable insurance for the loss exposures presented by the residence. If enough individuals experience similar problems, the problem becomes a social issue.

The social issue by itself can be enough to cause insurance companies to change the insurance products they offer. In response to the inner-city property insurance problem, some insurance companies voluntarily established programs to locate insurance producers in inner cities; to create loss control incentives for the homeowners in these areas, such as discounts for deadbolt locks on doors and smoke detectors; and to offer affordable homeowners or dwelling property insurance for inner-city residences.

Legislation

Social issues that insurers do not address can grow and eventually create enough public pressure to gain the attention of local council members, representatives of state congress, and state senators. At that point, the state legislature might react to the public need. The state legislature might develop bills and laws to address the social issues. Insurance availability and affordability are frequently the object of political platforms because they are subjects that gain attention. Campaign promises to reform insurance problems and lower prices are generally well received by the public.

The National Association of Insurance Commissioners (NAIC) establishes Model Acts that can be used by each state. Model Acts help to develop uniform laws among states. The topics addressed in Model Acts frequently address social issues. In addition, state commissioners may also introduce topics into legislation to address social issues.

If laws are passed regarding insurance issues, the insurance commissioner of the state and his or her staff act as regulators to enforce these laws. The commissioner and the commissioner's staff interpret the laws, and the laws are enforced through their regulatory authority. Political pressures often drive legislative decisions, resulting in regulations.

Regulation and Insurer Compliance

The property and liability insurance industry is intensely regulated. State insurance commissioners are given the primary responsibility for regulating the insurance industry under federal and state law. Complying with insurance regulation is an insurer's requirement. Insurance regulation is necessary to achieve two goals in the public interest:

1. To ensure that insurance companies remain solvent to pay claims when they arise
2. To protect insurance consumers from those in the insurance industry who are unscrupulous and engage in unfair treatment

The goals of protecting the public interest also restrict the personal insurers' activities and act as forces to change the personal insurance product. The following section describes how each of the insurance regulation goals that protect the public also changes the personal insurance product.

Solvency Regulations Affecting the Insurance Product

Solvency regulations deal with identifying insurers that might become insolvent, determining why the insurers encountered financial difficulty, and helping the insurers correct their financial problems.[5] Customers must be able to rely on their insurers to remain in operation for the long term. Because customers are generally unable to evaluate their insurers' ability to fulfill their financial obligations, regulators play an important role in helping to preserve the long-term operation of insurers by monitoring their solvency.

Activities to preserve insurers' solvency also restrict insurers' activities and the resulting insurance products. To assess insurer solvency, regulators evaluate insurer financial statements quarterly. They assess premiums received, losses paid and reserved, changes in policyholders' surplus, underwriting expenses, investments, and the degree of investment risk to which the insurer's reserves and surplus are exposed. Although many measurements are made based on these assessments, a rule-of-thumb of $3 in written premium to every $1 in surplus is generally applied to quickly assess an insurer's solvency. An insurer with a ratio that exceeds this $3:$1 ratio would be restricted from writing any new insurance policies. Although such a restriction protects the public from an insurer that might not be financially sound, the restriction also reduces the insurer's policy writing freedom and potential profitability. In addition, the availability of insurance is reduced.

Fair Treatment Regulations Affecting the Insurance Product

State regulators are obligated to ensure that insurers treat their customers fairly. Consequently, regulation plays an important role in creating a uniform level of quality in personal lines insurance products. Market conduct regulation deals with how insurers treat insurance applicants, insureds, and claimants.[6] When performing market conduct activities, regulators focus on four insurance company operations. Their work to protect the public also restrict insurers' activities and the products they offer.

1. *Marketing and advertising*. Regulators protect customers from misleading or false advertising about advantages, conditions, or terms of insurance policies by enforcing the provisions of the NAIC model Unfair Trade Practices Act.[7] The act also restricts statements that insurers can make about their own products and prices and those of competitors. As a result, an insurer could not caution a policyholder against replacing one of the insurer's policies with a policy from a competitor generally known to have slow claim service. However, this withholding of information could lead to the customer's dissatisfaction with insurance service and the insurance industry in general.
2. *Ratemaking*. Regulators try to control what insurers charge for coverage because charging an inappropriate amount for a policy runs contrary to public interest. Overcharging could make coverage unaffordable for some customers. Undercharging could

lead to insurer insolvency. The regulators' goal is to create fair, stable, and understandable rates. However, the ratemaking regulation process can delay approval of a rate increase that an insurer believes is warranted to pay for the losses and expenses it is experiencing. In addition, state regulators are sometimes reluctant to grant all of the rate increase that an insurer has requested. As a result, insurers are sometimes forced to withdraw a product line from the market or a geographic area rather than to experience a continual financial loss because of what the insurer perceives to be inadequate rates. Personal insurance can therefore become less available.

3. *Claims*. Claim activities are heavily regulated. Regulators try to protect claimants by enforcing regulations and laws, which prohibits specified claim activities that are considered unfair. These regulations or laws often include time limitations within which a claim representative must communicate, investigate, provide paperwork, or settle claims. These time limitations place more urgency on claim representative activity. This can result in higher claim payments (often stemming from rushed investigations) than might otherwise have been paid. The results are increased losses and lower profitability for insurers and higher premiums for policyholders.

4. *Underwriting*. Some state regulators require insurers to file their underwriting guidelines; other regulators review the guidelines when insurance department market conduct examinations are conducted. Although regulators do not specify which guidelines insurers can use, they are concerned that guidelines be implemented consistently among all customers to deter unfair discrimination. Other ways that regulators deter unfair discrimination include specifying how certain policy provisions must be worded and requiring that specific policy provisions, such as cancellation provisions, be included in all policies. In addition, some state regulators prohibit specific underwriting classification factors, such as gender in automobile insurance, if they believe such factors promote unfair discrimination. The activities also restrict insurer activity and what some insurers believe are sound underwriting selection criteria. For example, regulators in many states restrict the use of credit reports as a source of underwriting information because they think that the use of these reports unfairly discriminates against applicants and policyholders. However, insurers—armed with statistical data demonstrating the link between a poor credit history and an increased frequency of losses—believe that credit reports are a valuable tool in predicting risks with an increased chance of loss. As a result, insurers who are unable to use credit reports and desire to use them as a selection criterion incur increased losses that they believe they would not otherwise incur. The result is increased premiums shared with all of their policyholders.

Judicial Decisions and Case Law

Policy language, claim handling, and insurers' activities can be modified by the judicial responses to lawsuits involving the interpretation of the policy language, the settlement of claims, and the availability and applicability of coverage.

For example, case law changes the insurance product when a court decides that coverage exists under an insurance contract, which was not considered when the policy language or rates were developed. If the extracontractual coverage granted by a court is extreme, insurers might restrict future policy writings, eliminate coverage, or increase future premiums to generate sufficient premium to pay for such losses.

FYI

In the United States, a court of law cannot express an opinion or post a response to a problem unless it is in the form of an actual case or a controversy that requires resolution through the court system. A case must be brought into the court as a lawsuit. The resolution of the suit is based on prior cases, legislation, and regulation. When a case involves the resolution of an issue that previously has not been brought before the court, the case can become an important part of case law used to help resolve similar problems in the future.

Educational Objective 5
Explain how reinsurance affects the personal insurance products available from primary insurers and the price of these products.

Reinsurance in Personal Lines

Reinsurers are an influential force in the personal insurance market. Few primary personal lines insurers operate without reinsurance to provide a level of protection against large losses and catastrophes. When primary insurers experience extreme losses, and they are compensated by reinsurers, the reinsurers then include these losses in future prices charged to the primary insurers. Primary insurers, in turn, include the cost of reinsurance as a factor in the prices they must charge to the customers. In this way, reinsurance helps to spread evenly over time the prices customers pay for personal insurance.

Reinsurance allows primary insurers to stay in business through large fluctuations in loss experience. The personal insurance market could not operate in its current form without the reinsurance market. Reinsurance prevents insurer insolvency after catastrophes.

However, reinsurers can also place pressure on primary insurers and affect their ability to make insurance available at affordable prices. The following are some of those pressures:

- Reinsurance prices reflect the losses in a geographic area. This can result in high prices in some geographic areas or for some coverage lines.
- Availability of reinsurance can dramatically increase or decrease the availability of primary insurance coverage. If reinsurance is not available, or available only at a high price, a primary insurer might not be able to obtain a rate increase that sufficiently covers the increased cost of the reinsurance premium.
- Reinsurers might ask primary insurers to cease writing classes of business that have generated excessive losses. Such a request can be a condition of renewal of a reinsurance contract. Such pressure can reduce the availability of insurance to those classes of business.

FYI

The reinsurance discussed in this section is treaty reinsurance. A primary insurer purchases treaty reinsurance policies that cover entire product lines or portions of product lines such as liability or property. All policies written by the primary insurer that fall within the coverage provided under the reinsurance treaty are covered. Facultative reinsurance, which is written to provide coverage for a single account or policy, is rarely applied in personal lines.

Educational Objective 6
Given a case study, explain how insurers', customers', regulators', and reinsurers' actions can affect personal insurance.

Case Study: Forces Affecting Personal Insurance Products

A student of insurance can observe the forces that affect personal insurance products through a review of news events. The activity following Hurricane Andrew provides one opportunity to examine those forces.

Hurricane Andrew left a path of destruction across south Florida. The state's insurance industry was also devastated by the storm. The events during and after the storm demonstrate how insurers', customers', regulators', and reinsurers' actions change and redefine the personal insurance product. Many of the factors addressed in this chapter occurred in Florida as a result of Hurricane Andrew.

Before Hurricane Andrew struck Florida, personal lines property rates were inappropriately low.[8] Hurricanes in the 1980s were rare, and those that hit the mainland tended to stay far from densely populated areas. Insurance organizations were relying on dated catastrophe models. Insurance companies competed aggressively to insure the thousands of homes being built every year in Florida; Florida became the nation's third-fastest growing state. Many experts thought the worst possible windstorms would cause no more than about $8 billion in insured property damage. Before Hurricane Hugo in 1989, which cost insurers $4.2 billion, no hurricane had resulted in claims in excess of $1 billion.[9]

Hurricane Andrew: August 24, 1992

Hurricane Andrew swept through south Dade County on August 24, 1992, with wind gusts of 145 miles per hour. It was the most expensive natural disaster in U.S. history, causing about $16 billion in insured losses. Homeowners incurred more than half of those losses. The following statistics demonstrate the size of the event and the devastation that resulted from the storm:

- Eighty-five deaths were blamed on the hurricane.
- At least 28,000 homes were completely destroyed, and 45,000 homes were made uninhabitable.
- The insurance industry sent to the area one out of every four insurance claim representatives in the country. This amounted to a total of 17,000 claim representatives who settled 95 percent of the 700,000 claims within six months. This was the quickest, most extensive deployment of claim services in history.[10]

- Ten insurance companies were bankrupted, affecting 88,000 customers and creating an estimated $500 million in losses that these companies could not pay.
- Almost 100 insurance agencies went out of business.
- Thirty-four insurance companies planned to withdraw from doing any business in Florida.
- Twenty-nine additional insurance companies planned to restrict writings or withdraw from writing certain types of insurance in Florida.
- Sixty-four errors and omissions suits were filed against agents in Florida. The suits alleged miscommunication of coverages regarding law and ordinance coverage issues.

Aftermath of Hurricane Andrew

The total insured property loss for Hurricane Andrew was twice as large as the worst-case estimates for hurricanes before Andrew. If Andrew had hit Miami, property damage claims would probably have exceeded $50 billion.[11] Insurers had to reevaluate their exposures to catastrophic property losses. Insurance companies began to look at the future and assess the possibility and the potential severity of the next catastrophic event.

Insurance Availability and Affordability Suffer

Insurers cut back the number of policies they wrote in disaster-prone areas. They nonrenewed existing policies and stopped writing new ones. Some insurers even paid a year's worth of premiums to policyholders to place their business with another carrier.[12]

In response to the social pressure regarding the shrinking insurance availability, the legislature passed the 1993 Property Insurance Moratorium Act, which created a moratorium on nonrenewals of residential insurance and policies on condominium associations to spur recovery of the Florida insurance market. This moratorium was extended until 2001. To reduce hurricane exposures, the moratorium capped nonrenewals at 5 percent of policies statewide and 10 percent in any one county. Insurers could nonrenew the windstorm coverage provided on residential property policies in areas covered by Florida's windstorm pool. An insurer was exempt from the act if the insurance department determined that its solvency was threatened.

Some of the state's largest residential property insurers limited the sale of new policies, particularly for homes in the southern parts of Florida and along the Atlantic coast, or they required homeowners to purchase windstorm coverage separately from the windstorm pool.

Rate Increases and Computer Modeling

Failed attempts to withdraw from the market because of the moratorium led insurers to increase rates to recoup their losses. Following Hurricane Andrew, insurers began to reassess the likelihood of losses, using new computer models to pinpoint high-risk areas. In 1995, the Florida legislature created a commission to study the role of computer modeling in rate setting. In 1996, lawmakers set up a three-member arbitration panel to evaluate appeals by insurers whose requests for rate increases based on computer modeling had been rejected by the state's insurance department. The insurance commissioner vowed to abolish the panel after it recommended rate increases as high as 24 percent for some insurers; rates had already risen by as much as 170 percent in South Florida. However, a study commissioned by the Florida House Committee on Financial Services found that the computer model offered a more precise picture of wind hazards by geographic area than earlier traditional methods.

Coverage Surprises and Extracontractual Liability

Florida law requires residences located in flood zones and sustaining damage beyond 50 percent of market value to be elevated above flood plain levels. Elevating a dwelling requires lifting the building with a series of jacks placed under the support beams and securing the building on top of pilings that are driven in the ground or to other support structures that are built on the site. Elevating a dwelling is an expensive process. More than 3,000 homeowners in Dade County were informed that their residences needed to be elevated before they could rebuild.[13] Many homeowners policyholders discovered that they could have purchased an optional Ordinance and Law Coverage endorsement that would have compensated them for their increased costs of repairs needed to bring their residences up to current zoning ordinance building requirements. Errors and omissions suits against insurance producers were filed because of the producers' failures to offer the coverage.

Jargon Alert!

A *guaranteed replacement cost* policy is a homeowners policy with an endorsement such as ISO's Additional Limits of Liability for Coverage A, B, C, and D endorsement (HO 04 11) attached. If a loss occurs to a residence covered by a homeowners policy with this endorsement attached, the limits of liability will be amended to equal the current replacement of the dwelling. The term *guaranteed replacement cost* is frequently used in the insurance industry to describe this coverage.

Insurers had cited the *ordinance or law exclusion* to deny coverage for the increased cost of elevating homes. Dade County filed suit against some insurers, claiming the policy language was ambiguous and violated public policy. The county assumed that homeowners insurance under a *Guaranteed Replacement Cost* policy should provide the extra expense of elevating residences.

The outcome of the case required insurers to cover the cost of building code upgrades for heavily damaged residences under the *guaranteed replacement cost* provisions of the homeowners policy. This extracontractual liability is in direct opposition to the contract's *ordinance or law exclusion*. Barring a reversal on appeal, the cost to elevate the thousands of residences that were in the flood plain and that were more than 50 percent damaged could have run as high as $30,000 to $40,000 each. The court also held that it was the insurers' duty to cover electrical and structural upgrades in thousands of other residences.[14]

The Windstorm Pool and the JUA

The Florida Windstorm Underwriting Association, also known as Florida's *windstorm pool*, issued 50,000 policies before Hurricane Andrew and grew to issue over 400,000 policies as insurers excluded windstorm coverage from policies they had previously accepted. Legislators voted in 1998 to freeze the geographical expansion of the windstorm pool indefinitely. The windstorm pool has a claim-paying ability of $4.2 billion. The pool had asked for an average rate increase of 20 percent annually, but it was granted only an average 12 percent rate increase. As this average rate increase is spread over the state, rates in southern Florida—where current rates were considered extremely inadequate—increased as much as 40 percent.[15]

The insurance commissioner created the Florida Residential Property and Casualty Joint Underwriting Association (JUA) as an expansion of the Florida Windstorm Underwriting Association. The JUA was intended to be the insurer of last resort in the state for homeowners insurance. After Hurricane Andrew, the JUA grew to nearly 900,000 homeowners policies and became the state's third largest insurer, covering 18 percent of the residences in Florida. Its potential loss exposure grew to more than $4 billion for a storm with the intensity of Andrew. The JUA's policy writings were heavily concentrated in windstorm-prone areas, and questions arose over its ability to respond to claims if another big hurricane occurred. The JUA collected about $400 million in premium a year; however, it paid them out almost immediately in routine claims. The JUA could borrow money to pay claimants, and the state would then repay those debts by assessing all insurance companies doing business in the state. These costs would then be passed on to property insurance policyholders in the state. It was estimated that, following another devastating storm, policyholders could count on a 35 percent premium increase to pay off those debts, with continuing increases of 20 percent per year.[16] Securing the initial sums for a huge catastrophe loss to the JUA became a concern. If the state exhausted its line of credit, it would have to turn to the bond market, which could be expensive and time-consuming. Many homeowners who have had to place coverage with the JUA are dissatisfied because the policies do not cover many items such as jewelry and silverware that policies issued by private insurers will cover. As a result of some media coverage, these homeowners also have concerns about the financial status of the JUA. In May 1996, state regulators created incentives for insurance companies if they would assume policies that would otherwise be written by the JUA.

Jargon Alert!

The Florida Windstorm Underwriting Association is commonly referred to as the *windstorm pool.* Other common references for such programs are beach plans and windstorm plans. These programs were developed in the 1960s and 1970s in the states along the Gulf of Mexico and the Atlantic Ocean to provide windstorm coverage for coastal properties. The purpose of those plans was to ensure an adequate market for coverage and a method of distributing coverage responsibility among insurers. In coastal areas, an insurer deletes coverage from homeowners and dwelling policies by endorsement. The insured then purchases a windstorm policy from the state program. Losses incurred under the program, which are not covered by the premiums collected, are shared by all the insurers writing property insurance in the state according to proportional formulas determined by the state.

Reinsurance and the Catastrophe Fund

After Hurricane Andrew, reinsurers raised the price of reinsurance coverage and restricted the limits of coverage they would provide to primary insurers. With ceilings for each layer of reinsurance reduced, primary insurers were forced either to limit the amount of property insurance they would sell or to take on the exposure to losses above the ceiling themselves. The increased cost of reinsurance and the decreased availability caused primary insurers to reassess their business strategies.[17]

The Florida Hurricane Catastrophe Fund was created in 1993 as a state-run catastrophe reinsurance program designed to encourage insurers to stay in the Florida market. It is financed by residential property insurers doing business in the state based on each insurer's exposure to hurricane losses. The premiums insurers are assessed to pay for the catastrophe fund can be passed on directly to policyholders in the rates charged for property policies. The Catastrophe Fund has accumulated about $2.5 billion in cash, and its bonding capacity available to finance future catastrophes is about $6 billion, bringing its total capacity to nearly $11 billion.

The insurance commissioner ordered insurers to roll back rates following a ruling by the Internal Revenue Service (IRS). The IRS ruled that bonds that would be sold by the Catastrophe Fund to pay for some of the damage suffered by homeowners in a major hurricane would be tax-free. The fact that interest on Catastrophe Fund bonds is tax-exempt will make them more attractive to investors, allowing the state to sell bonds at a lower interest rate and thus raise the amount of bonds it sells. The commissioner believes that the additional bonding capacity, set at $1.7 billion, would provide increased protection to insurers. This increase in protection would reduce the amount of reinsurance that insurers would have to purchase. As a result, they could afford to roll back rates.[18]

Some insurers cut their rates, but others expect the actual savings from the IRS ruling to be minimal. Nevertheless, in June 1998, the commissioner ordered the state's two largest insurers and the windstorm pool to cut their rates. The insurers are seeking alternatives to what they believe are already inadequate rates.

Changes to the Insurance Product as a Result of Hurricane Andrew

Hurricane Andrew has affected policyholders and the insurance business in the following ways:

- Policyholders have repeatedly expressed public outrage at the difficulty in obtaining insurance coverage at affordable prices.
- In a poll taken by the *Miami Herald* newspaper in March 1997, 70 percent of the policyholders reported that they have received fair treatment in their loss settlements.
- State regulators have stopped companies from nonrenewing policyholders en masse.
- State regulators have restricted rate increases.
- State regulators have funded loss control projects aimed at reducing the hurricane damage through the use of stronger shutters, windows and doors; hurricane straps; and improved building codes.
- Insurance companies have committed to assuming policies previously written by the JUA.

Overall, Hurricane Andrew and the forces that followed the storm have substantially changed insurance in Florida. Dramatic changes affected the following in a short period of time:

- *Insurers*. Insurers lost profitability and attempted to withdraw from the market. Prices increased dramatically when insurers were unable to withdraw.
- *Customers*. Customers' expectations were not met in the areas of affordability, availability, or fair treatment. Service expectations were met only in the area of claim settlements.
- *Social issues, legislation, regulation, and judicial decisions*. Social issues regarding insurance affordability and availability became extreme as some policyholders received rate increases from their insurers and other policyholders experienced policy cancellations when their insurers withdrew from the state. Both legislators and regulators responded by enacting laws and regulations to control the insurance industry. The judicial system responded by requiring extracontractual liability for ordinance or law exposures.
- *Reinsurance*. Reinsurers raised rates and limited coverage in response to the losses they suffered. To help prevent a mass exodus of insurers from the state, the legislature created a state-run catastrophe reinsurance program encouraging insurers to stay in the Florida market.

Summary

The personal insurance product is a combination of the coverage features in the insurance contract, the services provided, and the price at which personal insurance is sold. The following forces act together to define personal insurance products:

- *Personal insurance companies operate to generate a profit.* Some of the factors that affect an insurer's profitability are the changing nature of claims, catastrophes, claims consciousness of insureds, and extracontractual liability. In addition, personal insurers strive to meet service goals in order to meet customers' needs and to acquire and retain policyholders.
- *Personal insurance customers expect, at a minimum, to have their expectations met regarding insurance affordability, availability, service, and fair treatment.* Beyond minimum expectations, customers have individual needs according to their interest, time, and mood. Customers expect that interactions with insurers contain no surprises. The media have a role in influencing customer expectations regarding insurance.
- *Social issues can become the focus of legislation.* Legislation regarding insurance becomes regulations implemented by the states' insurance departments. Conflict regarding insurance coverages or insurer activity can be resolved through the judicial system to become case law.
- *Reinsurance allows insurers to remain in business after catastrophes; however, premiums create affordability and availability problems.* Reinsurance premiums can reflect losses in a geographic area, resulting in high premiums for customers in those areas. Insurers

might have difficulty obtaining adequate rates to cover the high cost of reinsurance.

One relatively recent event that demonstrates many of the forces that define personal insurance products is Hurricane Andrew. That catastrophe changed residential property products in the state of Florida.

Chapter Notes

1. Insurance Information Institute, *The Fact Book 1997: Property/Casualty Insurance Facts* (New York: Insurance Information Institute, 1998), p. 49.
2. Insurance Information Institute, p. 53.
3. L. L. Berry, V. A. Zeithaml, and P. Parasuraman, as quoted in Arthur R. Tenner and Irving J. DeToro, *IIA Edition of Total Quality Management: Three Steps to Continuous Improvement* (Reading, MA: Addison-Wesley Publishing Company, 1994), pp. 48-49.
4. Kathleen Seiders and Leonard L. Berry, "Service Fairness: What it is and Why it Matters," *The Academy of Management Executives*, May 1998, pp. 1-11.
5. Kathleen Heald Ettlinger, Karen L. Hamilton, and Gregory Krohm, *State Insurance Regulation* (Malvern, PA: The Insurance Institute of America, 1995), p. 3.
6. Ettlinger, Hamilton, and Krohm, p. 3.
7. For more information about this act, please refer to Chapter 4 of the API 28 text.
8. Leslie Scism and Martha Brannigan, "Florida Homeowners Find Insurance Pricey, If They Find It at All," *The Wall Street Journal*, July 12, 1996, sec. 1.
9. Ruth Gastel, "Catastrophes: Insurance Issues," *Insurance Issues Update*, August 1998, p. 1.
10. Russ Banham, "Hurricane Andrew—One Year Later," *Independent Agent*, August 1993, p. 54.
11. Gastel, p. 1.
12. Scism and Brannigan, p. 2.
13. *The Miami Herald*, "County Goes to Court Against Insurance Companies," January 26, 1993, p. 2B.
14. James C. Docs, Mary F. Connley, Helun K. Docs, June Feuillerat, Mary L. Harrington, Philip E. Horst, Nancy Krepczynski, Melvin Miller, Scott M. Shepard, Paula L. Blair, Jeffrey Hay, Daniel Radvansky, and Chad Smith, "How Have the Catastrophes of 1992 Affected Solvency, Capacity, and Reinsurance in the Property and Casualty Industry?", *CPCU Journal*, June 1995, p. 80.
15. Gastel, p. 5.
16. Scism and Brannigan, p. 6.
17. Ruth Gastel, "Financial and Market Conditions," *Insurance Issues Update*, August 1998, pp. 3-4.
18. Gastel, p. 4.

The Personal Insurance Market

Chapter 2

Educational Objectives

1. Describe the characteristics of the personal insurance market. (pp. 2-3 to 2-4)
2. Describe underwriting cycles and their effects on personal lines insurance; explain the importance of understanding underwriting cycles. (pp. 2-5 to 2-9)
3. Describe the stages in market development; explain the importance of understanding stages in market development. (pp. 2-9 to 2-12)
4. Explain how the personal insurance market is segmented. Describe benefits and limitations of market segments. (pp. 2-12 to 2-16)
5. Describe technology applied in personal insurance, and explain the effects of technology on the personal insurance market. (pp. 2-16 to 2-18)
6. Explain why personal lines insurers seek strategic alliances. (pp. 2-18 to 2-19)
7. Describe fraud in personal insurance, including the following issues: (pp. 2-19 to 2-29)
   a. Public attitude toward insurance fraud
   b. Forms of fraud in personal insurance
   c. Antifraud measures

Outline

I. Characteristics of the Personal Insurance Market

II. Personal Lines Underwriting Cycles
   A. What occurs in an underwriting cycle
   B. Why underwriting cycles occur
   C. The effects of underwriting cycles on personal lines insurance
   D. The importance of understanding underwriting cycles

III. Stages in Market Development
   A. The importance of understanding stages in market development

IV. Personal Insurance Market Segmentation
   A. National market
   B. Regional markets
   C. Customer group markets
   D. Niche markets

V. Technology
   A. Automated processing
   B. Database applications, data mining, and data modeling
   C. Internet communications and sales

VI. Strategic Alliances in the Personal Insurance Market

VII. Fraud in the Personal Insurance Market
   A. Public attitude toward fraud
   B. Forms of insurance fraud
   C. Antifraud measures

VIII. Summary

Chapter 2

The Personal Insurance Market

Chapter 1 described the forces that define personal insurance products. Once created, these products are sold through the personal insurance market. Personal lines now represent half of the entire property-liability market. Bringing personal insurance products to customers would be relatively simple if insurers offered their insurance products within an open market in which supply and demand controlled prices and if insurers marketed insurance products as other industries market theirs. However, many factors affect the personal insurance market to create a challenging environment for personal lines insurance companies.

The personal insurance market is not a static environment. Some of the same pressures that influence insurance products also influence the market. Also, larger economic factors have sent this market into extreme cycles of availability, affordability, and price; insurers are uncertain whether these cycles will continue, change, or stop completely. In addition, the personal insurance market has been affected by elements often found in a best-selling novel: powerful players, huge sums of money, unexpected twists, segmented areas of operation, technology, strategic alliances, and crime.

This chapter addresses the characteristics of the personal insurance market. These characteristics are governed by the economics of personal lines insurance and the influence of regulations, customers, and insurers. The discussion includes the factors within the market. These factors are displayed in Exhibit 2-1. The dimensions of the personal lines market are supply and demand. Within the market, underwriting cycles create fluctuations in profitability and price of insurance. Also within the market, insurers segment portions of the market, build technology, and form strategic alliances to gain advantages. Fraud in the personal insurance market creates significant losses. These losses are passed on to policyholders in the form of increased premiums. The insurance industry is allied with consumer groups, state and federal government, and law enforcement to combat insurance fraud.

Exhibit 2-1
Factors in the Personal Insurance Market

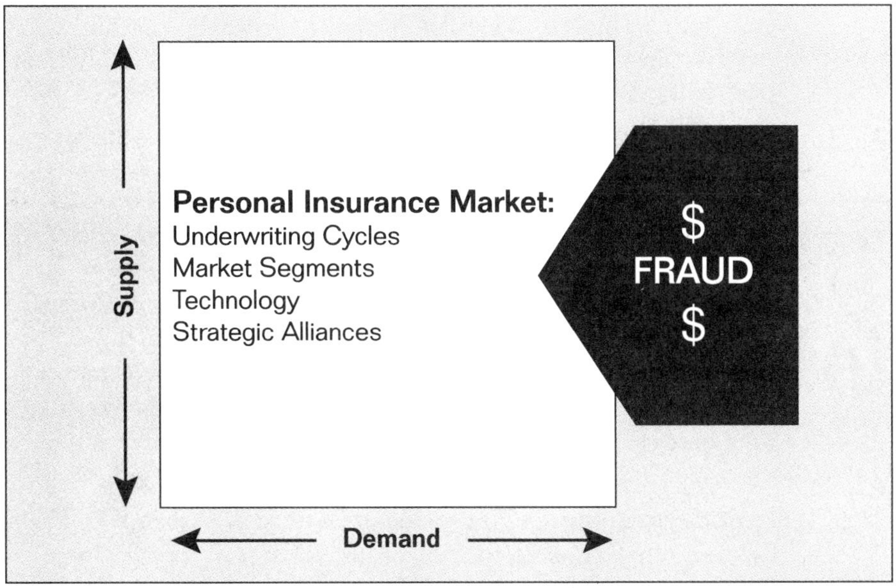

Educational Objective 1
Describe the characteristics of the personal insurance market.

Characteristics of the Personal Insurance Market

The personal insurance **market** is unique in some aspects from other insurance markets such as the commercial insurance, bond, surplus lines, or reinsurance markets. The following are some of those unique characteristics:

A **market**, as it relates to insurance, is an environment in which insurers and policyholders interact and trade.

- *Personal insurance supply.* **Supply** refers to sellers' market intentions. The supply in the personal insurance market and the number of insurers competing in the personal insurance market are huge. In 1995, there were 3,354 property and liability insurance companies in the United States.[1] Although the United States has some very large insurers, no single personal lines insurer controls the market.

Supply refers to sellers' market intentions.

- *Personal insurance demand.* **Demand** reflects buyers' market intentions. The demand in the personal insurance market is immense. Personal lines insurance policies accounted for over $133 billion in premium in 1996. Over $107 billion of that premium came from personal auto insurance alone.[2]

Demand reflects buyers' market intentions.

- *Personal insurance regulation*. The personal insurance market is highly regulated, which restricts to some degree the easy entry and exit of insurers in the market.

Inelastic and elastic refer to the sensitivity of demand in relationship to changes in price. The demand for personal insurance is inelastic because the quantity of product demanded does not fluctuate greatly in response to price changes. In other words, personal insurance customers purchase the same amount of insurance whether prices fall, rise, or stay the same.

- *Inelastic demands*. Demand for personal insurance is generally **inelastic**. This means if the prices of these insurance products rise, policyholders might purchase coverage from another insurer, complain, or protest to legislators, but they usually continue to purchase insurance coverage. Personal auto insurance and homeowners insurance are the two largest personal lines. Personal auto owners in states with financial responsibility laws are required to purchase personal auto liability insurance. (The option, which is available in some states, of purchasing a bond to meet financial responsibility requirements is rarely exercised by individuals or families.) Personal auto owners who have loans on their vehicles are required by the lienholder to purchase physical damage coverage. Homeowners must purchase property insurance to satisfy the mortgage requirement. Even if homeowners do not have a mortgage, they usually protect this valuable asset; 95 percent of all homeowners insure their homes.[3]
- *Market segments*. The personal insurance market is so large that most insurers only attempt to operate within a portion of it. They define strategic niches, focuses, or limited areas of operation—which are referred to as market segments.

Homogeneous products, in the marketing context, are products perceived to be the same by consumers. This perception occurs when the market has many undifferentiated suppliers.

- *Perception of homogeneous insurance products*. Personal insurance products are perceived by many customers to be **homogeneous products**. Many customers do not have *brand loyalty*; they do not care who their insurer is. Some insurers are working very hard to create improvements in services provided to their customers to differentiate their products from those of other insurers.
- *Easy automation*. Insurance contracts and services offered by an insurer are fairly standard; therefore, they can be easily automated. Changes in technology can dramatically improve an insurer's profitability.
- *Distribution systems*. Distribution systems are necessary for communication between customers and insurers. Sudden changes in access to the market through new distribution systems and through strategic alliances can create dramatic shifts in the market.
- *Fraud*. The personal insurance market is riddled with fraud. Because of the high volume of insurance applications and claims processed by insurers, the market is susceptible to unscrupulous policyholders and claimants.

Educational Objective 2
Describe underwriting cycles and their effects on personal lines insurance; explain the importance of understanding underwriting cycles.

A **profit cycle** is a recurring rise and fall in profits, usually profits in just one industry.

The **underwriting cycle** is a commonly used term for a recurring rise and fall in profits and prices in the property and liability insurance industry. Underwriting cycles are the property and liability insurance industry's profit cycles.

Personal Lines Underwriting Cycles[4]

The **profit cycle** within the property and liability insurance industry, which is referred to as the **underwriting cycle**, is the pattern of rising and falling underwriting profitability that occurs over a period of time. The following section describes underwriting cycles and their effects on personal lines insurance. Also included is a discussion of the importance of understanding underwriting cycles and their importance to insurance professionals.

What Occurs in an Underwriting Cycle

An underwriting cycle is a series of increases and decreases in a measure of underwriting profitability, such as dollars of underwriting profit, percentage of underwriting profit growth, or some other measure. As demonstrated in Exhibit 2-2, the high points of the series are referred to as peaks, and the low points are referred to as troughs. A complete cycle is the interval from peak to peak or from trough to trough.

FYI

The terms *peak* and *trough* are not equivalent to the terms *hard market* and *soft market* that insurance people often use to refer to market conditions at different times during a cycle. *Hard market* refers to an insurance market in which buyers have difficulty finding coverage and must pay higher prices for the coverage they are able to buy. *Soft market* refers to an insurance market in which coverage is widely available and insurers reduce prices to write the policies. A hard or soft market can persist for a long period of time.

Exhibit 2-2
Underwriting Cycle Example

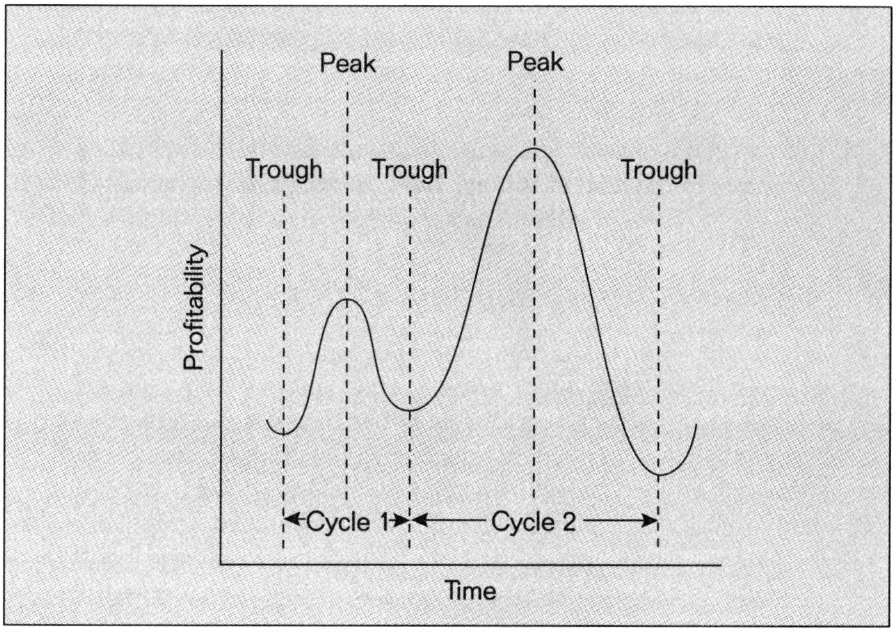

Barbara D. Stewart, *The Profit Cycle in Property and Casualty Insurance* (Malvern, PA: American Institute for CPCU, 1997), p. 2.

The **combined ratio** is the sum of the loss ratio and the expense ratio. It compares operating funds that flow into and out of an insurance company. The combined ratio is the traditional measure of underwriting profitability in the property and liability insurance business.

Peaks and troughs are turning points. Profitability declines until it reaches a trough, and it rises until it reaches a peak. Underwriting cycles can be analyzed for one product line, such as personal automobile insurance, or for a combination of lines, such as personal lines insurance. Underwriting cycles can also be analyzed for the whole insurance industry. Exhibit 2-3 shows the industry's profitability based on **combined ratios** for all property and liability insurance lines from 1945 through 1995. A definite recurring pattern can be observed.

Exhibit 2-3
Combined Ratios for all Property and Casualty Lines

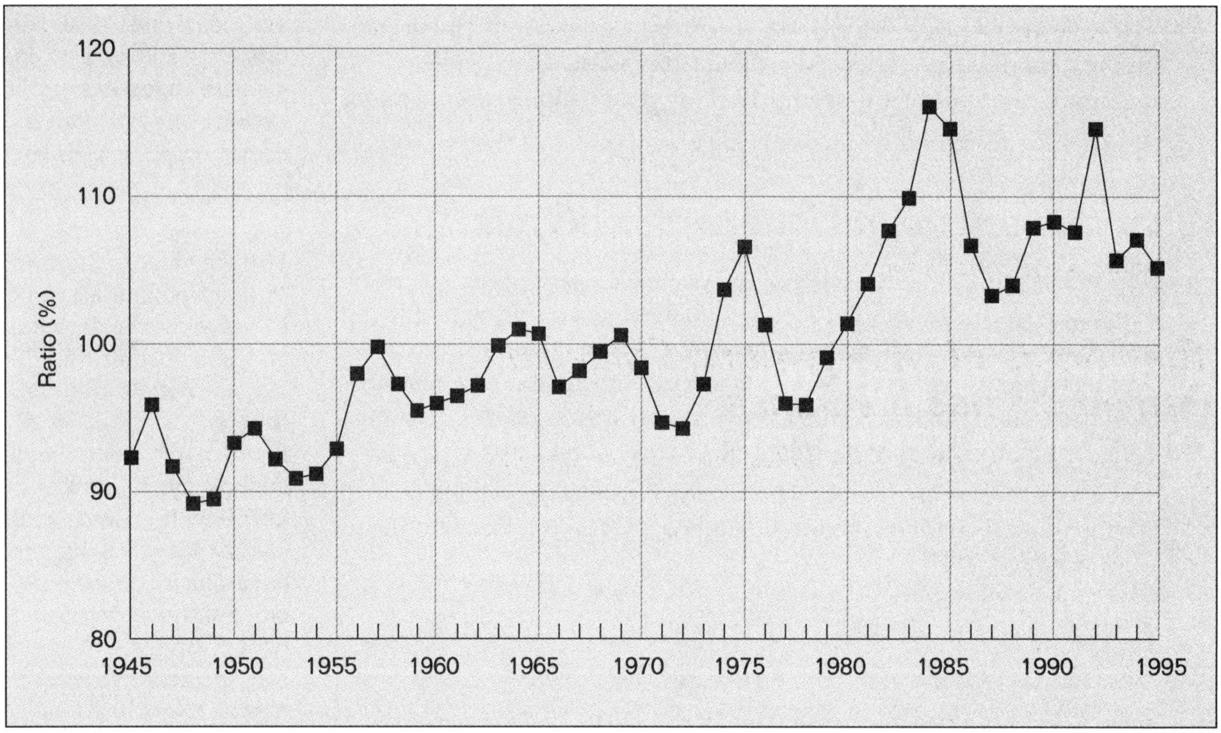

Barbara D. Stewart, *The Profit Cycle in Property and Casualty Insurance* (Malvern, PA: American Institute for CPCU, 1997), p. 3.

Why Underwriting Cycles Occur

Supply is a key factor in underwriting cycles. When expected profits in an insurance market are attractive, insurers attempt to increase their sales, and other insurers enter the market. The supply of insurance expands. Because demand does not generally change in personal insurance, supply exceeds demand. Insurers drop prices to increase their market share. Insurance buyers move their policies to insurers with lower prices, resulting in those insurers increasing their market share. Other insurers, however, do not want to lose their business, so they also cut prices. Consequently, every insurer's prices fall.

Price cutting squeezes profit margins so that insurers no longer want to write business at existing prices or they are forced out of business. As insurers curtail their writings or drop out of the market, the supply of available insurance shrinks. Buyers, however, still need to obtain insurance coverage. Supply is less than demand, so prices rise until expectations of profits once more become attractive enough to encourage sellers to increase market share and others to enter the market. The whole process then occurs again.

Other factors that can cause insurers to withdraw from the market and reduce the supply of insurance include the following:

- Unforeseeable and devastating events—such as hurricanes and winter storms—that deplete profit margins to unacceptable levels and cause a general withdrawal from the market
- Large inflation rates that cause increases in loss payments
- Reinsurance **capacity** that decreases following significant catastrophes and in turn increases the price of reinsurance and reduces primary insurers' profit margins
- Sudden erosion of surplus that occurs when the stock market collapses

Capacity is the volume of business (written premiums) that an insurer is able to handle relative to the size of its policyholder surplus.

Such events make insurers believe that they need more capital to support the policies they write.

The Effects of Underwriting Cycles on Personal Lines Insurance

From the 1950s through the 1970s, insurance cycles followed a distinct pattern of peaks and troughs. Cycles encompassed all major personal lines; commercial lines sometimes moved independently from personal lines.

In the 1970s and 1980s, the insurance industry's profitability went through two sharp swings. Deep premium cuts were abruptly succeeded by huge premium markups. Coverage, especially commercial liability coverage, which had been overabundant one day, became scarce or unobtainable the next. In both instances, once the crisis had passed, the competition for business began in earnest again. Personal lines were affected, but premium fluctuations were not as drastic as those experienced in commercial lines. For many insurers, personal lines emerged as a preferred line of business because of the relative stability it offered.

Jargon Alert!

In the late 1970s and early 1980s, high interest rates affected the underwriting cycle. Insurers slashed premiums because they were able to compensate for underwriting losses with increased investment income. Insurers accused one another of *cash flow underwriting,* which meant cutting prices to get cash from premiums to invest at the then-high interest rates.

In the late 1980s, some commentators predicted a major catastrophe would scare companies into reducing their writings and raising prices across the board. The catastrophes came, but the awaited reaction did not. In 1992, Hurricane Andrew hit the industry with the worst losses ever from a single event. Yet only Florida and other coastal area homeowners insurance and property catastrophe reinsurance markets were affected.

Some commentators now say the underwriting cycle is dead, but many insurance managers do not talk about the cycle at all. Rather than speculate about a cyclical turn, they have concluded that they are better off addressing what might be a permanent state of relentless competition. Many economic indicators suggest that the cycle is not dead but that the insurance business will experience it differently in the future.

One fundamental element of the underwriting cycle has remained constant. In personal lines, insurers' expectations of profits have consistently influenced the supply of insurance. However, insurers have continually changed their expectations regarding the size of the profit margin they can achieve because of competition in the market.

The Importance of Understanding Underwriting Cycles

The information presented so far has addressed insurance cycles of the past forty years. But is that information useful for looking ahead? The following are reasons why insurance professionals should study underwriting cycles:

- *Studying underwriting cycles teaches how the market works*. Underwriting cycles have brought profound change and challenge to insurers, customers, producers, and regulators. Taking action in the future first requires understanding the nature of the cycles in the past. Cycles are the inevitable result of the competitive dynamics from within the insurance market. No matter how forcefully controls are brought to an insurance market, the market will eventually win out. Market forces are currently pushing prices down in many personal lines markets. Those forces in personal lines include (1) profitable investments, and (2) better information permitting pricing closer to expenses and reducing profit margins. What market forces will push prices up? If history is a guide, rising prices will involve something that no one expects.
- *Understanding underwriting cycles helps in developing the business strategy of a company or an agency*. Understanding the economics of competitive markets helps an insurer develop a competitive strategy. A competitive strategy is a plan to become distinct from the competition. The plan might be to become the only seller, to sell a different product, and to erect as many barriers as possible to protect that position. The competitive strategies include product differentiation and lowest possible costs. Competition in personal lines insurance will be discussed in Chapter 3 of this text.
- *Factors that drive insurance cycles still exist and affect the personal insurance market*. The insurance industry has debated about the importance of underwriting cycles, whether underwriting cycles have gone away, and whether underwriting cycles have changed substantially. Even if cycles have stopped, the factors that drove the cycles still exist, and they can still affect the personal insurance market.

- *Understanding the causes of underwriting cycles can lead to appropriate prevention.* The fiercely competitive environment that emerged in the 1970s made it clear that the ups and downs of prices and profits in property and liability insurance had more to do with market economics than with regulation, industry consensus, or change. Much of the economic analysis that has resulted has been directed at finding causes of the underwriting cycle and the wide fluctuations in the markets in recent decades. Understanding the causes might suggest appropriate regulatory action and insurer strategy to prevent similar market swings from occurring in the future. To date, insurance professionals, financial experts, and regulators have had little agreement on the causes and cures of the underwriting cycle. The problem is not the quality or quantity of the analyses performed but is the constant changing of the insurance business and its markets. Specialists in personal insurance should identify the market events in the media that apply to the property and liability insurance business and consider how they affect the continuing evolution of insurance cycles.[5]

How Past Underwriting Cycles Can Help Guide Decisions Today

Cycles can provide lessons regarding the results that can come from some decisions made about personal insurance products. Assume that you are the underwriting manager for an insurance company, and you are losing market share in your personal auto insurance line. You have determined that your competitors are reducing their prices. Interest rates are currently very good. You could reduce prices or loosen underwriting guidelines to write more personal auto policies. If you do so, you could invest the additional premium and make up for the lost premiums and increased losses. If you followed underwriting cycles in the past, you know that this decision could lead to larger problems such as marginal profits and potentially inadequate premiums in the future. You might decide instead to take a more conservative course of action or target a customer group that is inadequately served to develop a larger market share without reducing premiums or loosening underwriting guidelines.

Educational Objective 3

Describe the stages in market development; explain the importance of understanding stages in market development.

Stages in Market Development

Markets for the major lines of insurance followed a similar pattern of evolution. The pattern consisted of four stages of development, which are displayed in Exhibit 2-4.

Each stage is a reaction to the one preceding it. The following is a description of the stages:

1. *Emergence stage*. The first stage of market evolution occurs when a new insurance coverage is introduced. An insurance need is recognized, and a new coverage is developed to meet the need. Insurers compete fiercely for market share. Insurers have little experience in emerging markets; therefore, statistics on the newly recognized insurable risks are not yet available. Because the nature of the exposures and the scope of coverage might not be understood, pricing coverage for such risks is more guesswork than science. When pricing and risk selection turn out to be inaccurate (as they often are), the subsequent corrections in pricing and coverage terms are often abrupt and severe. For example, the automobile insurance market was chaotic when it first emerged around 1900. It involved a new form of insurance, and loss statistics for the auto insurance market did not exist. The market had no standardized coverages, policies, or rates. Insurers competed for market share based on price. This often resulted in underwriting losses because premiums were inadequate to pay for covered losses. Rates were subject to frequent and violent changes.
2. *Control stage*. The second stage of market evolution occurs when industry participants (often with the help of government regulation) try to control the market. Control requires elaborate systems to establish rules and enforce conformity. Problems created in the emergence stage by competition require efforts to keep competition from disrupting the market again. Suppressing competition requires control of supply, which is done by restricting insurer entry into the market, stabilizing market shares, and standardizing products. Continuing the automobile market example, ratemaking bureaus were established in the early 1900s to help bring some control to the wildly fluctuating prices for the existing insurers.
3. *Breakdown stage*. The third stage of insurance market evolution occurs when controls stop working because they are undermined by change. Change can come from new laws, from new needs, or from new ways of meeting needs. Change typically opens the way for insurers and other organizations to compete against the insurers subject to the implemented controls. In the automobile market example, insurers were forced by regulation to charge the high rates developed by the ratemaking bureaus. Some insurance applicants recognized that they were being grossly overcharged, so they organized their own insurance companies. They began writing policies directly for people they knew or associated with, so they did not need independent agents as distributors. (Thus began the direct writers.) The lower premiums offered by the direct writing insurers gave them a significant price advantage over the established insurers. The direct writers were able to pass their savings to policyholders in the forms of dividends, which were not regulated.
4. *Reorganization stage*. The fourth stage in the evolution of insurance markets occurs when the control systems break down and the order in the market also breaks down. In the new competitive environment, inefficient, undifferentiated firms are absorbed or

forced out. The quest for competitive advantage leads to the reorganization of insurance markets into smaller, differentiated segments and around companies with compelling cost advantages. Market segmentation occurs as individual companies attempt to secure a competitive advantage by differentiating themselves from their competitors. Low cost is a powerful competitive advantage. Reorganization brings new market leadership. In personal auto insurance, direct writers charging lower prices assumed market leadership.

Exhibit 2-4
Four Stages of Market Development

Emergence Stage:
- New insurance products are introduced.
- Coverages, policies, and rates are not standardized.
- Rates are subject to frequent and violent changes.

Control Stage:
- Industry participants establish elaborate control systems.
- Regulators suppress competition and control supply.
- Rates and products are standardized.

Breakdown Stage:
- Controls stop working because of changes in the market.
- Change opens the way for competition.

Reorganization Stage:
- Evolution occurs when control systems break down.
- Order in the market is disrupted.
- The market reorganizes itself.

The Importance of Understanding Stages in Market Development

The history of the stages in market development provides useful insights for thinking about the future of insurance. The following describes insights that make the stages important to the insurance professional:

- *What new events could lead to a breakdown stage?* The current competitive situation in most property and liability insurance markets is forcing profit margins to be too thin for every participant to survive. Insurers wonder if the entry of banking into the market or the use of the Internet for insurance sales might be a catalyst for the breakdown stage and might result in the next change in underwriting cycles.
- *What events in the personal insurance market can change the economics of personal lines insurance?* A substantial change in the stock market, technology, competition, or the global market might be significant enough to create a breakdown stage.

If an event is identified that might lead to a breakdown stage, the following questions can help in analyzing the event's possible effects on the personal insurance market:

- *How might each event change the supply of insurance that personal lines insurers are willing to offer?*
- *How might each event be controlled by the current systems (regulations)?*
- *If a breakdown stage occurs, what might the eventual outcome be during a reorganization stage?*
- *How might my organization react or recover in the reorganization stage?*

Educational Objective 4

Explain how the personal insurance market is segmented. Describe benefits and limitations of market segments.

Personal Insurance Market Segmentation

A **niche market** is a group of customers with specialized needs.

The personal insurance market is so large that many insurers select a specific strategic market segment for operation. They focus on specific groups of customers, geographic regions, or **niche markets** based on customers or products. Insurers limit the scope of their market based on their history and expertise, the regulatory climate of the states in a geographic area, the competition, and specific customer needs. Only very large insurance companies approach the personal insurance market on a national basis.

National Market

Companies in the national market serve all or most of the United States. Many national insurers offer all personal insurance product lines. Insurers capable of offering personal insurance products must be large enough to offer their products over the extensive geographic territory. The following are the benefits to an insurer of operating in a national market:

- *Geographic spread of risk.* A national spread of risk decreases the likelihood that an insurer will have a single loss that threatens its continuation. A national insurer can concentrate policy writings in areas having a history of favorable loss results.
- *National product offering.* As policyholders physically move across the country, the national company can continue to offer insurance to the policyholder regardless of location. As individuals' lifestyles change or as they make career moves, the insurer maintains the customers.

Operating in a national market has some limitations. The following are those limitations:

- *Establishing and maintaining a national presence.* Establishing a national presence is an expensive process. An insurer must maintain visibility through continuous television, magazine, newspaper, and billboard advertising.
- *Maintaining service countrywide.* A national insurer incurs service expenses countrywide. Customers expect loss adjustment and customer service response regardless of their location. Service must also be available regardless of time zones.

Regional Markets

Regional markets can be composed of any grouping of states. A region might be limited to a geographic area such as the Northwest states or the New England states. Often, regional insurers start business in one state and expand into neighboring states. The following are the benefits to an insurer of operating in a regional market:

- *Knowledge of the local hazards.* Insurers that concentrate within a specific geographic region develop knowledge of the hazards unique to that region. For example, residential property underwriters recognize the problems inherent in specific types of heating and cooling systems used in the region, which allows them to underwrite with a high level of expertise and recommend effective loss control measures. Knowledge of the local hazards allows a regional company to select and price risks more effectively than an insurer who does not know the region. Regional insurers can be powerful competitors in their geographic areas.
- *Local recognition.* Regional companies can concentrate their marketing dollars in a smaller area than can national insurers, creating more recognition in a region. The physical presence of

the company also creates recognition. Producers or independent agents can develop a closer relationship with regional company representatives and underwriters because they can visit the insurer's office and establish personal contacts.

- *Dealing with limited or selected state regulations*. Dealing with regulations in many states requires a staff to interpret regulations and ensure company compliance. Limiting the number of states also limits the number of sets of regulations and the time required to ensure compliance in each state.

Operating in a regional market has the following limitations:

- *Regional loss concentration*. Regional concentration exposes an insurer to a significant number of losses from a single catastrophe. Freezing, windstorms, hail, forest fires, and floods can create losses that might jeopardize the regional insurer's ability to survive the loss. Regional concentration increases an insurer's need to purchase catastrophe reinsurance, which can be a substantial expense.
- *Expansion problems*. For regional companies, growing requires entry into new product lines, entry into new states, or use of new distribution channels. Expansion and the addition of new customers bring with them the costs of uncertainty and experimentation.
- *Loss of customers from the region*. When a customer leaves a regional insurer's territory, the customer must cancel his or her insurance with the insurer and establish insurance with another insurer. Some people move frequently because of their jobs. Many others change jobs and move for career advancement. The regional insurer will lose a percentage of its policyholders because it cannot move with its customers.

Customer Group Markets

A customer group market can consist of selected groups of customers based on occupation, affiliation, or risk characteristics. For example, teachers, military officers and enlisted personnel, and high-risk drivers are customer groups that have been targeted by insurers as customer group markets.

The following are the benefits to an insurer of selecting a customer group market:

- *Knowledge of customers' needs*. An insurer that concentrates on a particular group of customers can identify the needs of those customers with more accuracy than can an insurer that seeks customers from the general population.
- *Products specific to the customer*. By identifying customers' needs, an insurer can tailor products and services to better meet those needs, increasing the chance of obtaining and retaining those customers.
- *Selection of customers known to be profitable*. As an insurer selects a customer group, it can select those customers known to be profitable. For example, if college graduates are identified as policyhold-

ers with a low frequency of losses, an insurer can target this group, reduce premiums accordingly, and increase the chance of obtaining and retaining these customers. High-risk automobile insurance can also be a profitable customer group for an insurer; the insurer prices the risks appropriately, gains efficiencies in claim settlement, and writes coverage for the customer group profitably.

A customer group market has some limitations:

- *Limitations in expansion*. Once an insurer has absorbed a large portion of a customer group market, it might have difficulty expanding. If the insurer is offering homeowners and personal auto insurance to the customer group, the addition of other personal insurance product lines will not create significant premium increases. Personal umbrella, inland marine floaters, and watercraft policies either have low premiums, or they are required by a limited number of customers. To expand, the insurer must broaden the customer group; to do this, the new group must have the same needs and risk characteristics as the original group, or the insurer must develop new products and price structures for the new group. A differentiation of this type might be difficult to justify to state regulators if the differences are not statistically obvious. For example, an insurer attempting to justify a different set of rates based on an insured's occupation or school affiliation might be prohibited from doing so on the basis of unfair discrimination.
- *Dealing with countrywide service problems*. If the customer group that the insurer has selected is located countrywide, the insurer might encounter the difficulty of addressing regulations and customers' service needs in all states without a customer base that is large enough to support the expense.

Niche Markets

Some insurers elect to service a niche market. Personal insurance customers have a wide variety of interests, hobbies, activities, and possessions that can create exposures requiring insurance protection. Many of these can be an opportunity for a niche market.

The following are keys to niche marketing:

- Understand the customer.
- Understand and customize the product to meet the customer's needs.
- Determine the best distribution channel(s). Evaluate the distributors' needs, strengths, and areas for cooperation. Create strategic partnerships.
- Maintain competitive advantages in the face of copycat competition.

As examples, substandard personal automobile business was a niche market for many insurers in the 1980s. (It has now grown to a product line for many standard insurance companies, so it is no longer considered a niche.) Urban homeowners business markets are addressed by some insurers with homeowners products with limited coverages and perils. Antique collections, special event insurance (such as that for weddings and graduations), and home businesses are niche markets for some insurers.

Identifying a niche requires some skill in identifying and locating profitable specialty areas that allow an insurer to build on its strengths. For example, an insurer might employ several underwriters with years of nautical experience. Their own personal experiences with boat ownership and their understanding of watercraft insurance could help an insurer develop a niche for large yachts, jet skis, or bass-fishing boats.

Insurers can also develop strategic partnerships that assist them in marketing a niche. Using the previous watercraft example, an insurer could establish a contract with an independent agent located near the marinas of several pleasure craft harbors. The insurer might also form a partnership with a boat manufacturer, providing insurance applications at sales offices.

The following are the benefits to an insurer of selecting a niche market:

- *Knowledge of customers' needs*. An insurer in a niche market can gain an understanding of customers' coverage requirements and service needs.
- *Specific product features and services*. The insurer can translate customers' needs into related products that address those needs. This product tailoring can build loyalty among customers and increase policyholder retention.

A niche market has some limitations:

- *Limitations in expansion*. Expanding a niche market might require entering additional states or entering other niche markets. If a niche market becomes obviously profitable for an insurer, there is an increased chance that other insurers will attempt to enter the market.
- *Dealing with countrywide service and advertising problems*. If potential policyholders and customers are located across the country, the insurer must find a way of effectively advertising to these customers and servicing their needs.

Educational Objective 5

Describe technology applied in personal insurance, and explain the effects of technology on the personal insurance market.

Technology

Technology has become increasingly powerful and easy to use. Technology has also become a factor in the personal insurance market. Because personal insurance products and services are relatively homogeneous, they are easily automated. Insurers who largely automate their personal insurance operations are able to improve their profit margins, pass savings to customers in the form of lower premiums, and improve the services that they offer to policyholders. Companies that have not taken steps to automate their operations are falling further and further behind the competition. The need to automate has even been a factor in insurance company mergers. Companies that thought they were too far behind in the automation process merged with companies that were more highly automated rather than attempt to develop their own automation system.

The three key areas of technology for the personal insurance market are automated processing, database applications, and Internet communication and sales.

Automated Processing

Automated processing is the use of technology to streamline the tasks performed by producers, underwriters, and other insurance company and agency staff members. Tasks that were once performed manually are eliminated. The process usually begins when a producer enters an application for insurance into a computerized system. The application is then transferred electronically to the insurer, from whom the system can obtain necessary external reports that the system analyzes. Applications are then accepted, rejected, or referred to an underwriter. Finally, the policies or cancellation notices are generated by the system and mailed to the parties.

Automation creates databases of information that can reveal patterns for fraud detection. This is described later in this chapter.

Automated processing systems allow insurers to move information more efficiently and serve customers more effectively. Automated processing is a significant advantage in insurer competition. Because policies can be processed with reduced activity, expenses can also be reduced. Automated processing and work flow are addressed in detail in later chapters of this text.

Database Applications, Data Mining, and Data Modeling

Databases are banks of information that can be searched for information. Data mining is the process of selecting elements of information from a database for analysis. Data modeling is the application of **predictive models** that analyze the selected information for patterns and trends that help insurers make decisions. The following are some of the ways that data modeling can be used in personal lines insurance:

- Underwriters and producers can predict the risks and characteristics presented by prospective policyholders by comparing their characteristics to a database of policyholders with known risks and loss histories.[6]

Predictive models statistically map the relationships among data elements for a specific purpose. The resulting statistics can be used to predict outcomes, which can help to guide decisions.

- Marketers and underwriters can select prospective customers with historical loss data to determine the level of predicted losses.
- Marketers can predict the probability of a prospective policyholder responding to an advertisement.
- Underwriters can analyze a portfolio of policies to determine the probable retention rate of those policies.

This type of modeling system allows a company to pursue new business that is more profitable and to eliminate some underwriting costs by reducing declinations. Data modeling also provides guidance for marketing activity and helps to reduce the cost of ineffective marketing and advertising efforts.[7]

Internet Communications and Sales

Direct response is marketing that takes place directly between the customer and the insurer through mail, phone, and the Internet without an agent as an intermediary.

Many companies are exploring Internet communication and advertising, but a very small percentage of insurance policy sales actually take place over the Internet. Although the actual extent of Internet insurance sales is only estimated, **direct response** insurers wrote only 7 percent of the personal lines market based on written premium in 1996 through all media, including Internet sales.[8] However, insurers watch this market carefully to determine if the number of direct response sales will increase. One impediment to selling insurance over the Internet is that many customers are not as comfortable with buying insurance as they are with banking and purchasing consumer goods. They have more difficulty comparing policies or are uncomfortable with completing such a personal and important transaction online.

Some customers are inherently interested in the Internet, and they will try insurance purchases over that medium just for the experience. In response, many companies and agencies are experimenting with sales over the Internet to gain experience in the event that it becomes a significant medium for insurance sales, for insurance leads for prospective customers, and for advertising, and a source of information and quotations.

Many insurers are using the Internet to communicate and to maintain a presence for their customers. Insurer Web sites containing corporate and marketing information are common.

Educational Objective 6
Explain why personal lines insurers seek strategic alliances.

Strategic Alliances in the Personal Insurance Market

Some insurers seek strategic alliances to increase market share. They seek to form these alliances with organizations—in a related market—that already have a customer base. For instance, an insurer might select a credit card company for reaching potential customers. Suppose that an insurer has determined that policyholders with good credit ratings have fewer losses and are potentially profitable for the insurer. The insurer could form a strategic alliance with the credit card company. Through this alliance, the credit card company can select from its database of customers those who have a good credit history. The insurer would then solicit applications from these credit card holders. The insurer might offer a policy with a lower premium based on the lower amount of losses anticipated from these individuals. The credit card holders would identify with the name of the credit card company appearing on the mailings they receive. This identification would increase the likelihood that the credit card holder would read the material and complete an application. The insurer increases its chances of obtaining customers with a lower potential of having losses, and the insurer can potentially increase its customer base. The credit card company gains by providing a service to its customers and by receiving a fee for each insurance policy secured.

Still other insurers are taking a more active role with banks by purchasing or creating an alliance with a bank as part of their organizations. This gives the insurers the opportunity to offer an expanded array of services to their customers as part of the insurance product and as part of the event marketing process. As an example, assume that an insurance company has a bank as part of its organization or as part of its strategic alliance. An insured who has had a total loss to his or her home will not only need to settle a claim but will also need to finance the reconstruction of the home. An insurer can provide the additional service to the customer of providing access to a loan officer who is immediately aware of the insured's circumstances, history, and needs. That loan officer can provide information and advice to the customer regarding loan availability and effective methods of financing the reconstruction. Insurance companies and banks, whether they are affiliated through ownership or strategic alliances, must take steps to ensure that services offered are not contingent upon the insured's acceptance of the array of products. For example, a loan should not be contingent upon the insured's purchase of the insurance policy, and an insurance policy should not be contingent upon the insured's acceptance of a loan.

Educational Objective 7

Describe fraud in personal insurance, including the following issues:

a. Public attitude toward insurance fraud
b. Forms of fraud in personal insurance
c. Antifraud measures

Fraud in the Personal Insurance Market[9]

Fraud in insurance has probably existed since the industry's beginnings, but it received little public attention until the 1980s. Law

Fraud is misrepresentation intended to induce another to part with something of value or to surrender a legal right. **Insurance fraud** is committed if (1) information in an insurance application is falsified in an attempt to obtain lower premium rates, (2) the amount of the loss in a claim is falsified, or (3) a claim is falsified.

enforcement agencies had other priorities and were thus reluctant to provide the training needed to investigate and prosecute cases of **insurance fraud**. And given the fine line between investigating suspicious claims and harassing legitimate claimants, some insurers were afraid that a concerted effort to eliminate fraud might be perceived as an anticonsumer activity. In addition, the need to comply with the time requirement for paying claims imposed by fair claim practice regulations in many states made it difficult to adequately investigate suspicious claims.

However, in the mid-1980s, the rising price of insurance, particularly personal automobile insurance, together with the growth in organized insurance fraud, prompted many insurers to reexamine the issue. They began to see the benefit of strengthening antifraud laws and more stringently enforcing them as a means of controlling escalating claim costs. The insurance industry found many allies who had been adversely affected by fraud and were willing to help. These allies included the following groups:

- Consumers who were paying for fraud through increased insurance premiums
- People (some of whom were convicted) used by organized fraud groups to file false claims
- Chiropractors and other medical professionals who were concerned that their reputation as a group was being tarnished by organized fraud ringleaders who had recruited their members to make fraudulent claims for medical treatment

Exhibit 2-6 provides a list of some of the organizations that have become involved in the fight against insurance fraud and their role. Many of these organizations' activities are discussed in the following section of this chapter.

The size of the insurance fraud problem is staggering. In 1994, fraud was estimated to have cost the property and liability insurance industry about $20 billion. Consider the effect of Hurricane Andrew with approximately $16 billion in insured losses; then consider that insurance fraud is larger and reoccurs *every year*.

The dollar amount of fraud might be declining as increased antifraud activity on the part of fraud bureaus and special investigation units (SIUs), along with the growth in funding for fraud-fighting personnel, has resulted in increased prosecutions. Successful fraud prosecutions not only block future fraudulent activities by individuals who are repeat offenders, but news of increased successful prosecution also acts as a deterrent to others who might be contemplating committing fraudulent acts.

Public Attitude Toward Fraud

In a 1995 survey conducted by the Insurance Research Council (IRC), almost a quarter of the respondents said that they think it is acceptable to pad their insurance claims to make up for their insurance premiums paid in previous years. Twenty-eight percent reported that padding a claim to make up for the deductible that they would have to pay is acceptable. These percentages have increased since the IRC began tracking attitudes towards padding claims in 1981. The American public thinks that fraud is a serious problem, but when asked about specific fraudulent practices, it seems to be more lenient.

Exhibit 2-6
Organizations in the Fight Against Insurance Fraud

The Organization	Its Role Against Insurance Fraud
American Insurance Services Group (New York)—a wholly owned subsidiary of the American Insurance Association	Developed the Index System, the Property Insurance Loss Register, and the Automated Property Loss Underwriting System (A-PLUS).
Coalition Against Insurance Fraud (Washington, DC)	An alliance of consumer, law enforcement, and insurance industry groups dedicated to reducing all forms of insurance fraud through public advocacy and education.
Coalition to Reduce Auto Theft and Fraud (Schaumburg, IL)	An alliance of insurance organizations that has designed model bills to combat auto fraud and theft.
Insurance Committee for Arson Control (Indianapolis)	All-industry coalition that serves as a catalyst for insurers' anti-arson efforts and a liaison with government agencies and other groups devoted to arson control.
Insurance Cost Containment Service (Gary, IL)	Assists insurance companies with property claim adjustment and arson and fraud claim investigations.
Insurance Research Council (Malvern, PA)	Provides the public and the insurance industry with timely research information relevant to public policy issues affecting risk and insurance.
Insurance Services Office (New York)	Integrated the American Insurance Service Group and the National Insurance Crime Bureau's databases into a single all-claims database that permits analysis of claim trends and patterns.
International Association of Insurance Fraud Agencies (Kansas City, MO)	An association of more than 3,300 insurance company special investigation unit (SIU) professionals representing the largest property and casualty insurance companies in the country. The organization acts as an education and communications resource in the industry's fight against fraud.
National Fire Protection Association (Quincy, MA)	Independent, nonprofit source of information on fire protection, prevention, and suppression; develops and publishes consensus fire safety standards.
National Insurance Crime Bureau (Palos Hills, IL)	Not-for-profit organization dedicated to combating crime and vehicle theft.

Adapted from Insurance Information Institute, *The Fact Book 1998: Property/Casualty Insurance Facts* (New York: Insurance Information Institute, 1997), pp. 125-138.

In a 1994 poll conducted by Gallup for the National Insurance Crime Bureau (NICB), survey respondents ranked fraud 8.9 on a scale of 1 to 10, where 10 represented a serious violation of the law. However, responses regarding specific questions yielded the following information:

- Twenty-three percent of the respondents did not consider lying about the annual number of miles driven in order to receive a lower premium a serious violation.
- Twenty percent thought that the process of finding and submitting the highest estimates possible for car repairs to make up their deductibles was not a serious problem or violation.
- Fourteen percent of respondents did not think that lying about the number of traffic violations for speeding and other violations, or lying about home addresses, was a serious violation.

Forms of Insurance Fraud

Jargon Alert!

Exaggerating claims is also referred to as *padding*. Examples of padding include increasing the estimated values or numbers of items lost in a fire or theft, exaggerating injuries to increase work absence following an auto accident, or increasing repair estimates on an automobile to include the amount of the deductible. These actions are taken with the intention of increasing insurance claim payments.

Fraud is more prevalent in some lines of insurance and in some geographical areas than others. For example, fraud schemes that might involve networks of professionals such as lawyers and doctors appear to be concentrated in urban areas, like Los Angeles and Philadelphia. Automobile insurance is also a fraud target because of the large number of relatively small claims that must be processed by insurance companies within a short period of time; this provides opportunities for insureds to submit fabricated medical and automobile repair bills or automobile theft reports that could go undetected in the volume of processing. Fraud committed by individuals—in incidents such as staged accidents or claim padding—does not seem to be limited geographically.

Fraud can be committed by several parties in the insurance transaction: applicants for insurance, third-party claimants, and professionals who provide service to claimants. Common frauds include padding or inflating actual claims, misrepresenting facts on an insurance application, submitting claims for injuries or damage that never occurred, and staging accidents.

Automobile Insurance Fraud

According to the NICB, 10 percent of all auto insurance claims are at least partially fraudulent. Fraudulent activities include the following:

- Staging auto accidents or claiming for accidents that did not occur
- Claiming for nonexistent injuries in actual accidents
- Exaggerating or padding claims for actual injuries to reach a specific dollar amount so that the claimant can sue for noneconomic damages (in states that have a dollar threshold for bodily injury claims before a lawsuit can be filed—states with verbal thresholds seem to have less medical claim padding)

How Much Do You Pay for Automobile Insurance Fraud?

According to the RAND Institute for Civil Justice, between 35 and 42 percent of medical care claims for motor vehicle crash victims under the bodily injury portion of auto insurance are "excess." RAND found that between 1980 and 1991, bodily injury costs incurred by insurers grew by 167 percent. Because motor vehicle crashes are declining, the increase in costs is attributed to health-care inflation (which accounts for 60 percent of the increase) and the increase in the number and size of bodily injury claims (which is responsible for the remaining 40 percent of the increase). If these excess costs were passed on to consumers as proportional increases in premium, then each American auto insurance policyholder paid between $100 and $300 more for auto insurance in 1993 because of excess medical claiming.

Arson

Based on data reported by fire departments in its survey, the National Fire Protection Association (NFPA) estimates that 85,500 of the structural fires that occurred in the United States in 1996 were of an incendiary or suspicious nature. Property damage from these fires totaled $1.4 billion.

In 1996, there were 47,000 vehicle fires of incendiary or suspicious origin. These fires caused an estimated $202 million in property damage.[10]

Insured property losses of a suspicious nature cause unique problems for insurers. Generally, residences and new automobiles have a mortgage or lien. The insurance contract language provides loss payment to a mortgagee or a lienholder (up to the limit of his or her interest in the property) even if the claim is denied to the policyholder. Therefore, an insurer might identify a residential property or vehicle loss to be caused by arson committed by the policyholder, and the insurer could deny claim payment to the policyholder on that basis. However, the insurer would still owe claim payment for damages to the mortgagee or lienholder.

In addition, insurers must approach any suspected arson loss with great care. An insurer cannot slander or libel a policyholder who is suspected of an illegal act, or else the insurer could face a lawsuit based on defamation of character. An insurer must also comply with requirements for adjusting losses promptly or face a lawsuit from a policyholder for failing to fulfill its obligations under the policy contract.

Antifraud Measures

Insurance companies are not law enforcement agencies. They can only identify suspicious claims, withhold payment when fraud is suspected, and collect information sufficient for use as evidence in a court of law to justify their actions. The success of the fight against insurance fraud depends on the resources devoted by the insurance industry to detecting fraud, and the level of priority assigned by legislators, regulators, law enforcement agencies, and society as a whole to eliminating it. Antifraud measures taken by insurers as well as state and national legislation and law enforcement to reduce fraud are discussed in the following section.

Insurer Fraud Detection

Insurers attempt to detect fraud by identifying patterns, by controlling underwriting at the point of sales, by detecting problems during claims, and by using special investigation units.

Identifying Patterns

Index systems are computerized databases that provide access to a bank of information through search inquiries.

Computerized databases, also known as **index systems**, have been established to help identify patterns of suspected criminal activity. By providing information on a policyholder's claim history, including the names of others involved in a claim, witnesses to an accident, and professionals rendering services, an insurer can prevent payment of duplicate claims. An indexing system can also be used to identify the recurrence of witnesses, attorneys, or physicians appearing in multiple suspicious claims. An indexing system must include information from many insurers to be effective. Without information that spans the history of many companies, a criminal could commit the same type of insurance fraud with several insurers without detection.

Insurance Services Office (ISO) is building a single, integrated all-claims database designed to benefit its customers by cutting operating costs and increasing the industry's capacity to fight fraud. The database will consolidate databases now maintained separately by the American Insurance Services Group (AISG) and the National Insurance Crime Bureau (NICB). AISG, which has been a leading provider of property and liability claims information, has become part of ISO. The NICB is an insurance industry-sponsored organization that has special expertise in preparing fraud cases for trial and serves as a liaison between the insurance industry and law enforcement agencies. In addition, it publicizes the arrest and conviction of the perpetrators of insurance fraud to help deter future criminal activities.

The NICB, insurers, and law enforcement agencies will use the consolidated claims database to help identify questionable claims, reduce insurance fraud, and speed payments of valid claims. Fraud investigators can cross-reference several identifiers and are more likely to obtain leads that might result in prosecution. For instance, in an auto fraud investigation, investigators can search by vehicle identification numbers, drivers' licenses, license plate numbers, Social Security and tax numbers, as well as previous claim information. Exhibit 2-7 provides specific examples of how a database can be used to fight insurance fraud.

Expert systems (also called knowledge-based systems) are sets of computer programs that perform tasks at the level of a human expert. Expert systems are created on the basis of knowledge collected from human experts, and they imitate the reasoning process of a human being.

Control at the Point of Sale

Expert systems can identify the red flags that indicate possible fraud. For example, an expert system can identify an applicant who lives fifty miles or more away from the producer submitting the application or a cellular telephone number provided by an applicant. However, it is easy to overlook detection of possible fraud indicators through the implementation or complication of expert systems that screen applicants and application data. The NICB checklist is an excellent point to begin the identification of indicators and add them to a system. This checklist as it relates to personal insurance is presented in API 28.

Exhibit 2-7
How a Database Is Used To Fight Insurance Fraud

In the past, much of an insurance investigator's time was spent physically retrieving information. Using new technology, investigators now mine databases for patterns of prior claims by name search and address combinations, Social Security numbers, or license numbers to detect suspicious patterns that can point out complex fraud cases, such as organized fraud rings. The following are examples:

Example 1: A major insurer suspected that staged auto accidents were increasing in the New York area. The insurer's investigators conducted a database search that identified common denominators of the members of the fraud ring. For example, the search revealed accidents that involved claims by unrelated people who received medical treatment from the same provider. The outcome was that forty-two claim cases were identified as fraudulent, generating $700,000 in fraudulent claims. With the end of the fraud ring, the future claims savings are projected to be millions of dollars.

Example 2: A slip-and-fall claimant demanded payment of $200,000, hired an attorney, but refused to disclose her identity, her medical records, or the complete nature of her injury. The investigators used the claimant's Social Security number to search the database for past claims. The search revealed that the claimant had filed twelve bodily injury claims using the same Social Security number but different names. Further database mining uncovered a relationship among the claimant's treating physicians and attorneys.

"NICB Turns Its Claims Databases Over to ISO to Move to Fight Insurance Fraud by Building One All-Claims Database," *News from ISO,* February 1998.

Claim Control and Special Investigation Units

Special investigative units (SIUs) exist to determine the facts about suspicious claims, to provide evidence of fraud when it can be proven, to avoid improper and unfounded accusations by insurers, and to pay claims that the investigation deems worthy. Insurance company surveys conducted by the NICB confirm that SIUs dramatically improve the financial results for many insurance companies. The administrator of the International Association of Special Investigation Units says that although the results might vary from company to company, on an average insurers save $10 for every dollar they invest in an SIU.

A special investigative unit (SIU) is a unit within an insurance company specially dedicated to investigating suspicious claims and other possible frauds. SIUs also exist within the insurance departments in some states.

Most claim departments are staffed for routine claims. This type of staffing makes devoting more time or effort to suspicious claims difficult. The appropriate investigation of suspicious claims is time-consuming. Some insurers develop their own SIUs while other insurers outsource the SIU operations. SIUs can range from a small team whose primary role is to train claim representatives to deal with the more routine kinds of fraud cases to teams of trained investigators—including attorneys, accountants, claim experts, and former law enforcement officers—who thoroughly investigate fraudulent activities. More complex cases involving large-scale criminal operations or individuals who repeatedly stage accidents might be turned over to the NICB.

SIUs investigate many aspects of fraud other than claim fraud. For example, SIUs might be assigned to investigate the following:

- Misrepresentation on policy applications, including identity and use of vehicles and claim history
- Wrongdoing by agents, including the failure to place coverage
- Internal fraud, including collusion by claim personnel with outsiders, embezzlement, and kickback schemes[11]

Increasingly, states are setting up their own fraud bureaus, often with insurance industry funding. Many have law enforcement power. In some states, laws require insurers to establish SIUs and to file antifraud plans with the insurance department.

Legislation and Law Enforcement Activities To Reduce Insurance Fraud

After insurers identify and document fraud, they turn their evidence over to the court system for action. Without effective legislation and law enforcement to fight fraud, prosecutors have a difficult time in taking action against the perpetrators or winning severe enough penalties to act as a deterrent.

National Developments

In September 1994, President Clinton signed the Violent Crime Control and Law Enforcement Act, which makes insurance fraud a federal crime when it affects interstate commerce. One of the law's provisions specifies that people engaged in insurance on an interstate basis who knowingly make false statements or intentionally overvalue any aspect of their business with the intent to deceive can be fined or imprisoned for up to fifteen years.

Other federal laws that help combat insurance fraud include the following:

- The federal mail fraud statute prohibits the use of the U.S. Postal Service to defraud or obtain money or property by means of false or fraudulent pretenses.
- The federal Racketeer Influence and Corrupt Organizations (RICO) statute (and similar state laws) is regularly used to prosecute insurance fraud cases. In addition to criminal penalties, RICO statutes may provide for civil actions (with triple damages) against those involved directly or indirectly in a pattern of criminal activity. Before this statute was enacted in 1970, the principals of organized crime operations could escape prosecutions by removing themselves from direct participation in criminal activities.

State Developments

Key laws that can effectively deter insurance fraud are discussed in the section that follows. Each state must pass the laws individually, and although some laws are based on model legislation, some provisions might be stronger or better defined than others. Appendix 2-A of this text provides information regarding the acceptance of these key laws by state.

Insurance Fraud Classified as a Crime Although insurance fraud, like other types of fraud, is illegal in all states, some laws are more effective at thwarting it than others. Prosecuting cases of insurance fraud is easier in states where it is identified as a specific crime in the state penal code and where what constitutes insurance fraud is defined, along with the penalties that can be imposed. Defining the crime specifically helps educate law enforcers about insurance fraud and provides prosecutors with clear-cut cases. Raising the level of the crime from a **misdemeanor** to a **felony** not only increases the penalties but also acts as a deterrent to future crimes.

A **misdemeanor** is an offense that is lower than a felony and generally punishable by fine, penalty, or imprisonment in a facility other than a penitentiary. A **felony** is a crime of a grave or serious nature punishable by death or imprisonment for a term exceeding one year.

Where insurance fraud is not specifically mentioned, it falls under general fraud provisions such as theft by deception. The level of seriousness attached to the crime also varies by state. Some states classify insurance fraud or certain types of insurance fraud as a felony, and others as a misdemeanor, a lower level of crime. Some classify insurance fraud as a felony when more than a specified dollar amount is involved.

Civil and criminal penalties for insurance fraud have been increased since the insurance industry has stepped up its fight against fraud. The following are some of those activities:

- Thirty states have passed laws that specifically define the crime of insurance fraud.
- Twenty-seven states now have laws that classify insurance fraud as a felony, either at a specified monetary level or after multiple offenses.
- Several states list insurance fraud as unprofessional conduct in statutes regulating doctors, lawyers, and other professionals. The consequences of unprofessional conduct would be determined by organizations conferring professional designations.

Immunity Statutes Privacy laws protect the rights of policyholders and claimants against the release of information considered confidential; insurance and claim information is considered confidential. However, to successfully bring a case to trial, insurers must be able to provide information to prosecutors on individuals suspected of fraud. Individuals and insurers must be exempt from libel or unfair trade practices lawsuits, which could be brought against them for releasing information on prior claims.

Immunity laws now exist in all states; however, not all of the laws cover insurance fraud specifically or allow information to be reported to law enforcement agencies as well as to state departments of insurance. The National Association of Insurance Commissioners (NAIC) has developed model bills for immunity as well as model insurance fraud laws to encourage states to address the problem of insurance fraud and to assist them in formulating appropriate legislation.

Immunity laws provide protection to insurance companies for the good-faith exchange of information required to provide information to state insurance departments or law enforcement officials without fear of criminal or civil prosecution.

Fraud Bureaus Special units have been established in some states' insurance departments to identify fraudulent acts, collect information on repetitive offenders, and investigate cases. The main purpose of the bureau is to set up documented criminal cases that can be readily prosecuted. Some bureaus have law enforcement powers. Twenty-five states have enacted legislation creating fraud bureaus; twenty of them are within the state's insurance department.

Jargon Alert!

In some insurance companies, nonexistent vehicles are referred to as *paper vehicles* because they exist only on paper.

Mandatory Insurer Fraud Plans In the states where mandatory insurer fraud plan laws exist, insurers are required by such laws to set up a specific program that identifies insurance fraud and outlines remedial actions taken to reduce it. At least seven states have initiated such laws.

Mandatory Photo Inspection Where mandatory photo inspection laws have been enacted, photographs must be taken of used cars before collision or other than collision insurance is issued. These laws are designed to eliminate claims for damage sustained before the issuance of personal automobile insurance and the purchase of insurance for nonexistent vehicles.

Chop shops are garages or lots where stolen vehicles are brought to be stripped of their components.

Vehicle Chop Shop, Stolen and Altered Property Act This bill and the ones that are subsequently discussed combat auto fraud and theft. They are model bills, which were developed by the Coalition to Reduce Auto Theft and Fraud (CRAFT). These bills, which have become laws in some states, are widely endorsed by insurers and other insurance organizations.

Injunctions are court orders that prohibit someone from committing a specified act or that command someone to undo a wrong or an injury.

The Vehicle Chop Shop, Stolen and Altered Property Act imposes criminal sanctions on persons involved with **chop shops**. It provides for forfeiture of the tools and equipment involved in the chop shops and allows for civil remedies, including treble damages and **injunctions**, against those involved in the chop shop operations.

Salvage Certificate Junk Vehicle Act When a vehicle is totaled, the title is changed in many states to indicate its salvage or junk status. However, criminals can alter these titles in a number of creative ways to falsify claims. For example, a salvage title might be transferred to another state that does not use a salvage classification. The title then appears to be proof of ownership of an operable vehicle. A criminal could then register the vehicle, insure it, and submit another claim for the damages.

The Salvage Certificate Junk Vehicle Act helps to standardize salvage or junk vehicle documents, whether the vehicle is insured or not. It also provides an effective procedure for eliminating the titles of unrepairable junk vehicles and mandates the surrender of a junk or salvage vehicle's title. This ends the title chain of junk vehicles and establishes a paper trail to detect and prevent fraud and theft.

An **owner give-up** is a term used to describe a vehicle owner who conspires with others to commit fraud.

Vehicle Owner Fraud Act This legislation combats **owner give-ups**, in which the vehicle owner conspires with others to file a fraudulent claim. Knowingly making or assisting in making a false claim for theft destruction or damage, or illegally obtaining vehicle ownership by making false statements is classified as a felony.

The False Police Report Act This law makes it a crime to knowingly file or assist with a false report to a law enforcement agency of theft or of destruction or damage of any property. Generally, the first offense is a misdemeanor, and subsequent offenses are felonies.

Gaining Public Attention in Fighting Fraud

The 1994 Gallup poll previously mentioned provides information regarding public awareness about the cost of fraud and the insurance industry's actions to combat it. Poll respondents gave the insurance industry a rank of 6.5 (on a scale of 1 to 10, whereby 1 represents no activity and 10 represents as much activity as possible) for doing everything possible to minimize fraud. However, about 75 percent of the respondents said they had never received any literature on fraud from their insurance companies, and only 6 percent of respondents said they were aware of any antifraud program.

Given the size of the fraud problems, the cost to insurance customers, and the public's general acceptance of claim padding, gaining public attention in the fight against fraud should have positive effects. Many fraud-fighting organizations are using advertising campaigns to communicate the cost of fraud losses to individuals, to provide warnings regarding the penalties for insurance fraud, and to provide rewards to help identify and prosecute insurance fraud.

Summary

The personal insurance market is not a static environment. Economic factors have created characteristics in the market that make personal insurance unique from other coverage lines. The following factors characterize the personal insurance market:

- Underwriting cycles are a series of increases and decreases in insurer profitability driven by the supply provided by insurance companies. Underwriting cycles are driven by many competitive forces. Insurance company pursuit of profit is the commonality throughout the cycles. The underwriting cycles have changed as products progress through stages of market development.
- Personal insurance market segmentation allows insurers to focus on specific groups of customers, geographic regions, or niche markets based on customers or products.
- Technology is a driving factor in the personal insurance market. Automated processing, database application, and Internet use reduce expenses and potentially increase sales.
- Strategic alliances between insurance companies and other organizations such as credit card companies or banks are providing insurers new avenues for sales within the market.
- Fraud is now an annual insurance industry cost that exceeds the losses experienced in Hurricane Andrew. These costs are passed directly to the insurance customer. Insurers are acting in conjunction with many other organizations and legislators to remove or reduce fraud's effect on the market.

Chapter Notes

1. Insurance Information Institute, *The Fact Book 1998: Property/Casualty Insurance Facts* (New York: Insurance Information Institute, 1997), p. 7.
2. Insurance Information Institute, p. 15.
3. Insurance Information Institute, p. 10.
4. Adapted from Barbara D. Stewart, *The Profit Cycle in Property and Casualty Insurance* (Malvern, PA: American Institute for CPCU, 1997).
5. Stewart, p. v.
6. Scott Price, "Where Marketing and Underwriting Converge," *Underwriting Trends*, December 1997, p. 3.
7. Price, p. 3.
8. "IIAA Study Compares Insurer Expenses and Marketshare," *Independent Agent*, November 1997, p. 48.
9. Adapted from Ruth Gastel, ed., "Insurance Fraud," *Insurance Issues Update*, March 1996, pp. 1-2.
10. Insurance Information Institute, p. 65.
11. James J. Markham, *Property Loss Adjusting*, vol. 1 (Malvern, PA: Insurance Institute of America, 1995) pp. 198-203.

Competing in the Personal Insurance Market

Chapter 3

Educational Objectives

1. Describe and analyze the competitive environment in the personal insurance market. (pp. 3-3 to 3-5)
2. Explain how insurers strategically position themselves within the personal insurance market. (pp. 3-5 to 3-10)
3. Given a case situation, analyze an insurer's strengths, weaknesses, opportunities, and threats; describe how an insurer might position its products within the personal insurance market based on that analysis. (pp. 3-5 to 3-10)
4. Explain how insurers compete on the basis of product features, price, and service. (pp. 3-10 to 3-19)
5. Given a case situation, describe actions that a personal lines insurer could take to compete in the personal insurance market. (pp. 3-10 to 3-19)
6. Describe team approaches to improve insurer service and gain efficiencies; describe elements of effective team management. (pp. 3-19 to 3-20)
7. Describe the benefits to an insurer of increasing customer retention and persistency; explain how insurers can increase retention and persistency. (pp. 3-21 to 3-25)

Outline

I. The Competitive Market

II. Developing Competitive Strategies
   - A. SWOT Analysis
   - B. Market Positioning

III. Product Features, Price, and Service
   - A. Enhancing Product Features
   - B. Using Pricing Strategies
   - C. Using Service Strategies

IV. Improving Retention and Persistency
   - A. Why Insurers Lose Customers
   - B. Methods for Retaining Customers

V. Summary

Chapter 3

Competing in the Personal Insurance Market

Chapter 1 defined insurance products as the combination of product features, price, and service created by forces in the insurance environment. That chapter also defined operating profit for insurers as the sum of investment income (or loss) and underwriting income (or loss).

Chapter 2 described characteristics of the personal insurance market, including underwriting cycles. Within underwriting cycles, insurers' profit expectations drive the supply of insurance products that the insurers are willing to offer in the market. Insurers operate in the market because they expect to generate a profit.

This chapter discusses the forces and characteristics described in Chapters 1 and 2 along with competition in the personal insurance market. Personal lines insurers are not free to bring all products to the market because they are controlled by the forces that define personal insurance products and the personal insurance market. Within these constraints, insurers strategically determine what their insurance products will be and how they will generate an operating profit. To obtain better advantages in the market, insurers develop competitive strategies; develop and refine their product features, prices, and services; and work to improve the retention of existing accounts.

Educational Objective 1

Describe and analyze the competitive environment in the personal insurance market.

The Competitive Market

Competition is the effort of two or more parties acting independently to secure the business of a third party by offering the most favorable terms.

Competition is the force that works to define which personal insurance products are available in the market. Competition is characterized as either perfect competition or imperfect competition. Exhibit 3-1 compares perfect and imperfect competition and analyzes the personal insurance market.

Exhibit 3-1

Comparison of Perfect and Imperfect Competition—Analysis of the Personal Insurance Market

Perfect Competition	Imperfect Competition	Analysis of the Personal Insurance Market
Perfect competition exists when individual buyers and sellers cannot affect the market price.	Imperfect competition exists when individual sellers can charge a price that is greater than the full cost of the product. These sellers are said to have market power because they are price setters.	Personal insurers rarely gain market power because many competitors are in the market. Occasionally an insurer will gain market power in a specific market segment or in a product line for a period of time.
The market has a large number of buyers and sellers.	Only a few buyers and sellers control the market. The most extreme situation occurs when there is only one seller: this is called a monopoly.	The personal insurance market has many buyers and sellers. Any market control gained is only temporary.
Customers believe that products are the same (that is, homogeneous). The customers have no brand loyalty.	The product is nonhomogeneous. Customers have brand loyalty, and a significant amount of advertising intends to convince consumers that the advertised product differs from similar products.	In personal insurance, auto and homeowners insurance contracts are generally homogeneous. However, the price and the service delivered as part of the insurance product can vary significantly. Generally, personal lines insurers compete in the personal auto and homeowners markets based on price and service. Insurers attempt to create brand loyalty through service. In other smaller personal insurance lines (such as umbrella, inland marine, or watercraft), the personal insurance contracts are nonhomogeneous. Insurers compete based on product features, services, and price.

Continued on next page.

Perfect Competition	Imperfect Competition	Analysis of the Personal Insurance Market
Perfect information is available. Buyers know everything about the quality of the product and the price and conditions of sale. The sellers know who and where the buyers are and how much they are willing to pay.	Imperfect information keeps buyers from understanding prices and important characteristics of competing products. Imperfect information also prevents sellers from having complete information to price their products accurately.	Both personal insurance customers and insurers have imperfect information. Customers do not fully understand the insurance product they are purchasing or the services they should expect to or will receive. Although advisory organizations collect and disseminate large amounts of claim data, individual personal lines insurers do not have enough information—regarding each risk they insure—to price their products with absolute accuracy. In addition, customers do not always supply correct information to allow insurers to price individual policies with accuracy.
There is free entry into and exit from the market. New sellers enter the market easily. Existing sellers leave easily. If prices become excessive, new sellers enter the market and offer the product for a lower price. This market entry keeps the price of the product from becoming too high. Sellers leave the market if prices become too low to be profitable, causing the remaining insurers to raise prices. This market exit keeps prices from becoming too low.	Barriers exist that limit competitors' entry into and exit from the market. Those competitors in the market keep prices inflated without the fear of new competitors entering the market and offering lower prices.	Regulatory restrictions for personal lines insurers can be significant, but not insurmountable. The initial costs associated with trying to enter the market are very high. Internet sales and strategic alliances with banks might be factors that reduce the marketing costs.

Adapted from Yung-Ping Chen, Robert C. A. deVos, and Lowell Young, *Choices and Constraints: Economic Decisionmaking* (Malvern, PA: American Institute for CPCU, 1994), pp. 46-49.

In several respects, the personal insurance market meets the characteristics of both perfect and imperfect competition. These characteristics are part of the economic environment that defines competition in the personal insurance market.

The characteristics of the competitive environment are the following:

- The personal insurance market has many customers and insurers, and the products offered by insurers overlap.
- Personal lines insurers compete on the basis of product features, price, and service.
- Insurance products are generally available for most of individuals' or families' personal insurance needs unless external forces (such

as regulation or catastrophe exposure) prevent insurers from generating enough premiums to offer the products profitably.

- Personal lines insurers offer relatively homogeneous product features in auto and homeowners coverages. Other product lines such as umbrella, inland marine, and watercraft are nonhomogeneous.
- Personal lines insurers compete most frequently in personal automobile and homeowners insurance on the basis of price and service. The insurer's distribution system is an integral part of service.
- Personal lines insurers price their products based on available information, but the pricing mechanism is imperfect; personal lines insurers base their prices on incomplete information.

Educational Objective 2
Explain how insurers strategically position themselves within the personal insurance market.

Educational Objective 3
Given a case situation, analyze an insurer's strengths, weaknesses, opportunities, and threats; describe how an insurer might position its products within the personal insurance market based on that analysis.

Developing Competitive Strategies

Each insurer approaches competition in the market as part of its **strategies**. The comprehensive statement of an organization's strategies, along with its **mission** and **goals**, constitutes an organization's strategic plan. Strategic planning is important for the following reasons:

- It helps insurers identify and develop **competitive advantages**.
- It provides a sense of direction so that insurance company employees and stakeholders know where to expend their efforts.
- It can help highlight the need for innovation and provide an organized approach for encouraging new ideas related to strategies.
- The process of developing the strategic plan can be used to involve managers at various levels in planning, thus making it more likely that they will understand and support the resulting plan.[1]

Strategies are large-scale action plans for interacting with the business environment in order to achieve long-term goals.

A **mission** is an organization's purpose or its fundamental reason for existence.

Goals are major planning components that are the target or end result that an organization wishes to achieve.

Competitive advantage is a significant edge over the competition in dealing with competitive forces.

SWOT Analysis

As part of strategic planning to gain a competitive advantage, insurance company managers carefully analyze the company's competitive

A **SWOT analysis** is a method of analyzing an organization's competitive situation that involves assessing organizational strengths (S), weaknesses (W), opportunities (O), and threats (T).

situation. This analysis involves assessing the environmental and organizational factors that influence an organization's ability to compete effectively.[2] One approach used by insurers either formally or informally in the strategic planning process is an analysis of the insurers' Strengths, Weaknesses, Opportunities, and Threats. This is called a **SWOT analysis**, and it can be used to help an insurer determine its position in the market and the actions it will take. Each insurer conducts its own SWOT analysis and determines how it should respond to remain profitable. Exhibit 3-2 displays guides for a SWOT analysis and sample SWOT analyses for two insurers.

Exhibit 3-2
SWOT Analysis and Examples for Personal Lines Insurance

SWOT Analysis Guides	Example: Insurer A	Example: Insurer B
Strengths. A strength is an internal characteristic that gives a competitive advantage or has the potential of improving the organization's competitive situation. The following are some personal lines insurers' strengths: • A distinctive competence (for example, technical expertise, knowledgeable staff) • Significant financial resources • Positive reputation • Effective implementation of technology • Effective advertising campaigns • Product innovation skills • Effective management • Effective geographic spread of risk • Effective service processes • Strong market distribution • Low expense ratio	Insurer A offers personal lines in all states. It offers only standard insurance products in homeowners and personal auto. It offers umbrella and watercraft policies as accommodations. Insurer A has a positive reputation and is recognized internationally. Insurer A is a direct writer with producers' offices located throughout the United States. Insurer A has several managers who have developed international products for previous employers.	Insurer B specializes in pleasure-use watercraft insurance for boats of all sizes. It writes insurance in all states that border the Atlantic Ocean, the Gulf of Mexico, and the Great Lakes. Insurer B is recognized as one of the leaders in the watercraft insurance market. Insurer B has automated its policy processing with independent agents located in its states of operation. Insurer B's underwriters have remained abreast of watercraft industry developments. For example, they are aware of the resurgence of wooden-hull sailboat construction. Some of the underwriters are instructors at the boat-building schools for these sailboats.
Weaknesses. A weakness is an internal characteristic that leaves the organization vulnerable to strategic moves by competitors. The following are some personal lines insurers' weaknesses: • No clear strategic direction • Problems in implementing strategies • Obsolete technologies	Insurer A's management style and technology have become out-of-date in the last two decades. Key employees have left the company for better opportunities at other insurance companies. Insurer A is having difficulty maintaining talented staff.	Insurer B has been a watercraft insurer for over 100 years and has never entered another product line. It is unknown outside of the watercraft market. Other than the use of automated policy processing, Insurer B's management style has not

SWOT Analysis Guides	Example: Insurer A	Example: Insurer B
• History of unprofitability • Lack of managerial depth and talent • Missing key skills or competencies • Too narrow a product line • Weak market image • Weak market distribution • High expense ratio	Insurer A's traditionally low expense ratio has been increasing as new employees are hired and trained.	changed since its founding. Insurer B's management hierarchy makes changes difficult to implement. As a result, Insurer B is slow to react to required change. Insurer B has a very high expense ratio because of the high commission rates it offers.
Opportunities. An opportunity is a condition external to the insurer that offers significant prospects for improving an organization's situation relative to competitors. The following are some potential opportunities for personal lines insurers: • Serving additional customer groups • Entering new market segments • Expanding a product line to meet a broader range of customer needs • Marketing through strategic partnerships or strategic alliances • Experiencing falling trade barriers in attractive international markets • Experiencing complacency among competitors	Insurer A has been approached by several college alumni organizations that would like to offer insurance products to members at a discount. Insurer A has been approached by a number of organizations in other countries that have suggested an alliance to offer limited insurance in their countries.	Insurer B has been exploring a number of new watercraft markets including boat clubs, marinas, and jet ski rental agencies. Insurer B's competitors have not changed their product features, prices, or services in twenty years.
Threats. A threat is a condition external to the insurer that offers significant prospects for undermining an insurer's competitive situation. The following are some potential threats for personal lines insurers: • Entry of new competitors into the market • Increasing use of alternative distribution systems by competitors • Costly regulation requirements • New products, services, or product features offered by competitors • Significantly lower prices charged by competitors	Some of Insurer A's competitors have begun adding new product features for affluent customers. Competitors have also begun experimenting with Internet advertising and sales.	Watercraft insurers from other countries have become licensed in some states and have begun advertising in sailing magazines. They offer low-priced insurance for large privately owned yachts.

Bulleted items in column 1 are adapted from Arthur A. Thompson, Jr., and A.J. Strickland III, *Strategic Management Concepts and Cases,* 6th ed. (Homewood, IL: BP/Irwin, 1992), p. 89.

As part of the SWOT analysis, insurers should consider the unique aspects of the market they are engaged in. For example, Insurer A has a national marketing approach; it offers standard personal lines products in a broad geographical area. Other insurers such as Insurer B carve out niche markets with a specialty product. Either approach can have its benefits or limitations. In a broad market, an insurer has a larger customer base to draw from; however, other large insurers also compete in the same large market. A niche market can be an excellent market to control if an insurer is one of the few insurers in the market. However, other insurers might enter the niche and begin competing for the same relatively small market. This occurred in the 1990s in the substandard auto market. What was a profitable niche market for a small group of insurers became a competitive market with many insurers vying for customers.

By performing a SWOT analysis, an insurer can better identify those areas that require improvement and activities that are necessary for the organization's continuity. For example, Insurer A is facing management and staffing problems. Without strong human resources, Insurer A will find it difficult to develop the products and services required to remain profitable and competitive. Insurer B operates in a small market area and has done little to broaden its market, enhance its product, or gain market share.

In addition, the SWOT analysis can identify opportunities that an insurer might have overlooked. Opportunities can be identified in an insurer's internal strengths and in its external opportunities. Strengths and opportunities that align create unique marketing opportunities such as the following:

- Insurer A has a nationally and internationally recognized identity. It is also positioned throughout the United States. Some of its managers have experience developing international products. Insurer A has been contacted by organizations in other countries that would like to form an alliance to offer insurance products in their countries. Insurer A is uniquely positioned to offer coverage internationally. International insurance would probably not be affected by Insurer A's current threats from other competitors that are experimenting with Internet sales.
- Insurer B is recognized in the watercraft industry, and its underwriters have remained informed of trends and practices in the watercraft industry. Insurer B has the opportunity to expand into new market areas such as insuring marinas, boat clubs, boat-building schools, and boat-rental agencies. These new product areas would probably not be affected by the international insurers that have entered the large yacht market.

Note that in the SWOT analysis, insurers' strengths have many facets, including the strengths of their employees. However, organizations sometimes overlook employees' strengths that might be in the form of activities and interests that take place outside of the workplace or experiences that employees have had in previous jobs.

Market Positioning

An insurer might also consider its position within the market and its competitors within that market. Generally, market positioning is considered by product line. An insurer might profile its position within the market as part of a SWOT analysis or as part of a marketing effort. **Market positioning** is demonstrated in Exhibit 3-3 for a group of insurers offering personal auto insurance.

Market positioning is the act of designing a set of meaningful differences to distinguish an insurer's products from the competitors' products so that the insurer's products occupy a distinct and valued place in the market.

Exhibit 3-3
Market Positioning Example for Personal Auto Insurance

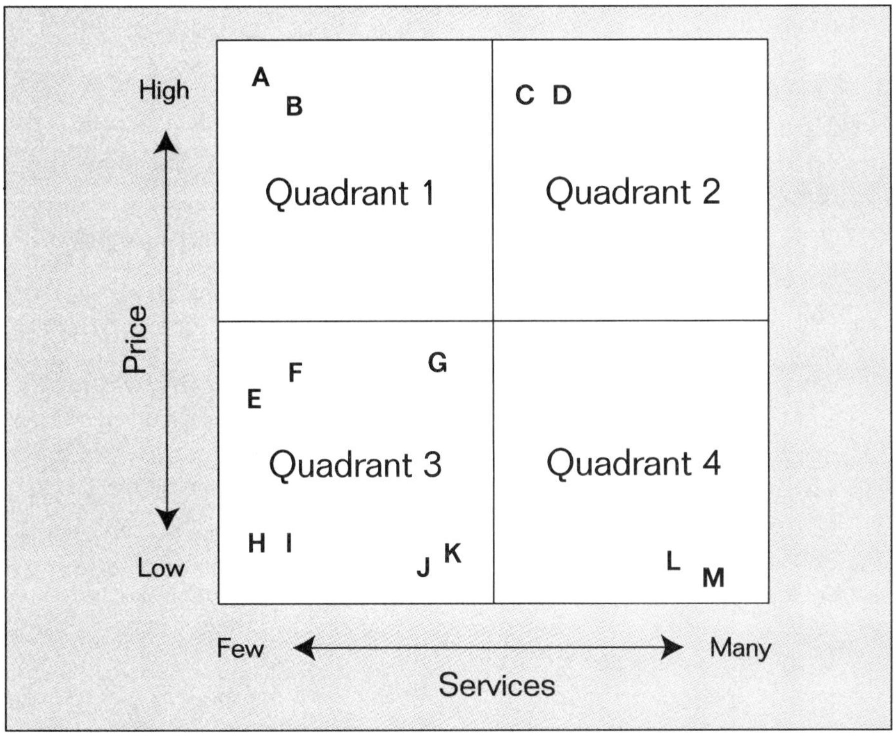

Exhibit 3-3 indicates market positioning, based on price and service (which is a comparison often made in the personal auto insurance market), for Insurers A through M. (Each letter represents an insurer plotted according to its position in the market regarding price and service.) The quadrants could represent the following:

- Insurers in Quadrant 1 (A, B) offer high prices and few services; they might be insurers of high-risk drivers.
- Insurers in Quadrant 2 (C, D) offer high prices and many services; they might be insurers specializing in affluent customers.
- Insurers in Quadrant 3 (E, F, G, H, I, J, K) offer low prices and few services; they might be insurers offering coverage through Internet distribution.
- Insurers in Quadrant 4 (L, M) offer low prices and many services; they might be insurers that have developed highly automated databases and processing systems.

When an insurer considers its competitors in a market as large as personal insurance, it cannot reasonably compare itself to all personal insurance companies in the market. Instead, an insurer should consider its market position and the competitors in a similar market position. For example, Insurers L and M do not compete with all of the other insurers plotted in Exhibit 3-3; they compete only with each other, just as Insurers A and B compete only with each other. These companies compare their prices and services as well as their product features against those of their immediate competitors to determine what strengths, weaknesses, opportunities, and threats appear in that comparison.

When factors such as price and service are very close, as they are with some insurers plotted in Exhibit 3-3, product features can become key competitive differences among insurers' products. For example, Insurer L is in close competition with Insurer M. Insurer L could offer expanded product features such as coverage in additional countries, such as Mexico. Insurer A is in close competition with Insurer B. Insurer A could offer a monthly payment plan for policy premiums as a competitive product feature.

In personal lines, auto and homeowners product lines are by far the largest coverage lines, and they are highly competitive markets. However, specialty product lines such as insurance for motorcycles, mobile homes, watercraft, and recreational vehicles are equally competitive within their own markets. Insurers specializing within a specific market segment are highly competitive among themselves for market share. Occasionally, an insurer can experience a period of time when it holds the largest share of the market within a geographic area. However, these periods are usually short-lived. For example, an insurer specializing in mobile homes might be strategically located in a city with booming industrial growth. Residential contractors might be unable to keep pace with construction demands. Mobile homes could be in extreme demand to meet immediate housing needs. That insurer might experience a near monopoly in that area in mobilehome insurance. However, competitive advantages in the United States do not usually last. Other insurers discover the opportunity and also take advantage of the lack of competition.

Educational Objective 4

Explain how insurers compete on the basis of product features, price, and service.

Educational Objective 5

Given a case situation, describe actions that a personal lines insurer could take to compete in the personal insurance market.

Product Features, Price, and Service

Insurers compete in the market through product features, price, and service. These competitive factors are fundamentally important in personal lines insurance. The actual development of insurance products and prices is described in detail in later chapters of this text. This chapter addresses these topics only as they apply to an insurer's competitive strategy.

Insurers balance the cost of the product with the potential profit that could result. For example, in competing with other insurers, an insurer might design its product to meet the needs of a market segment. The insurer could offer twenty-four-hour-a-day claim service to meet the needs of and attract customers who travel globally and require this type of service. The insurer must balance the cost of this expanded service with the potential revenue in premiums added or insurance policies retained to determine whether there is enough return to change the service it offers.

Jargon Alert!

Many insurers are moving to services provided twenty-four hours a day, seven days a week. Some insurers refer to this as *24 by 7* service, or simply *24-7*.

Enhancing Product Features

A product innovation can be a competitive advantage. For example, the insurer that was the first to package personal auto and homeowners insurance together with options for additional coverages such as personal umbrella or watercraft coverage gained a competitive advantage because value was added for the customer. The value added included the ease of having all insurance located in one contract. As another example, an insurer might provide a policy that is guaranteed not to be canceled or nonrenewed for a period of time such as five years; this adds the value of peace of mind for the customer.

Insurers frequently copy innovative ideas that are successful; therefore, insurers find it difficult to maintain a competitive advantage through product innovations that can be implemented easily. Only if a product advantage is difficult for other insurers to copy or if there is some barrier against other insurers applying the innovation can an insurer sustain an advantage for a prolonged period. As an example, the relationship-building databases described in Chapter 1 that allow insurers to engage in event marketing are difficult and expensive to construct. An insurer that invests in that technology will have a competitive advantage for a prolonged period of time. The expense of the construction is a barrier that prevents other insurers from copying the product feature. As another example, an insurer who develops and implements a product feature before regulation restricts other insurers from implementing a similar feature enjoys a competitive advantage while other insurers face a regulatory barrier prohibiting them from applying the same feature.

The following are additional examples of product features that could enhance preferred auto policies:

- Increased liability limits up to $10 million and up to $1 million in uninsured or underinsured motorists coverage
- Worldwide automobile liability coverage
- Agreed-value physical damage insurance that allows the customer to lock in the amount at which the car will be valued in the event of a total loss, eliminating the factor for depreciation used in settling most automobile insurance claims

- Original equipment coverage providing manufacturers' parts instead of after-market parts used in many vehicle repairs
- Lease gap options that cover the dollar difference between a car's current value at the time of a total loss and its lease buyout value
- Coverage to replace car locks if keys are lost or stolen

Again, any changed or added product features should provide a value added to the customer. This might be a need the customer has expressed or a feature that would fill a need that the customer has not recognized.

Using Pricing Strategies

Reducing prices while remaining profitable is difficult for an insurer. An insurer with an 85 percent renewal retention rate that cuts prices by 10 percent must increase new business sales by almost 60 percent just to keep the same written premium level it had before the price cut.[3] To effectively reduce prices, insurers must reduce one of the components of the costs associated with the premiums. Those components were displayed in Exhibit 1-3 in Chapter 1.

A company that can reduce its expenses can generate more profit and reduce prices as a competitive advantage. Remember from Exhibit 1-3 that the premium dollar allocation for property and liability insurance includes claims and claim expenses, operating expenses, taxes, and dividends. An insurer takes little direct action to reduce taxes, and dividends are an expectation of stockholders and policyholders that are also difficult to reduce without loss of financial support or loss of policyholders. The two components that an insurer can address are claims and operating expenses. Expense reductions can be achieved more easily in personal lines than in other areas of insurance because the policies and processes are relatively standard. Many of the claim handling functions and policy processing functions can be mechanized. Efficiency reduces expenses and increases an insurer's competitive advantage.

Controlling Claims and Claim Expenses

Because claims are such a significant portion of insurers' expenses, any change in claim expenses or controls that can be taken that is even marginally effective has a large effect on insurance company results and the premiums that insurers charge.

Insurers can act to reduce claims and claim expenses before losses occur and after they occur. Before a claim occurs, an insurer can take the following actions:

- Continually encourage effective underwriting to select risks with a lower loss frequency
- Implement a catastrophe management plan
- Educate insureds regarding their coverages to eliminate unnecessary claims or conflict when claims occur

- Encourage policyholders to engage in loss control activities by providing education about loss control and providing discounts for loss control measures
- Create a special investigative unit (SIU) to investigate potentially fraudulent claims
- Before a catastrophe occurs, create catastrophe teams, develop customer response centers at catastrophe locations, and train teams at the site of catastrophes

After a claim occurs, an insurer can take the following actions to reduce claim expenses:

- Act promptly to minimize claims
- Process claims efficiently
- Outsource claim investigation when necessary

Controlling Operating Expenses

One of the largest expenses for an insurance company is employee salary. Insurers attempt to maximize the efforts of employees through technology. When necessary, insurers reduce staff, reduce rent, reduce facilities, reduce expense accounts, centralize functions, and add more work requirements. This reduction can sometimes occur without the company's making sufficient changes to handle the additional work. The downside of staff reduction is the loss of expertise. Underwriting staff can be reduced too much to maintain the level of service that company strategy requires.

In an effort to control expenses, insurers might centralize functions and close branch offices. Again, these activities to control expenses must be carefully weighed against the lost services and expertise that can occur. Consolidating offices can create economies of scale by eliminating duplication in the management ranks and duplication in roles. Companies can go too far, however, in attempting to gain efficiencies by reducing costs; the net effect can be the opposite, that is, efficiencies are lost rather than gained. For example, an insurer attempted to gain efficiencies in policy processing. The insurer introduced automation in its processing system so that the system automatically ordered and reviewed motor vehicle reports. The insurer introduced the automated system and team activity in the processing center at the same time. The company estimated the number of employees that would not be needed as a result of the changes made, and the insurer laid off one-fifth of the policy processing staff members. However, the changes took longer to implement than the insurer anticipated. Also, the changes did not yield the efficiencies that were expected. In addition, it took longer than expected to train the staff in implementing the changes. As a result, the remaining policy processing staff members were frustrated, and many left the company. Those staff members who stayed with the company were expected to work overtime to process the applications and endorsements. Many employees were working parents who were unable to work additional hours. As a result, the insurer was unable to process many of the applications.

Some applications were over sixty days old before underwriters were able to review them. Some applications could not be canceled within the first sixty days, and they were, therefore, written regardless of underwriting intent. New policyholders were upset with the insurer, and the insurer was so late in processing premium payments that the net income of the company was reduced for months. In an effort to gain efficiencies, the company decreased service, expertise, and income.

Exhibit 3-4 demonstrates the potential benefits and drawbacks of cost-reduction activities and lists questions insurers can ask to help determine whether to undertake the activities.

Exhibit 3-4
The Benefits and Drawbacks of Cost-Reduction Activities

Activities	Potential Benefits	Potential Drawbacks	Questions To Ask
Reducing staff	Salary and benefits costs are reduced.	Expertise might be lost. The staffing cut could be too large.	• Do these employees have expertise that will be difficult to replace later? • Are we certain that the number of employees being reduced is not too large? • Are the remaining staff members sufficiently trained or otherwise available to handle any changes or increased responsibilities? • If training staff is reduced, who will assume responsibility for training employees?
Centralizing and consolidating offices	Salaries of employees performing duplicate functions are eliminated. The cost of maintaining multiple locations is eliminated.	Insurer loses local presence and expertise.	• Can we remain a competitive force in the market if we do not have a physical presence in the geographic area? • Is there duplication of effort that eliminating branch offices will resolve? • Are there any essential services offered at the branch office that cannot be duplicated at a central office? • Will centralization negatively affect loss experience through a lack of immediate knowledge of conditions in a geographic area? • Can increasing field travel by underwriters and insurer representatives offset the negative effects of centralization?

Activities	Potential Benefits	Potential Drawbacks	Questions To Ask
Reducing budget	Immediate savings	The short-term and long-term losses that result from budget cuts such as loss in benefits, reduction in capital expenses, or reduction in staff might be intolerable.	• What were the short-term and long-term benefits of the products and services no longer being purchased? • What is the worst-case scenario that can result from the budget reduction? • Is there another way to gain the benefits that might be lost?

Decreasing operating expenses does not always fit a company's strategies. Some large expenses are necessary to gain efficiencies or market share later. For example, an insurer that is focusing on services to policyholders might make a huge investment in a computer system for policy processing and record storage. A large investment in employee training would also be required to operate the new system. In addition, the human resource department would be investigating ways to retain the employees in whom the company has made a substantial training investment. All of the costs associated with this type of investment are made with the strategic plan of recouping the costs in the long run through reduced operating expenses with the use of the new system.

Merger is the combining of two or more companies into one organization.

Acquisition is the purchase of all or part of one organization by another.

Mergers and Acquisitions

In the last two decades, the trend among insurance companies has been toward **mergers** and **acquisitions** as growth strategies. With growth, the insurer can strengthen and build its internal resources. The new larger organization can gain technology, marketing, processing, and product line advantages that combine the strengths of the former separate organizations. The joined organizations can also eliminate redundant activities and functions to increase profit margins.

A **strategic business unit (SBU)** is a division within an organization that is defined for the purpose of measuring that division's productivity. These units are called *business units* or *profit centers*, or *silos*, by some insurers. (Note that the term *"silo"* can have negative connotations when it indicates divisions that have isolated objectives.)

Strategic Business Units

As insurers become larger, some insurers have implemented **strategic business units (SBUs)** within their organizations as a method of determining the productivity of segments of an insurer's organization. The purpose of creating SBUs is to measure the productivity of a unit, such as a line of business, a department, or a corporate division, and to compare it to the expenses required to operate that unit. Some SBUs are expected to operate at a financial break-even or to generate a profit. Some SBUs—such as human resources—operate to serve other SBUs. These units that serve others are sometimes called *shared-services*; they allocate portions of their expenses to other SBUs such as underwriting. In some organizations these allocations are called *bill-backs*. In this case, human resources would include the allocation as income while underwriting would include the allocation as an expense. **Zero-based budgeting** is often used in this type of system.

Zero-based budgeting is an internal budgeting process in which each business unit begins with no debt or credit. Each unit begins every fiscal year new with a zero balance in the budget.

An insurer can use SBU budgets and SBU results to determine whether it could save money by outsourcing an activity rather than operating the business unit or whether other changes are required. For example, if the cafeteria SBU estimates that its operating expenses for the year will be $250,000 but its income for the year will be $150,000, the insurer has the following choices:

- Outsource the cafeteria services to another vendor that can provide the same services for $150,000 per year.
- Allow the cafeteria to allocate the $100,000 loss to all other SBUs.
- Increase prices in the cafeteria to cover the $250,000 expenses per year.

A cafeteria provides a simple example of how decisions could be made based on SBU budgeting. Decisions involving integral insurer systems such as underwriting and claim handling SBUs are much more complicated.

SBUs can help companies determine whether the individual units within the organization are competitive or could be more efficient. This type of measurement can help the entire organization become and remain competitive. From a negative standpoint, SBUs can be cumbersome to manage, and they can create bickering between the SBUs over allocation charges without delivering value that reduces expenses or enhances the insurer's ability to compete. Exhibit 3-5 provides additional pros and cons of SBUs.

An insurer that is able to control expenses through increased efficiencies has a greater competitive advantage. An insurer might absorb financial gains as profit, invest in capital expenses to further increase efficiencies, or reduce premium to the policyholders. Any efficiencies that the insurer gains create more options for the insurer in meeting strategies.

Exhibit 3-5
Pros and Cons of SBUs Observed in Insurance Companies

Pros	Cons
• Each unit within the company is accountable for productivity. • Healthy competition between departments can result. • Units seek efficiency in operations. • Unit results can be compared from year to year. • Business decisions are improved. • Some services are shared to help manage expenses. • Units develop an awareness of how expenses affect results. • SBUs providing services to other SBUs will be pressured to offer effective services for the allocation charges, or the other SBUs will outsource to obtain the services they require.	• The implementation and tracking can require substantial effort. • The allocation process can create internal confrontation. • Accommodating risks whose policies cross over SBU lines is difficult. This can reduce service to customers. • The self-interests of the SBUs can block activities that benefit the entire company and the customers. • If an SBU does not like services that are allocated from another department, the SBU might build its own internal services, creating redundancies. The ultimate result is increased costs.

Using Service Strategies

Many service issues are not new. Insurers have traditionally addressed service by promoting customer service through improved interaction between employees and customers. This approach to service remains important; however, insurers are now taking strategic approaches to make service more comprehensive. The following are descriptions of some of those approaches that insurers use to improve service:

- *Event marketing.* As described in Chapter 1, event marketing involves collecting comprehensive information about a customer so that an insurer can anticipate triggering events in a customer's life. These triggering events indicate loss exposures and risks that might require advice and insurance coverage.
- *Event contact perspective*. Every contact with a policyholder, including renewal notices, billing notices, claim reporting phone calls, and policy changes, will be a positive, neutral, or negative experience for the policyholder. If a policyholder has enough neutral or negative contacts, he or she will consider changing to a company that potentially offers more positive contacts. Every contact (also called a *moment of truth*) is an opportunity to positively influence the customer's perception of the insurer. Every point of contact should be, if possible, a positive contact.
- *Service recovery*. When a contact with a policyholder is negative, some insurers perform a service recovery, which is a second contact with the policyholder to attempt to correct a problem or mistake. Positively handled, these service recovery activities can effectively build customer loyalty. For example, a policyholder calls a producer to complain about an error in a billing notice. The producer initiates the correction. One week later the producer performs a service recovery by calling the policyholder to ensure that the problem was corrected to the policyholder's satisfaction. The follow-up telephone call will leave the policyholder with a more positive impression regarding the insurer.
- *Call center management*. The objective of call center management is to make the insurer employee with the necessary expertise available to the customer when the customer is ready. One policyholder might require advice regarding auto insurance coverage after normal working hours. Another policyholder might need advice following a claim in the middle of the night. Call center management establishes the appropriate link between offices across the country or to an office that was established to handle after-hours questions and claims. After-hours services can also be outsourced.

Service is provided at many different levels in the insurance industry: from one department to the next, within departments, and from insurers to producers. The policyholders are the ultimate customers of the insurance company, and all service should be focused on meeting their needs. For example, a producer who is an employee of the insurer has a meeting with a policyholder. Just before the meeting, the vice-president of marketing schedules a mandatory conference call for all

> **FYI**
>
> *Best practices* describe the optimum ways to perform a business process. They are the means by which leading organizations have achieved top performance. They also serve as goals for other organizations striving for excellence.
>
> Many times, however, there is no single "best" way to perform a business process. *Best practices* should be evaluated in the context of an organization's business strategy. Therefore, *best practices* function more as a source of ideas rather than prescribed activities.

producers. A company with a customer focus will understand that the producer should attend the meeting with the policyholder. A company without that focus might believe that the conference call takes precedence over the client meeting.

Exhibit 3-6 provides *best practices* developed by the Independent Insurance Agents of America as guidelines for increasing efficiency and service in a personal lines agency. These guidelines are equally helpful for insurance companies.

Exhibit 3-6
Best Practices in Personal Lines

Hire the right people and train them:

- Your employees are an investment; hire people who can share the vision of the agency.
- Foster employee growth: Give employees a good work environment.
- Open communication is key. Hold staff meetings weekly.
- Share the agency's success with your employees. Pay for performance. The annual increase and/or bonus should be tied to sales and service goals, use of automation, retention of business, educational accomplishments, and teamwork.
- Customer service representatives (CSRs) should be coached to do a better job of meeting customers' needs. Help them role-play in asking questions about customers' insurance programs and recognizing cross-selling opportunities.
- Consider hiring retirees as part-time producers for your agency.

Focus on customers:

- Be selective. Do business with customers you can properly and profitably serve. The best agencies do not lose many clients.
- Adequately staff your agency to properly service your clients. Encourage your employees to think customers are their bosses.
- Be a consultant to your customers—not just a salesperson.
- Work as a risk manager on all accounts. Look out for the interest of your clients with an annual review on all accounts. Record all contacts with customers.
- Make sure your staff responds to every customer inquiry. Never hang up on a caller until all parties understand the next step. End every telephone conversation with, "Are you satisfied with us?"
- If you lose an account, find out why and solicit the account again for the next few years.

Focus on sales:

- Referrals are key: The warmest leads are your own customers. Soliciting referrals as a matter of doing business means you won't need to spend much time on cold calls.
- Think new business. Aggressively seek the kind of business and niches you want.
- Cross-sell. If you have a large portfolio of commercial lines, why not launch an effort to market personal lines to your business clients or the

employees of these clients? Ask every auto customer for his or her homeowners or renters insurance business. Other possibilities: floaters, flood, umbrellas, marine, RVs, disability and life, and financial services products.

Look for win-win relationships:

- Choose four or five carriers that make it easy for the agency to do business, offer some added value, and are competitive and committed to the market.
- Treat your companies with respect. Communicate with them clearly. Set firm performance expectations.

Evaluate your systems:

- Automation means a quick turnaround on work, cross-selling support, and faster service. Take advantage of it.
- Every employee in the agency should know how to access the computer system.
- Ask your employees to identify ways to improve your systems. Empowering them to take ownership of the improvements will give you better results.

Be a leader:

- Set an example for your employees. Successful agents work hard, and they emphasize integrity and honesty.
- Develop a clear vision or mission statement in cooperation with your staff. Allow that vision to influence every decision that is made.

Write it down:

- Put your sales strategies on paper. How will you assist your producers with warm leads? Where will new sales come from? List specific tactics you will take to complete your mission. For example, identify the number of new referrals and contacts your agency needs on an average day.

Set up profit centers:

- Organize your data to know exactly what you make in personal lines.
- View your commissions as value to your agency over time, rather than just annually. That will help you focus on long-term potential.

Adapted from Nadia R. Schulman, "Profiting in Personal Lines," *Independent Agent*, August 1998, p. 31.

Educational Objective 6

Describe team approaches to improve insurer service and gain efficiencies; describe elements of effective team management.

Team Approaches

A **team approach** is currently a popular method used by insurance companies to improve service and gain efficiencies. Teams are often made up of individuals who are involved in different functions within an insurance company. Each team member brings his or her expertise to the group to resolve a problem or to assist a customer.

A **team approach** is the use of temporary or ongoing task groups whose members are charged with working together to identify problems, to form a consensus about what should be done, and to implement necessary action in relation to a particular task or organizational area.[4]

Types of teams used in insurance companies depend on the need being addressed. The following are types of teams identified in insurance companies:

- *Cross-functional teams*. A cross-functional team includes members from two or more functions. A cross-functional team might be used to review a new insurance product being implemented to ensure that the insurer has addressed all possibilities that can affect service.
- *Virtual teams*. Virtual team members are not present in the same location. Using a common database and electronic correspondence, virtual team members can assist a customer, develop products, complete projects, and interact in many of the ways that teams in the same location can.
- *Process centers*. Some functional areas naturally fit well together to complete a specific type of transaction. For example, customer service representatives might work together as team members with underwriters to expedite customer requests for additions to coverage or policy changes. The request received by the customer service representatives can be immediately reviewed and processed by the underwriter.

Insurers consider which functions work together to achieve their strategies. Some combinations include underwriting and marketing, underwriting and customer service, and customer service and policy processing.

Team Management

The benefits of a team approach are efficiency and improved service to the customer. The drawback of a team approach is that it can cause infighting that reduces the service provided to customers. Key requirements for successful teams are the recognition and rewards that are given to the group as a team. Team members should have common team goals. Without them, team members will be more likely to work toward those goals that will individually provide each member with the greatest reward. The following are elements of effective team management:

- *Managers should expect, not reward, individual competence*. Competitive salaries, profit-sharing bonuses, and professional development opportunities are basic work force needs, not incentives. When used as rewards, they promote competition, not teamwork.
- *Recognition is often the best reward*. Recognize exceptional performance as long as it contributes toward the team's goals and objectives.
- *Develop broad-based team incentive plans*. Team financial incentive plans should reward all team members based on benchmarks that are measurable and have genuine value to the team. Less tangible organizational assets like learning, growth, and positive customer relationships should also be rewarded.[5]
- *Training*. Train individuals to work as a team. Team members should receive adequate training in interpersonal skills and team-building skills.

Educational Objective 7

Describe the benefits to an insurer of increasing customer retention and persistency; explain how insurers can increase retention and persistency.

Improving Retention and Persistency

Insurers recognize that new policies generate more losses than existing policies. Insurers generally anticipate a 5 to 15 percent higher loss ratio with new policies within their first two years compared to policies written for customers whom they have served for a longer period of time. The reason for this is that no matter how carefully underwritten, individuals prone to losses will apply and be issued insurance policies. Insurers include in their strategies activities aimed at increasing policy **retention** and policyholder **persistency** to reduce claim frequency and to continue to write those accounts that are known to be profitable.

Retention is the percentage of policies that are renewed at an anniversary. **Persistency** is a measurement of retained policies over a long period of time.

In addition, insurers reduce expenses by improving policy retention. Acquisition costs to initially write a policy are higher than the maintenance expenses to renew and retain the policy. Exhibit 3-7 indicates the importance of policy retention and policyholder persistency in reducing expenses.

Exhibit 3-7
Policy Retention Example

Each company initially has 1,000 personal auto policies with $1,000 premium per policy.		**Year 1**	**Year 2**	**Year 3**	**Year 4**	**Year 5**	**Cumulative five-year results (premiums-costs)**
Company X retains 90% of renewals.	Policy count	1,000	900	810	729	656	
	Premium	$1,000,000	$900,000	$810,000	$729,000	$656,000	$3,957,850
	Acquisition cost	$90,000	$0	$0	$0	$0	
	Maintenance cost	$0	$9,000	$32,400	$7,290	$6,560	
Company Y retains 80% of renewals.	Policy count	1,000	800	640	512	410	
	Premium	$1,000,000	$800,000	$640,000	$512,000	$410,000	$3,229,180
	Acquisition cost	–$90,000	$0	$0	$0	$0	
	Maintenance cost	$0	$8,000	$25,600	$5,120	$4,100	
Company Z retains 70% of renewals.	Policy count	1,000	700	490	343	240	
	Premium	$1,000,000	$700,000	$490,000	$343,000	$240,000	$2,650,570
	Acquisition cost	$90,000	$0	$0	$0	$0	
	Maintenance cost	$0	$7,000	$19,600	$3,430	$2,400	

In the example shown in Exhibit 3-7, each insurer began a five-year period of time with 1,000 personal auto policies. Each policy has a $1,000 premium. Acquisition expenses in the first year include external reports such as motor vehicle reports and credit reports, inspection and photographs of the automobiles by the producer, processing by the underwriter or automated screening system, and policy processing. In the second year, maintenance costs drop to $10 per year for policy issuance and routine policy changes. During the third year, the maintenance cost increases by an additional $30 when motor vehicle reports are rechecked. The only variable among the companies is the policy retention rate shown in the first column.

Over a five-year period, the results of Companies X and Z will vary by over a million dollars based only on policy retention differences. This does not even take into consideration the probable differences in claim losses experienced by the companies, the differences in investment income, or operating expenses. To maintain 1,000 policies, Company Z must incur the expense each year of acquiring 300 policies to replace the policies being lost. Because new policies in their first two years generally have more losses than an insurer's existing policies, Company Z will experience far more losses than Company X.

Based on analysis performed in 1996 by Tillinghast-Towers Perrin,[6] a 2 percent point improvement in retention, for example, from 85 percent to 87 percent, contributed up to 6 percent added value (increased premiums, in-creased capital for investments, reduced expenses, and improved loss ratio) for auto insurance product lines. For an insurer with $1 billion in premium, this improved retention translates into an additional $60 million in added value. A 5 percent improvement contributes added value up to $140 million.

Increased costs and increased losses prompt insurers to discover why they lose customers and to find effective methods for retaining those customers.

Why Insurers Lose Customers

Insurers lose customers for the following reasons:

- The insurers nonrenew the policies.
- The policyholders die.
- The policyholders move geographically.
- The policyholders have a change in lifestyle and no longer need the policies.
- The policyholders move their policies to another insurer.

The key for insurers is to retain those policies that the insurer wishes to retain. This might mean finding ways not to lose the policyholder to a competitor, or it could mean finding creative ways to retain policyholders through geographic changes and changes in lifestyles.

Methods for Retaining Customers

Insurers use a variety of methods to encourage policyholders to renew their existing policies. The following are incentives insurers use to encourage policy renewal:

- *Cross-selling.* One of the keys to customer retention is providing multiple policies so that the customer is not forced to purchase coverage from another insurer.

- *Persistency discounts*. Discounts might take the form of increasing percentage discounts for anniversaries of policy renewal or a flat percentage for policies renewed after a fixed anniversary year such as the second or fifth year.
- *Loss-free discounts*. Insurers reward policyholders who have experienced loss-free periods when their policies renew.
- *Multiple policy, combination, portfolio, and package policy discounts*. Discounts for multiple policies or policies that are combined in some form will encourage the policyholder to retain the policies with the same insurer. It is more effort for a policyholder to move a group of policies to another insurer than to move a single policy. The discount provides an additional incentive to renew the group of policies with the current insurer.

All of these efforts are aimed at encouraging retention of policyholders. Insurers are considering even more creative incentives and services that will encourage policyholder retention. Some insurers view their policyholders as members of an association and develop services that extend beyond traditional insurance policies. These services, such as procurement of a driving service (a service purchased for an annual fee that provides an established number of rides to the doctor's office, to the grocery store, or to other locations) when a member is no longer able to drive, establish a relationship between an insurer and a policyholder that is very difficult for another insurer to duplicate. The key is to focus on customer needs and to provide allied services, even if those services are beyond the services traditionally offered by insurers.

Tillinghast reported information in its study regarding effective measures to increase policy retention. That information is summarized in Exhibit 3-8.

Exhibit 3-8
Retention-Focused Activity

Retention-Focused Activity

In the contest to retain customers, there is a big difference between what effective companies know and do and what ineffective companies know and do. The following section describes examples of practices that clearly affect policy retention and examples of promising activities that might affect policy retention but are under-exploited or unexploited.

Proven Practices in Retaining Policies

The following practices have been used by insurers and have clearly increased policy retention:

- *Corporate-level commitment.* A commitment that begins in an insurer's executive offices is one of the best indicators that a company will be successful at customer retention.
- *Retention goals.* Explicit retention goals should be included in the insurer's corporate strategy.
- *Accountability and authority.* Accountability and authority should be given to a chief retention officer and/or a small group of senior managers

Continued on next page.

(usually regional managers and a senior management committee) to make changes.

- *Key measurements.* Customer retention should be made a key measure in an insurer's corporate objectives.
- *Initiatives.* Ongoing initiatives should be sponsored by the executive levels that are particularly focused on improving customer retention. These initiatives include maintaining a customer satisfaction index in a score card, training programs focused on customer service, household marketing campaigns, economic-value-added analysis of individual customers, and affinity marketing programs.

People Strategies To Strengthen Retention

A strong and positive correlation exists among customer retention and employee and producer tenure. Insurers with relatively low levels of turnover have superior customer retention results. In general, insurers that are effective at fostering loyalty in their own employees and producers follow effective practices for the following:

- Selection and deployment of employees in the organization
- Learning and development
- Rewards and recognition
- Performance management

Customer Focus as Part of All Operations

All insurers say they are customer-focused, but relatively few take action with programs that keep their attention squarely on their customers. Insurers with superior retention results do the following:

- Institute customer satisfaction measurement programs that survey policyholders, new customers, competitors' customers, claim customers, and lost customers to better understand how to meet or exceed expectations.
- Contact new customers in many ways before the first renewal, when customer retention is normally the lowest, using such methods as new customer orientation programs.
- Have specific customer service levels and standards in place to measure agent and employee performance.
- Offer multiple billing and payment options, including electronic funds transfer.
- Provide account billing for their customers.
- Offer extended service hours.
- Identify leading indicators of customer loss and develop programs to minimize it.

Practices Likely To Retain Policies

The following section describes practices that hold great promise to increase policy retention, but they have been under-exploited or unexploited by insurers.

Some insurers have begun using a flatter commission structure for new or renewal business, thus recognizing the value of ongoing customer relations and sharing the additional value with producers who have had higher retention rates.

Other suggestions for creating incentives that foster policy retention are the following:

- Bonuses for producers contingent on reaching or surpassing retention goals.
- Bonuses for producers contingent on increasing the number of policies written per household.

Retention-Focused Rate-Level Changes

Rate-level activity does affect retention, but few insurers actively measure the different effects a rate change will have on particular customers, and even fewer insurers attempt to explain rate changes to their customers. There is strong evidence that some large statewide rate increases have an adverse impact on retention that negates the gain from the rate increase. Smaller rate increases that are carefully communicated to policyholders could be more effective.

Adapted from Bruce C. Bassman and Jaimie Pickles, "Customer Defection: Into the Valley...," *Best Week—Property and Casualty,* May 4, 1998, pp. 29-30.

Summary

Forces that define the insurance product and characteristics of the personal insurance market combine with competition to form the environment in which personal lines insurers operate. An analysis of competition in personal lines insurance reveals characteristics of both perfect and imperfect competition.

Within the competitive environment, personal lines insurers compete on the basis of product features, price, and service. Insurers first decide how they should compete. A SWOT analysis is one method for making that decision. In a large market, insurers also analyze their market position. Market positioning can reveal additional information to add to the SWOT analysis. These or similar analysis tools help insurers develop their competitive strategy.

Once an insurer has established a strategy, it can take the following steps to become or remain competitive:

- Enhancing product features
- Using pricing strategies of controlling claims, claim expenses, and operating expenses
- Using service strategies such as team approaches

Improving policy retention and persistency is an important competitive strategy for all insurers. Retained policies have fewer claims, cost less to process, and produce more income that can be invested. An insurer that can increase retention and percentage can significantly increase its competitive advantage through reduced expenses. Insurers have many possible options for increasing retention.

Chapter Notes

1. Kathryn M. Bartol and David C. Martin, *Management* (New York: McGraw-Hill, Inc., 1994), pp. 168-169.
2. Bartol and Martin, p. 171.
3. Risk Information, Inc., "Falling Auto Insurance Rates Force All to Think Differently," *Auto Insurance Report*, August 17, 1998, p. 2.
4. Bartol and Martin, p. 487.
5. "Reward Teams, Not People," *People @ Work*, September 15, 1998, p. 5.
6. Tillinghast-Towers Perrin, *Improving Customer Retention—Personal Lines*, May 1998.

Developing Personal Insurance Products

Chapter 4

Educational Objectives

1. Explain how personal lines insurers identify the need for new products and services or changes in existing products and services by monitoring the external environment. (pp. 4-3 to 4-7)
2. Explain how personal lines insurers identify the need for changes in their existing products and related services by monitoring policies in force, new policy count, and policy retention. (pp. 4-7 to 4-11)
3. Based on a change in a key indicator for a portfolio, explain how an insurer determines the reason(s) for the change. Describe the type of investigation an insurer might perform to determine the reason for a change. (pp. 4-11 to 4-17)
4. Describe the product, related services, or underwriting changes that can address problems identified in a personal insurance portfolio. Describe the limitations of the possible changes. (pp. 4-17 to 4-20)
5. a. Describe the costs and benefits associated with a new product or a product change.
   b. Explain how insurers choose among new product or product change ideas. (pp. 4-20 to 4-23)
6. Describe the purpose and the components of a product proposal. (pp. 4-23 to 4-26)

Outline

Chapter 4

Developing Personal Insurance Products

A **portfolio** is a group of policies with common characteristics, such as type of coverage or territory. As a group, these policies are analyzed for losses, change in the group size, and trends. A portfolio is also called a portfolio of policies, a portfolio of risks, or a book of business.

Portfolio management is broadly defined as the activity involved in developing new insurance products, changing existing insurance products, establishing profitability goals, pricing products, managing profitability, and managing operations associated with a portfolio of insurance policies.

The first three chapters of this text presented a view of the environment in which personal insurance operates. All insurance companies that offer personal insurance products deal with market pressures, competition, and other forces in the personal insurance arena. This section of the text examines actions taken by individual insurance companies to operate within the dynamic personal insurance market. As the forces, pressures, and competition in the market change, insurance companies' staff members monitor changes in the environment and changes in the profitability of the insurer's **portfolios**. The staff members can then act to increase company profitability. This text uses the term **portfolio management** to describe this activity by insurance companies.

The term portfolio management has no universally accepted definition. In it broadest sense, it is any activity associated with a portfolio of insurance policies directed at establishing and achieving the financial goals of the insurer. Mutual and reciprocal exchange insurers might also have goals and activities aimed at meeting their customers' insurance needs. Some insurers use the term portfolio management only in association with the problem correction processes, while other insurers use the term to encompass pricing, product development, monitoring, and problem correction.

However the term portfolio management is used, it is the activity that differentiates underwriting in commercial lines from underwriting in personal lines. The focus of underwriting for large commercial policies tends to concentrate on the specific loss exposures of individual accounts and the appropriate application of coverages and pricing for the individual accounts. However, the focus of personal lines underwriting tends to concentrate on the management of a portfolio. Personal lines policies are highly standardized with little modification available. As a group, policies are priced, monitored, and modified to meet established goals. This approach to personal lines insurance does not diminish the need to understand the specific coverage, loss exposures, or hazards associated with personal lines policies. On the contrary, insurance company staff members who make portfolio management decisions must thoroughly understand the underwriting of individual policies to effectively manage a portfolio. Further, insurance companies that have automated underwriting processes for personal lines rely on staff members who can manage a portfolio and correct computerized policy-screening criteria based on an understanding of the selection criteria used for individual policy underwriting.

This text describes portfolio management in its broadest sense and organizes the facets of portfolio management as follows:

- Chapter 4: Developing personal insurance products
- Chapter 5: Underwriting profitability for personal insurance
- Chapter 6: Pricing personal insurance products
- Chapter 7: Reunderwriting personal insurance portfolios
- Chapter 8: Gaining efficiencies in personal insurance operations

For the purpose of instruction, activities are described separately in these chapters. In reality, insurance company staff members may perform these activities simultaneously. For example, a staff member examining a portfolio of homeowners policies that is experiencing poor results compared to the goals established will consider many possible causes for the problems that might create the discrepancy. The staff member will consider product changes needed to attract customers, the rationality for the goals, the need for pricing adjustments, loss patterns that are damaging the profitability, and overall operations or processes within the insurance company that might improve results.

This chapter begins the examination of managing the profitability of an insurance portfolio. Insurers identify the need for new products and services or changes to existing ones by collecting information from internal and external environments. In addition, insurers monitor key indicators within a portfolio of policies. When changes are identified in key indicators, staff members determine the reasons and make any corrective changes needed. New products and services or changes to existing ones are undertaken only after significant research.

Educational Objective 1

Explain how personal lines insurers identify the need for new products and services or changes in existing products and services by monitoring the external environment.

Identifying Customer Needs

Insurers identify the potential need for new products or services, or changes in existing products and services, by monitoring the following:

- Internal staff reports
- Current customer trends
- Emerging trends
- Marketing research

After insurers identify potential needs, they can determine the customer requirements and the extent of the customer demand through market research.

Internal Staff Reports

Insurers rely on all individuals within their organizations to provide information from customers and the insurance market that can lead to new product development. The following are examples of this type of information and possible product development indicated:

- Customer service representatives report repeated questions from customers about the difficulty in understanding payment plan options. This can indicate the need to develop new payment options, clarify current billing information, or provide Internet access to customers' billing and payment summaries.
- Producers report their increased use of premium financing to offer extended payment plans to customers. This can indicate the need to develop credit card options for payments, automated fund transfers from checking accounts, or payment plans offered directly from the insurer.
- Claim representatives report customers' confusion regarding the coverage provided by the homeowners policy for items located in rented storage units. This can result in a clarification of the of the policy wording or an endorsement providing coverage requested by customers.
- Underwriters report an increase in homeowners policy applications indicating that applicants are self-employed and work from their homes. However, the applications do not include requests for endorsements to extend liability or property coverages to the business exposures. This can indicate the need for products tailored to individuals who work from their homes, customer and producer education, and special assistance to new customers who are entrepreneurs.

For an insurer to collect and use the type of data that insurance company employees can provide, the insurer must do the following:

1. *Create an easy system for reporting.* An insurer should have a mechanism for employees to easily report this information as part of their regular activities. A system that relies on additional activities can overburden employees who must perform multiple steps for each transaction.
2. *Develop a system for collecting reported data.* The insurer should have a system for collecting and analyzing the data. Patterns of recurring events should be identifiable.

3. *Translate collected data into potential new products and services*. Staff members can analyze the recurring problems to identify the customer needs that are not being met, the potential new products or services the insurer could offer, and the advantage to the insurer of developing the new products or services.

Current Consumer Trends

Current customer needs can be identified by tracking consumer trends and demographics in the news media, journals specializing in demographics, consumer trend publications, and numerous other sources that provide information about purchasing patterns. The following are examples of current customer trend indicators:

- The sale of light trucks and sports utility vehicles makes up almost half of all private passenger automobile sales.
- The majority of baby boomers are in their late 40s or 50s.
- An increasing percentage of hotel customers are people age 50 and older.
- Over 50 percent of all college students are working adults.
- The cost of computers is dropping.

Such indicators can provide clues regarding needed insurance for property and liability loss exposures. For example, if over 50 percent of college students are working adults, it is likely that a high percentage of these individuals have computers to complete their studies, research, and required papers. Since the cost of computers is dropping, the demand for new specialized homeowners endorsements to cover computers has decreased. However, these individuals are probably becoming more Internet proficient through the completion of their studies. So, sales and services provided through the Internet might be more attractive to this group of individuals.

Using the same list of current customer trend indicators, another possible clue regarding the need for insurance can be found in the increased purchase of the sports utility vehicles, hotel spending, and the increasing age of the baby boomers. Some demographic journals indicate the baby boomers are seeking the safety afforded by larger and heavier vehicles, and they are seeking safe adventures in the form of cross-country road trips. If this is true, an insurer that specializes in personal automobile insurance and related services for the owners of these vehicles could attract this market. Possible product features might include lower premiums for mature drivers and increased coverage for transportation expense after an accident. Claim reporting and handling services throughout the United States could also be attractive to this group.

Emerging Trends

While current customers' needs can be identified from internal company sources and current customer trends, emerging customer or mar-

Environmental scanning is the process of (1) identifying factors that are crucial for an organization's success or failure in the marketplace, (2) defining signals or events that affect the factors, and (3) determining the implications of the signals or events.

ket trends require projections and assumptions based on **environmental scanning.** In an environmental scan, an organization will consider factors that are crucial in its success or failure in a marketplace. For example, Countdown Auto Mutual is an insurer with a large portfolio of nonstandard automobile insurance. Countdown might define the following success factors:

- At least 80 percent of all families in the United States will continue to drive individually owned or leased automobiles as their primary source of transportation.
- At least 15 percent of the population will not be able to purchase insurance through the standard personal automobile insurance market because of their driving record, loss history, or vehicle related exposures.
- State regulations involving personal automobile policies will not change substantially in the next five years.
- The number of insurers in the nonstandard auto market will remain unchanged.

Countdown will then look for signals or events that could change any of the factors. These could be economic, political, social, cultural, technological, competitive, distribution related, or consumer demand trends. Consider how the following hypothetical announcements could affect Countdown's success factors:

- A news release announcing a national bill to add a thousand commuter trains in major urban areas
- A publication by an insurance researcher announcing a decreasing trend in driving under the influence (DUI) violations
- An announcement by a large insurance competitor that it plans to withdraw from the nonstandard automobile insurance market within the next year

Each of these would alter Countdown's success factors and change its chances of successfully marketing its product. For example, the increase in commuter trains could decrease the number of individually owned automobiles; the decrease in DUI violations could increase the percentage of drivers who can purchase insurance from standard insurance markets; the withdrawal of a competitor from the market could open the available market to the remaining companies offering nonstandard automobile insurance. Countdown would then project the outcome based on the events occurring, identify a preferred outcome, and implement changes to improve the chances of the preferred outcome occurring. The outcome might be new products and services or changes to those that are already offered.

Marketing Research

When insurance company staff members identify current or emerging customer needs, they attempt to gather as much information as possible before taking any action. Changes in insurance products and services involve significant resources that could be used for other projects. Insurers perform marketing research to determine whether the assumptions made about the customers' needs and trends as well as any proposed products and services are correct.

There are many methods for performing marketing research. A common method is to conduct **focus groups** to test the customers' needs that have been assumed. Because focus groups involve a limited number of people, an insurer might follow up by surveying a large number of people to determine whether the opinions expressed in a focus group are held by a significant percentage of the customers or potential customers. For example, an insurer's marketing staff might hold a series of focus groups to ask for opinions about the need for a package policy combining personal auto and homeowners coverages, the appropriate discount to offer for a package policy, and the other endorsements or features that should be offered. The focus groups might indicate that package policies are unnecessary, but the people in the groups instead discuss their fear of being canceled for a small loss. They state that a guarantee that they would not be canceled after a loss-free period of five years would be an attractive product feature. Before the insurer invests money in developing such a feature, it surveys thousands of customers and potential customers to determine (1) whether they have the same fear of being canceled and (2) whether a guarantee would be an attractive policy feature.

A **focus group** is a small group of customers or potential customers brought together to provide opinions about a specific product, service, needs, or other issue. Focus groups provide qualitative data regarding customers' opinions through open discussion.

Educational Objective 2

Explain how personal lines insurers identify the need for changes in their existing products and related services by monitoring policies in force, new policy count, and policy retention.

Identifying the Need for Changes in Existing Products

In addition to the methods used for identifying the need for new products and services, insurers also identify the need to change their existing products and related services by monitoring their portfolio for indications of problems or opportunities. Insurers monitor many key indicators in a portfolio to identify changes over a period of time or differences from portfolios in the industry.

Key indicators and their measurements used for identifying needed product changes include policy in force (PIF) count, new policy count, and retention percentage. In addition, the **risk profile** of a portfolio is monitored to identify changes that can increase or decrease exposures to loss, which might require a product change.

The **risk profile** of a portfolio is a set of characteristics common to all risks in a portfolio.

Insurance company staff members might have data available only in a computerized list. Graphs and charts help to visually demonstrate changes and comparisons. Comparisons of key indicators to goals established for a line of business are also helpful to determine whether the insurer is meeting its goals in that product line.

Insurers collect and monitor many other data, such as premium and loss data. However, the key initial indicators of an insurer's success are its ability to attract and retain policyholders and increase the overall size of the portfolio. A portfolio of sufficient size can then be priced and managed to achieve an insurer's profitability goals. Without adequate size, a portfolio can have large fluctuations in results based on a relative small number of losses. Large fluctuations make managing and pricing a portfolio difficult as demonstrated in the following chapters.

Policies in Force: A Key Indicator for Product Changes

The PIF is the number of policies that are effective at any point in time. The PIF is measured monthly, quarterly, and annually. Annual goals for PIF are often compared to the actual count during a year to monitor the growth or reduction in a portfolio's size. Exhibit 4-1 provides an example of the PIF for the ABC Insurance Company. The PIF is plotted in a chart to visually demonstrate trends.

Exhibit 4-1
PIF Indicators of Effects of Product Changes

ABC's PIF Data (000s)

Year	Annual Goal	Actual Count
1998	10	12
1999	11	14
2000	15	24
2001	19	19
2002	22	23
2003	25	25
2004	29	33 (YTD)
2005	31	

ABC's PIF Chart

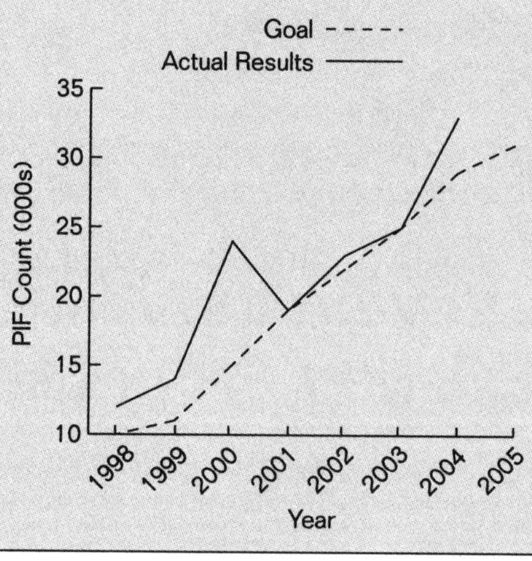

The data in Exhibit 4-1 might suggest that ABC's PIF far exceeded the annual goal in 2000. However, the chart comparing the overall actual results to the goals demonstrates a long-term increase in PIF that has paralleled the projected growth goal. The chart provides a clearer picture of the development of the portfolio. In addition, ABC's staff members can identify the effects of product changes on the PIF. For example, the sudden growth in ABC's PIF in 2000 might have been the result of another insurance company withdrawing from a state because of unacceptable losses. By tightening underwriting guidelines in subsequent years, ABC was able to restrict the addition of new policies with unacceptable loss exposures.

Jargon Alert!

YTD, a common abbreviation for *year to date* means that the data reflects only that information collected so far during a current year.

New Policy Count: A Key Indicator for Product Changes

The new policy count, also called the new business count, is the number of new policies that are written during a period of time, such as a quarter or a year. The counts for quarters and years are often depicted in a bar graph to demonstrate trends. Comparison of various portfolios, or segments within portfolios, is helpful in illustrating where growth is occurring. Exhibits 4-2 and 4-3 provide examples of new policy count data and a bar graph depicting the data.

Exhibit 4-2
New Business Count Indicators for Product Changes

ABC's New Business Count (000s)

Year	Total for Portfolio
1998	9.5
1999	9.2
2000	9.8
2001	10.3
2002	10.2
2003	11.6
2004	9.9 YTD

Bar Graph for Total

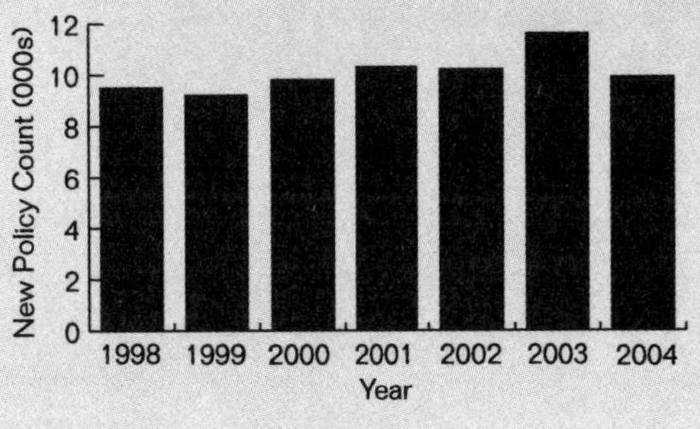

Exhibit 4-3
New Business Count Indicators for Product Changes Shown by Territory

ABC's New Business Count by Territory (000s)

Year	Territory I	Territory II	Territory III
1998	2.3	0.2	7.0
1999	1.8	0.6	6.8
2000	2.2	1.3	6.3
2001	2.4	2.3	5.6
2002	2.0	3.1	5.1
2003	2.2	4.0	5.4
2004	1.3 YTD	4.6 YTD	4.0 YTD

Bar Graph by Territory

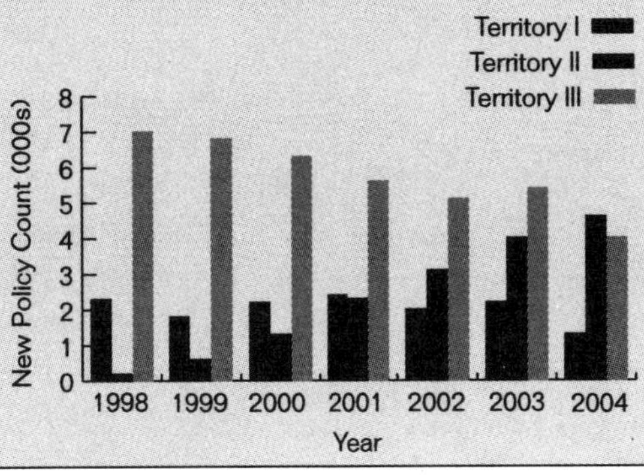

ABC's data provided in Exhibit 4-2, shows that the new business count for the entire portfolio appears to be growing steadily. However, an examination by territory within the portfolio, as shown in Exhibit 4-3, reveals that Territory I's new policy count is relatively stable, Territory II's new policy count is increasing dramatically, and Territory III's new policy count is steadily declining. Without an examination of the new policies by territory as demonstrated in a bar graph or chart, the changes in the territories would not have been apparent. ABC's staff members can now identify the reasons for the decline in

Territory III and the dramatic increase in Territory II. Based on the reasons identified, staff members might make product changes.

In addition, ABC staff members might consider other divisions of information to further analyze the new business growth in this portfolio. If this information represents personal automobile policies, an analysis of the new business by driver classification could indicate the types of drivers and vehicle uses that ABC is accepting on new policies. If, for example, an unusually high number of drivers were using their vehicles in their businesses, ABC's staff members would perform additional investigations to determine why this is occurring.

Policy Retention: A Key Indicator for Product Changes

Policy retention is usually shown as the percentage of policies that are renewed, and retention is most frequently measured on an annual basis. Insurers want to retain their current profitable business. Current policyholders have a known history with the insurance company, additional expense is not required to attract them to place their coverage with the insurer, and current policyholders represent a continuous stream of renewal premiums.

Changes in the insurance people purchase sometimes reflect customer trends. Demographics of the population, overall consumer attitudes, and property values can change the nature of loss exposures and insurance needs. These trends do not necessarily reflect customers' satisfaction or dissatisfaction with their insurer. For example, a growing segment of consumers might be renting their homes and moving into assisted living facilities. For this reason, all insurers that sell homeowners insurance could experience an overall drop in the retention of homeowners policies. Therefore, it is often useful to compare policy retention rates to industry retention rates. Results that are significantly higher or lower than retention rates experienced by the entire industry indicate possible problems or changes required.

Assume that you are a member of ABC's staff reviewing the policy retention data that appears in Exhibit 4-4. Further assume that this data is for a portfolio of homeowners policies, and the portfolio is for a territory covering six states. Viewed in isolation, ABC's data provides little information other than displaying a retention percentage that has dropped slightly over the last several years. However, when the data are compared to the industry results for the same time period, ABC's results become clearer. ABC is actually retaining more homeowners policies than the industry average in the last several years shown. However, as ABC's staff member, you should ask additional questions to fully understand the retention experienced by this portfolio:

- Is the industry's average retention for homeowners policies the same as the average for the six states in this portfolio?

- What is the retention rate for each state within the portfolio, and how does that compare to the state averages for the industry?
- Are there any other retention rates that we should monitor, such as retention by Coverage A limit? This would indicate whether we are losing homeowners policies for higher or lower valued homes.

Exhibit 4-4
Policy Retention Indicators for Product Changes

ABC's Policy Retention Data

Year	ABC's Retention
1998	76
1999	77
2000	77
2001	77
2002	76
2003	76
2004	76 (YTD)

Retention Compared to Industry Results

Retention (percentage)	1998	1999	2000	2001	2002	2003	2004
Industry Results (average)	77	78	77	76	75	75	74
ABC Insurance Company	76	77	77	77	76	76	76
ABC's Variance to Industry	−1	−1	0	+1	+1	+1	+2

Year

Educational Objective 3
Based on a change in a key indicator for a portfolio, explain how an insurer determines the reason(s) for the change. Describe the type of investigation an insurer might perform to determine the reason for a change.

Determining the Reasons for Changes in Portfolios

Based on the changes identified in the key indicators, insurers ask additional questions, make assumptions, and perform investigations to determine the reason for the changes. These activities guide corrective actions by staff members, if any change is required. The problem-solving activities are unique to each insurance company. While some insurers take an analytical approach by collecting and analyzing data in sequential steps, other insurers take a more intuitive approach by asking questions and investigating likely reasons for changes.

In the following section, two approaches are examined:

1. Risk profile analysis
2. Investigations based on questions

Risk Profile Analysis

A risk profile is a snapshot at a point in time that provides data about the characteristics of the policies in a portfolio. Such snapshots might be taken monthly, quarterly, or annually and might be compared to goals established by the insurer, although not all insurers establish goals at this frequency. By comparing these risk profiles over a period of time, an insurer's staff members can better understand changes in the portfolio. The staff members can then begin to analyze the importance of those changes. Exhibit 4-5 provides an example of such a risk profile for a homeowners portfolio. The data captured and displayed in a risk profile depends on the type of policies in the portfolio, the extent of the insurer's database, and the concerns of the insurer's staff members. For a portfolio of policies written in the Northeast United States, data about the roofs and ice dam prevention might be captured. For a portfolio of policies written in the Southeast United States, data about the distance to the ocean or gulf would be included. A risk profile for houses in arid areas might include data about cooling systems.

Exhibit 4-5
Risk Profile Indicators for Product Changes

ABC's Risk Profile for the Northwest Homeowners Territory
(Averages)

Year	Coverage A Amount	Age of Dwelling (in years)	Age of Policy (in years)	Percentage With Wood Shingles	Percentage of Losses per 100 Policies	Percentage in Protection Class 10
1998	150,000	10	5	9	.5	1
1999	151,000	11	5	9	.75	2
2000	153,000	11	5	10	.80	2
2001	155,000	10	4	11	.85	3
2002	157,000	11	5	12	.90	4
2003	156,000	12	6	14	1.1	5
2004	156,000	13	6	15	1.2	5

Making Assumptions and Verifying Information

Insurance company staff members must make assumptions based on data and attempt to verify that their assumptions are correct.

Exhibit 4-5 reveals several trends in the risk profile:

- Coverage A was increasing slowly; however, it has not increased in the last three years.
- The average age of the houses is increasing, and the average age of the policies is also increasing. This could mean that more policies are being retained, but fewer new homes are being written on new policies.

- The risk profile includes the percentage of homes with wood shingle roofs as well as the percentage of homes that are in protection class 10 areas, which are homes without fire protection due to their isolated locations. Houses in isolated and heavily forested areas are at high risk of losses from forest fires. This problem can be compounded when houses have wood shingle roofs that have not been properly treated with fire retardant chemicals. For this portfolio, the class 10 and wood shingle roof percentages are increasing, indicating a possible overall increase in loss exposures.
- The number of losses per policy is increasing.

If the retention information in Exhibit 4-4 and the risk profile information in Exhibit 4-5 is based on the same portfolio, you might come to an overall assumption:

> The retention for this portfolio is slightly better than industry average, but we are increasing our percentage of (1) older homes, (2) unprotected homes, and (3) homes with wood shingle roofs. Each of the factors can increase the fire loss exposure. In addition, the average Coverage A is dropping when compared to inflation and increasing construction costs. Therefore, the portfolio has an increasing loss exposure from fire and a decreasing Coverage A value.

Before recommending changes, you should ensure that your assumptions are correct and be prepared to answer questions that might be asked about your assumptions, such as the following:

- Are the houses in unprotected areas also the houses with wood shingle roofs?
- Is the increase in older homes a result of older homes being written as new policies or an aging of the policies that are being retained?
- Do the states where the houses are located have building codes requiring chemical treatment of wood shingle roofs, and how effectively are the building codes enforced?

These questions might require additional research of data available for this portfolio to confirm that the assumptions are correct. Staff members must also be informed regarding the relevant issues in the territory and states they are reviewing. Once the assumptions are confirmed or revised, with as much confidence as possible, corrective changes can then be made to reduce the loss exposures or increase the rates to reflect the increased potential for losses.

Working With Imperfect Data

Insurance company staff members must often work with less than perfect data. Data that would be ideal to test assumptions might be unavailable because it has not been collected on the policy applications or in a computer database. Also, data might be difficult to use because the collection techniques changed during the years being reviewed. Using Exhibit 4-5 as an example, assume that the ABC's homeowners applications have included a question about the type of roof material since 1995. However, ABC did not strictly enforce the completion of that question until 2002. As a result, the percentage of houses in the portfolio with wood shingle roofs might not have increased; the data collection method might be the only variable. Therefore, insurance company staff members work with a degree of uncertainty. Staff members increase their ability to accurately analyze data with experience and knowledge regarding the insurance company's history and activities, the portfolio, the territory, and the loss exposures involved.

Investigations Based on Questions

Exhibit 4-6 presents types of changes in the key indicators that insurers look for, the questions they ask, and possible investigations that staff members might perform as a result. Many possible questions and investigations can result from changes in key indicators. In the examples presented in Exhibit 4-6, notice that questions and investigations seek to answer the following global questions:

- Why have the key indicators changed?
- What are the possible reasons for the change?
- What are the possible consequences of the change?

Exhibit 4-6
Changes in Key Indicators, Resulting Questions, and Possible Investigations

Changes in Key Indicators *What change has occurred in the portfolio?*	**Questions**		**Possible Investigations**
The PIF is decreasing.	Does our current product meet our customer's needs?	Yes	☐ If both the new business count and retention are decreasing, identify possible changes in the demographics of customer population. Are fewer customers available for this portfolio? ☐ Identify the percentage of the available market that has been written in the portfolio over the previous years. If the portfolio is maintaining the same percentage of available market but the market is shrinking, consider expanding the current market or adding additional markets.
		No	☐ Graph the history of the PIF with the new policy count.
		Unsure	☐ Perform a focus group and/or survey to identify customers' needs and satisfaction with the current product. ☐ Contact customers who have nonrenewed or canceled coverage to identify the reason for the action. Compare the results with previous measurements.

Changes in Key Indicators *What change has occurred in the portfolio?*	**Questions**		**Possible Investigations**
The PIF is increasing faster than expected.	Are there any other factors in the market that we need to be aware of? Are competitors taking any of the following actions? ☐ Reducing PIF ☐ Withdrawing from the market ☐ Increasing their premiums ☐ Reducing coverage	Yes	☐ Identify the reasons for the competition's reduction in PIF. ☐ Identify loss exposures covered by the policies that might be underpriced. Seek adequate pricing for the loss exposures and hazards written. ☐ Judge the risk factors involved in writing policies that other companies are abandoning or repricing. ☐ Review underwriting guidelines and the adherence to those guidelines to avoid adverse selection.
		No	☐ Determine the marketing activities or product features that are generating positive results so that they can be duplicated, repeated, or reinforced.
		Unsure	☐ Obtain copies of state rate filings by competitors to identify the justifications for rate changes. ☐ Determine the justifications given by competitors for their withdrawals from the markets.
The new policy count is decreasing.	Have conditions in the market changed? Are any of the following present in the market? ☐ New competitors ☐ Lower prices offered by existing competitors ☐ More coverage services offered by competitors ☐ New innovations that better meet customers' needs ☐ Problems with the product that make it difficult for producers to understand or sell	Yes	☐ Benchmark a successful insurer's products or services and develop innovations to compete or exceed the competitor's efforts. ☐ Accept the decline in new policy count and work to retain the existing policyholders. ☐ Find other markets or market niches that offer better opportunities for new policy growth. ☐ Correct the problems that are preventing producers from selling the product.
		Unsure	☐ Compare the new policy count in a chart over the last decade or more if data are available. Compare the increase or decline in new policy count to the overall growth goals for the portfolio.
The new policy count is increasing faster than expected.	Are we accepting any loss exposures that might increase our loss ratio?	Yes	☐ Determine the loss exposures that are being accepted and the adequacy of the pricing for those exposures. If pricing is inadequate, (1) adjust underwriting guidelines to limit the extent of the exposures assumed or (2) increase the pricing for the exposures to adequately cover expected losses.

Continued on next page.

Changes in Key Indicators *What change has occurred in the portfolio?*	**Questions**		**Possible Investigations**
		No	☐ Graph and compare the history of the new policy count for segments (such as by territory, by producer, or by coverage limits) to identify segments of growth and decline within the portfolio. Project the overall risk profile change of the portfolio based on the new business. Determine whether the projected change will be favorable or unfavorable. For example, is all of the growth occurring in a territory that experiences a high or low frequency of losses?
		Unsure	☐ Gather data for all new policies written in the portfolio since the growth in new policy count began. Create a profile of the new policies to identify the characteristics of the new policies that are different from the existing policies. For example, if 40 percent of all new personal automobile policies are written for sports cars, but only 20 percent of the existing portfolio of policies are written for sports cars, the disparity might indicate a premium that is low compared to other insurers or underwriting guidelines that are not as rigorous as other insurers. ☐ Identify the prior insurance companies that customers are transferring from and detect any patterns. Insurance companies that are limiting policy writing or increasing premiums in a segment of policies might cause an increase in unexpected loss exposures.
The policy retention rate is higher than industry average.	Should we duplicate our activity in this portfolio in other portfolios?	Yes	☐ Identify the satisfying features that are retaining policyholders (such as price, service, coverage, and so forth). Determine the possibility of duplicating the features in other portfolios.
		Unsure	☐ Determine whether the portfolio profile is stable and if the accounts that are being retained are those that are profitable. ☐ Graph the retention rate by division (such as by territory, producer, or type of policy) within a portfolio over the past ten years, if possible. Graph the retention rate by the industry for similar policies over the same period of time. Note differences in the retention rates between the industry and the insurer. Determine whether any of the divisions with high retention rates represent an increase in loss exposure that has not been anticipated in the pricing.

Changes in Key Indicators *What change has occurred in the portfolio?*	**Questions**		**Possible Investigations**
The policy retention rate is lower than industry average.	Are the policyholders we are losing the ones who we would like to have retained?	Yes	☐ Identify the lost policies for the past several years. Tabulate the reasons for the attrition of accounts that the insurer would have preferred to retain. Beginning with the most frequently occurring reason for losses, identify methods for reducing future policy losses.
		No or Unsure	☐ Identify the lost accounts for the past several years that the insurer would have preferred to retain. Determine the reason the policies were nonrenewed or canceled.

Educational Objective 4

Describe the product, related services, or underwriting changes that can address problems identified in a personal insurance portfolio. Describe the limitations of the possible changes.

Making Corrective Changes

A portfolio that is losing PIF, failing to gain new policies, or deteriorating in policy retention could be failing to compete in one of the basic insurance marketing features: product, price, or service. If the insurer is marketing through independent agents, the product might not be competitive within the agents' available products. In addition, the underwriting guidelines might be too restrictive. The following is a description of corrective product changes an insurer might make to address the product, service, or underwriting problems identified in a portfolio. The issue of personal insurance pricing is often crucial in the competitive environment of personal insurance, and adjustments to prices require extensive examination. For these reasons, the subject of pricing personal insurance policies, as well as corrections in pricing, are addressed in Chapter 6 of this text.

Product Changes

If an insurance product does not meet the customers' needs, or if customers are being attracted to the policy coverage offered by another insurance company, an insurer can change the policy language, create additional endorsements to meet specific needs, or package coverages to better meet customers' coverage requirements. Each of these possible changes presents additional issues to consider within the personal insurance market.

Contract Change Issues

When the loss of customers is due to coverage needs that are not being met, the insurer might change the contract to better meet the customers needs. Insurers must be responsive to customers; however, insurers must also consider the following issues when making a change in the contract language:

- Will a change in the contract language introduce loss exposures that the insurer has not anticipated? The meaning of standard policy language has been examined and refined over many years. New contract language could contain ambiguities that the insurer has not anticipated, resulting in claims paid that are not anticipated in the pricing of the policy.
- Will regulators understand how products are priced? Innovative policy changes could include exposures and coverages that are difficult to assess, making the justification of the related pricing difficult for regulators to understand and approve.
- Could the change alter the statistical basis for the policy pricing? Because coverages on personal insurance policies have been consistent for years, the statistical credibility of premium and loss information is valuable in identifying trends and pricing coverages.

Additional Endorsement Issues

Insurers may respond to customers' needs by offering endorsements that extend current coverages or offer new coverages. For example, an insurer could meet the growing needs of people residing in assisted-living facilities by offering endorsements to tenant homeowners policies that (1) provide golf cart liability and property coverage, (2) extend property coverage to include service animals (such as seeing-eye or hearing-ear dogs), or (3) expand the limits of coverage for cash. An endorsement that adds coverage has the benefit of leaving the basic contract language and pricing unchanged. However, the insurer must address the issues of justifying the pricing of the coverage and wording the language in the endorsement to guard against providing coverage that was not anticipated.

Packaging Issues

Some insurers meet specific customers' needs by combining homeowners and personal auto policies with other coverages, such as personal umbrella coverage, personal articles floaters, and watercraft coverage, into a package of coverages. This package might combine the coverages with one liability limit for all exposures, or it might be a collection of standard contracts and coverage limits combined in a single policy jacket with a discounted premium. A package provides the policyholder the ease of combined billing and reduced gaps in coverage. A package also provides an insurer the potential for greater policy retention because policyholders are less likely to replace their automobile or homeowners coverage with another insurer if they must replace all of their previously packaged coverages.

When insurers package coverages, they must be aware of the potential problems they might encounter with state regulations. If a state has a compulsory automobile insurance program, assigned risk program, reinsurance facility, or another automobile insurance program, will the automobile portion of the package policy be subject to regulatory requirements that affect individually written automobile policies? Will the insurer be allowed to have different underwriting guidelines on the automobile portion of the package policy and the individually written automobile policies? The answers to these questions can affect the insurer's ability to select accounts that meet the underwriting guidelines for the wide range of loss exposures covered by the package.

Service Changes

If the services offered by an insurer do not meet the customers' needs, or if customers are being attracted to another insurance company because of the services the company offers, an insurer can change the services it offers to better meet customers' needs. Changes in services do not involve the issues that product changes might involve. However, additional services usually involve expenses for implementation and maintenance. The insurer must decide whether the additional expenses can be justified by the benefits derived from the policies that are written and retained. The following are some of the services that insurers offer to attract personal insurance customers:

- A variety of payment plans
- Premium payments through automatic fund transfers or credit cards
- Access to customer service and claim representatives 24-hours a day
- Drive-in claim services
- Telephone claim handling
- Telephone and Internet quoting services
- Internet access to respond to questions

Underwriting Changes

If insurance policies do not sell successfully because the underwriting criteria are too restrictive, or if unanticipated loss exposures are being accepted on new insurance policies, an insurer can change the underwriting guidelines. More restrictive criteria can be used to screen new policies or **reunderwrite** the existing portfolio of policies. Because reunderwriting to correct an existing problem in a portfolio can be a complex process, it is addressed thoroughly in Chapter 7.

Reunderwriting is the process of analyzing the characteristics of policies within a portfolio and the trends of those characteristics. Through this analysis, insurers identify common loss exposures that generate losses that were not anticipated at the time rates were established for the exposure units. Possible activity for correction are then identified and one or a combination of activities is selected for implementation. The portfolio is monitored to determine the effectiveness of the reunderwriting activity.

Changing the underwriting criteria for new policies might require filing the changes with the state insurance department, if the state requires this information to be filed. In addition, producers must be notified of the change so that they can modify the type of risk submitted on applications.

> **Educational Objective 5**
> a. Describe the costs and benefits associated with a new product or a product change.
> b. Explain how insurers choose among new product or product change ideas.

A **cost/benefit analysis** is a study that compares the likely costs of a product or service with the likely benefits, both to the customer (in meeting a customer need) and to the insurer (in meeting profit and growth objectives). Some organizations refer to a cost/benefit analysis as a C.B.A.

Determining Costs and Benefits of New Products and Product Changes

Insurers, like other organizations, have limited resources. An insurance company has many opportunities to implement new products and services; however, the costs associated with changes prohibit a company from taking advantage of all of the possible opportunities. Therefore, an insurer must have some method of choosing among the possible product changes. One method of making product change decisions as well as comparisons among many possible changes is to develop a **cost/benefit analysis** for each possibility.

To develop a cost/benefit analysis, an insurer's staff members must answer many questions to ensure that all of the costs have been considered and that the potential benefits have not been overstated.

Product Development Costs

To estimate the costs associated with creating or changing a product, an insurer's staff members consider the time needed for product development, changes in operation, systems development, regulatory filings and record keeping, external marketing, and training. All of these estimates of time are then translated into costs by multiplying the *average hourly cost* of the individuals involved by their associated overhead.

> **Developing Average Hourly Cost**
>
> The following is an example of a process used to develop the average hourly cost of individuals involved in product development:
>
> ABC Insurance Company's overhead for all employee benefits, office space, office equipment, and office materials equals $35 million per year. ABC's salaries equal $100 million per year. Therefore, employee-related benefits and expenses equal 35 percent of salaries.
>
> To ensure confidentiality of salary information, the human resources department averages the annual salaries of all actuaries who prepare rates for state filings. The average annual salary of $80,000 is divided by the

> 2,000 hours worked per year (50 weeks, or work weeks minus vacations, times 40 hours) to equal $40.00 per hour.
>
> Rather than identifying the benefit expenses, office space, equipment, and materials expenses just for actuaries, a standard overhead percentage of 35 percent of the hourly rate is added to the $40.00; therefore, the cost per hour of an actuary's time devoted to the project is $54.00.
>
> Similar costs are developed for all major categories of staff members involved in the project. The costs developed are used in all projects for consistency in comparisons.

The costs required for filings and advertising are also included in the overall cost of the project. The table in Exhibit 4-7 displays examples of questions that help to guide this process. Because the time of the staff members involved is a valuable and costly resource for an insurance company, emphasis is placed on the costs associated with the time required by people who will work on the project. Exhibit 4-7 can be used as a checklist and work sheet to develop the costs of a product development.

Product Development Benefits

The benefits associated with a proposed new product or change are based on the new policies, increase in policy retention, decrease in losses, or other positive results anticipated. The basis for determining such benefits will vary significantly depending on the project. The following are questions that can form the basis for determining benefits:

- What is the total available market? (In other words, how many insurance customers need or want the new product?)
- What percentage of the market can we capture? (How many of the total number of customers who need the new product could we reasonably expect to write policies for?)
- How many policies will we retain that we would otherwise lose without this new product or change?
- What is the annual increase in premium expected as a result of this project?
- What loss ratio can be expected for this product?

The total annual increase in the PIF from new policies and increased retention is multiplied by the average premium per policy to determine the annual increase in premium. The expected loss ratio is then applied to determine the expected annual losses. The expected annual losses are subtracted from the expected annual increase in premium to determine the benefits of the proposed new product or change.

Insurance companies such as mutuals and reciprocal exchanges that might measure benefits such as members' satisfaction or attainment of a customer benefit goal have an additional challenge in measuring the benefit of a new product or change. The benefit might be measured in terms of increased satisfaction expressed by policyholders in an annual survey. The benefit might also be the attainment of an objective or goal mandated by the members.

Exhibit 4-7
Product Development Costs

Questions (Check all "yes" responses.)	**People Involved**	**Number of Hours**	**Cost per Hour**	**Other Costs**
Development costs: What will it cost to initially develop the product or create the change?				
☐ Will the product change require marketing research?				
☐ Will the product change require a rate analysis?				
☐ Will the product change require outside contractors?				
☐ Will the product change require new contract forms, policy jackets, or endorsements?				
☐ Will an attorney review the new policy language, forms, communications, or other material?				
☐ Will other development costs be involved?				
Operational costs: What are the additional costs for administrative or operational procedures?				
(Develop annual hours and expenses based on the projected annual sales goals.)				
☐ Will the product change require additional processing steps?				
☐ Will the product change require additional documentation for applications?				
☐ Will the product change require additional processing by the producer?				
☐ Will the computer data system require changes to capture new or changed data?				
☐ Will processing, customer service, marketing, claim, or other staff members require training?				
☐ Will the product change involve other operational costs?				
Regulatory costs: What are the additional costs to meet regulatory requirements?				
☐ Will new or additional statistical information be reported?				
☐ Will the product be introduced in multiple states? Have the requirements of all states been considered?				
☐ Are there any limitations on canceling, nonrenewing, or limiting coverage that will require increased underwriting screening when an application is first written?				
☐ Will the product change require regulator approval before implementation that can result in unusual costs?				
Marketing costs: What are the costs to launch and maintain the product?				
☐ What budget is required to perform the initial advertising for the product?				
☐ What annual budget is required to maintain awareness in the market?				
☐ Will the sale of this product increase or decrease the sale of other products? What are the costs or benefits that can be associated with other sales?				

Choosing Among New Product or Product Change Ideas

Effectively prepared cost/benefit analyses can be used to determine which product has the potential of providing the most benefits to an insurer. The key to effective comparison is ensuring that the same criteria be used in each comparison. For example, Team A is calculating the product development costs for a new homeowners endorsement that will provide comprehensive physical damage coverage for small watercraft. Team A has included the initial and ongoing costs of training underwriters and producers in advanced watercraft risk selection techniques. However, Team B is calculating the product development costs for a similar endorsement for snowmobiles, but they have not included training for underwriters and producers. The question then follows: "Should similar training be included in the development costs for both products?" If the answer is "yes," similar costs should be added to Team B's product development costs in order to effectively determine the cost/benefit analyses.

The type and depth of evaluation required varies with the amount of resources needed to develop a product or implement a change. The larger the investment, the greater the intensity of the evaluation should be because more of the insurer's capital is invested in its success.

If a cost/benefit analysis supports the decision to make the change, a detailed proposal is created. The proposal describes the customers' needs, how the proposed change will respond to the need, what the costs are to develop and implement the change, and what the expected results will be for the insurer to justify the change. A proposed change that appears to be justified at the time of the initial cost/benefit analysis might fail to be justified after the details of the proposal are completed. The proposal process extracts details and expenses that might not have been initially considered because a close evaluation reveals that costs could outweigh any possible benefits.

Educational Objective 6
Describe the purpose and the components of a product proposal.

Writing Product Proposals

An insurance company's executive staff members have vested interests in their organization's success. Often they are compensated, at least partially, based on the financial success of the organization. In addition, they are charged with the responsibility of operating the company to meet the best interests of the stakeholders. Although executives encourage product ideas from all areas of the company, they do not have the time to investigate all possible product development ideas. Instead, they depend on the other staff members to research ideas and include the essential information about a new or changed product in a proposal. If an insurer can adopt a standard format for proposals, executive staff members can compare the relative merits of different product ideas more efficiently, regardless of where the idea originated within the company.

A proposal summarizes information that is crucial to the decision-making process. Brevity and powerful information are the keys to an effective and convincing proposal. Within an insurance company, many staff members might be promoting ideas. A product idea presented in a document that is clear, easy to review quickly, and convincing might be accepted over an equally beneficial idea that is presented ineffectively. An effective proposal contains the following primary components:

- *Proposal overview*. This section answers the question, "What is the purpose of this proposal?" The purpose of the proposal and the expected outcomes of the product development are summarized.
- *Customer need and identification*. This section answers the question, "How do we know that customers need this product, and how did we find out?" If, for example, customers have expressed a need for claim service availability around-the-clock, how frequently have requests been received? Has a survey been conducted to confirm that this is a widespread need among customers? Statistics about the number of policies canceled by customers because the claim service was not available would provide a powerful case for such a proposal.
- *Proposed product or change*. This section answers the question, "What is the proposed product or change, and how will it meet the identified need?" The proposed product must link directly to and address the need identified in the previous section. If the proposed product does not fully meet the need identified, an explanation should be included.
- *Marketing environment*. This section answers the question, "How many customers need the product, and who else is offering it?" For example, if an underwriter is proposing a new personal effects floater policy for students studying abroad, the proposal should include the annual number of students and a list of competitors and their products. A proposal will be more convincing if the underwriter can justify the percentage of the market that the company will capture. Letters from several large universities expressing a need for the product for their students and their willingness to promote the insurance coverage would also be convincing.
- *Cost/benefit analysis*. This section answers the question, "What will this cost, and what will we gain?" The summary of the cost/benefit analysis is included here. A brief explanation of the estimates or assumptions made is included.
- *Expected results and monitoring processes*. This section answers the question, "What should we expect as results, and how will the out-

comes be measured and monitored?" This section can be strengthened by providing brief but specific information about controls that will be implemented for monitoring the progress of the expected results and implementing corrective actions, if needed.

- *Recommended action*. This section acts as a summary of the previous sections and adds information about people who will implement or lead the project as well as the specific date for implementation.

Each of the sections in a proposal builds on the information provided in the previous sections. In addition, the proposal is linked to the overall strategies of the insurance company. A proposal might express a good idea but not an idea supported by the overall corporate direction. In such cases, the employee should consider the insurer's corporate culture. Some organizations encourage maverick ideas, while other organizations discourage ideas that do not follow the corporate strategies. Any additional or supporting documentation is included as appendixes to the proposal. This format allows an executive to locate specific supporting information, if needed. Exhibit 4-8 provides an example of how a proposal might appear based on the format described.

Exhibit 4-8
Sample Proposal for a New Endorsement

Proposal: Develop New Home Office Endorsement for Homeowners

Proposal Overview

Develop a new homeowners policy endorsement with supporting services to provide property and liability coverage for home offices. This product will meet an immediate need expressed by 9.5 percent of our current policyholders, and this market is projected to grow. The internal implementation cost will be $25,000 with continuing annual maintenance costs of $5,000. The expected annual benefits are $100,000 in additional premium projected over the next five years, an overall 1.1 percent increase in PIF and an overall 0.4 percent increase in homeowners policy retention. This proposal directly supports Strategic Objective II: "Identify and respond to customer needs to profitably increase PIF and policy retention."

Customer Need and Identification

Customer service representatives and producers have reported an average of 15 requests per week from existing customers for home office coverage. Two focus groups of current customers expressing such an interest were conducted in the first quarter of this year to identify specific loss exposures, customer concerns, and associated services required. Proposed product features and services were identified (see Appendix A). A survey was conducted to identify current customer interest in the proposed product. The outcome (shown in Appendix B) reflects that 10 percent of our current homeowners policyholders would purchase the endorsement, and 0.4 percent of our current customers were preparing to purchase their homeowners coverage through a competitor to obtain home office coverage.

Proposed Product

The proposed endorsement will provide an extension of liability coverages to premises and operations office exposures. In addition, the endorsement will provide property coverage for business property on the premises for a coverage amount selected by the policyholder. As part of the product package, we

Continued on next page.

will train our producers, underwriters, and customer service representatives in the new product and the specific needs of individuals with home offices so that they can provide insurance advice and referrals to other small business resources. Appendix C displays the product needs expressed by our customers in the focus groups and survey with the corresponding coverages in the proposed endorsement and supporting services.

Marketing Environment

As identified in Appendix B, 10 percent of our customers have expressed the need for this product. Reports in five leading demographic journals (shown in Appendix D) indicate that this percentage is found throughout the United States, and the percentage is projected to grow steadily over the next five years.

Our top four homeowners insurance competitors, as identified in the current year's marketing strategies (shown in Appendix E), offer endorsements for home offices. Appendix F exhibits a profile of the coverage and services offered by these insurers compared with our proposed product features and the needs expressed by our customers.

We will succeed with this product because of the related services we will offer. Although our proposed endorsement provides coverages similar to that of our competitors, our supporting services will be unique. These services represent an unmet customer need. These customers are largely new entrepreneurs who have insurance- and business-related questions. The resources available through the Internet and the U.S. Small Business Administration will provide answers. We will connect these customers to the appropriate resources.

Cost/Benefit Analysis

The proposed endorsement and services will cost $25,000 in the first year with a benefit of $100,000. In the four years that follow, the maintenance cost of the product will be $5,000 with a benefit of $100,000 annually.

Appendix G provides a detailed analysis of the costs and benefits with assumptions made in the projections.

Expected Results and Monitoring Processes

The following are the key indicators and expected results:

- 500 new home office endorsements written per year
- 93 percent annual policy retention for homeowners policies with the home office endorsements attached
- A loss ratio for the home office endorsements below 60 percent each year

Staff members will monitor key indicator results monthly and take corrective action to achieve expected results.

Recommended Action

Because (1) the proposed home office endorsement and related services fill a current and growing customer need, (2) the cost/benefit analysis provides a clearly positive return for the expenses required, and (3) the proposed product clearly supports our strategic objectives, we recommend that Jane Sterling act as project manager to initiate the activity required to implement this proposal in the first quarter of next year with a projected marketing rollout of the product in the third quarter of next year.

Summary

Insurers identify the need for new products and services or changes to existing ones by collecting information about customers' needs and market trends from their internal and external environments. Internal staff reports, current customer trends, and environmental scanning to identify emerging trends provide indications of required new products or product changes. Insurance company staff members perform marketing research to gather additional information to verify the need for the product or changes.

Insurers also identify the need for changes in existing products and related services by monitoring key indicators, such as PIF, new business count, and policy retention. Staff members use charts and graphs and compare industry and company data to analyze data for key indicators more effectively.

When changes are identified in a portfolio, insurers determine the reasons for the changes. The following are two approaches that can be used:

- Compare the risk profiles, which are characteristics of the policies in a portfolio, over a period of time to identify trends. From these trends make assumptions about the portfolio. Verify these assumptions through additional research.
- Ask questions about the changes in the key indicators to identify possible reasons for the changes, and the possible consequences of the changes.

Once the reasons for the change are determined, an insurer might modify its products and services. Additional issues should be considered for changes to products or services and related underwriting changes.

A cost/benefit analysis can help an insurer determine whether a proposed change is beneficial. Cost/benefit analyses can also help an insurer select among several possible proposed changes.

Product proposals are descriptions of customers' needs, how the proposed change responds to the need, the costs to develop the change, the expected results, and the recommended action. Insurance company staff members present proposals in a condensed, succinct format to executive staff members for easy review and comparison with other proposals.

Underwriting Profitability for Personal Insurance

Chapter 5

Educational Objectives

1. a. Describe the components of underwriting profit/loss.
   b. Explain how underwriting profit/loss affects policyholders' surplus. (pp. 5-2 to 5-4)
2. Explain how the components of underwriting profit are measured, and describe factors that can increase or decrease each component. (pp. 5-5 to 5-11)
3. Explain how an insurer establishes goals for overall underwriting profitability, and explain how it separates those goals to establish individual goals for product segments, product lines, and territories. (pp. 5-11 to 5-21)
4. Explain how insurers increase underwriting profit. (pp. 5-21 to 5-31)
5. Given a case study, describe actions an insurer might take to improve underwriting profitability. (pp. 5-31 to 5-34)

Outline

I. Components of Underwriting Profit/Loss
II. Measuring Underwriting Profit
   A. Measuring Premium Results
   B. Measuring Loss Results
   C. Measuring Expense Results
   D. Measuring Overall Underwriting Profit or Loss
III. Establishing Goals for Underwriting Profitability
   A. Establishing Projected Premiums, Losses, and Expenses
   B. Establishing Goals for New Product Lines
   C. Establishing Goals for Retiring Product Lines
IV. Improving Underwriting Profitability
   A. Increasing Premium
   B. Decreasing Losses
   C. Controlling Expenses
V. Improving Profitability—Case Study
VI. Summary

Chapter 5

Underwriting Profitability for Personal Insurance

Profitability is essential for the on-going strength and viability of any business. Underwriting profit or loss is the largest component of operating profit for most insurers. For insurers, there are three elements in the measurement of underwriting profits: premiums, losses, and expenses. To make an underwriting profit, companies must earn more in premiums from policyholders than they pay in claims and expenses.

Insurers establish goals to help achieve profitability. For example, a company will set sales goals in order to generate a specific amount of premium or target expense goals to control administrative costs. These goals are generally established during an annual planning session and are based on input from all areas of the organization as well as from an analysis of the insurer's current business environment.

There are a variety of ways in which an insurer can increase profitability. However, improving underwriting results can take time. As a result, insurers monitor their performance closely and respond quickly if results do not meet their objectives.

This chapter discusses the components of insurer underwriting profit, how insurers measure underwriting profit, how insurers establish goals for underwriting profit, and how insurers can improve profitability. A case study illustrates the practical application of the information presented.

Educational Objective 1

a. Describe the components of underwriting profit/loss.

b. Explain how underwriting profit/loss affects policyholders' surplus.

Components of Underwriting Profit/Loss

The calculation of **underwriting profit/loss** is essentially simple: an insurer subtracts its **incurred losses** and **underwriting expenses** from the premiums it earns. In other words, an insurer receives premiums out of which it pays losses and expenses and sets **loss reserves**. Exhibit 5-1 illustrates the calculation of underwriting profit.

Exhibit 5-1
Calculation of Underwriting Profit/Loss

Underwriting profit/loss = Earned premiums – Incurred losses – Underwriting expenses

Exhibit 5-2 illustrates the sources of funds available to insurers and the relationships among premiums, losses, and expenses that form the basis for calculation of both underwriting profit and **policyholders' surplus**.

As shown in Exhibit 5-2, an insurer's initial capital is raised from individuals, groups, other businesses, or venture capitalists. These funds are used to establish the company's underwriting operations. Subsequently, policyholder premiums are the insurer's major source of cash flow.

An additional source of income for insurers is earnings on investments. Insurers are required by regulation to keep large reserves available to pay claims or return premium payments on canceled policies. Insurers may invest these funds and profits from previous years in specific types of stocks, bonds, and investments. Any interest or dividends from such investments or any profits from their sale become part of an insurer's income. Investment income is not included in the calculation of underwriting profit.

After deductions for incurred losses and underwriting expenses, the insurer will post an underwriting profit or loss. In the case of an underwriting profit, these funds can be invested to generate additional income. The company may also choose to pay dividends, either to shareholders in the case of stock insurers or to policyholders in the case of mutual insurers. Any remaining profits are added to policyholders' surplus, which in turn is reinvested. If the company posts an underwriting loss, current investment income is used to make up the shortfall. Given the narrow profit margins on personal insurance products, this is quite common. If underwriting losses are large and current investment income is not sufficient to make up the shortfall, the insurer might draw from policyholders' surplus to meet its financial obligations.

Underwriting profit is income an insurer earns from premiums paid by policyholders minus incurred losses and underwriting expenses.

Incurred losses are the sum of paid losses and loss reserve adjustments (changes in the loss reserves) for a period of time.

Loss reserves are amounts designated by insurance companies to pay claims for losses that have already occurred but are not yet settled. A loss reserve for a claim is the insurer's best estimate of the total amount that it will pay in the future for a loss that has already occurred.

Underwriting expenses include an insurer's costs for acquiring new policies, general expenses for operations, taxes, and fees.

Policyholders' surplus of an insurance company is equal to its total admitted assets minus its total liabilities.

Exhibit 5-2
Insurers' Financial Overview

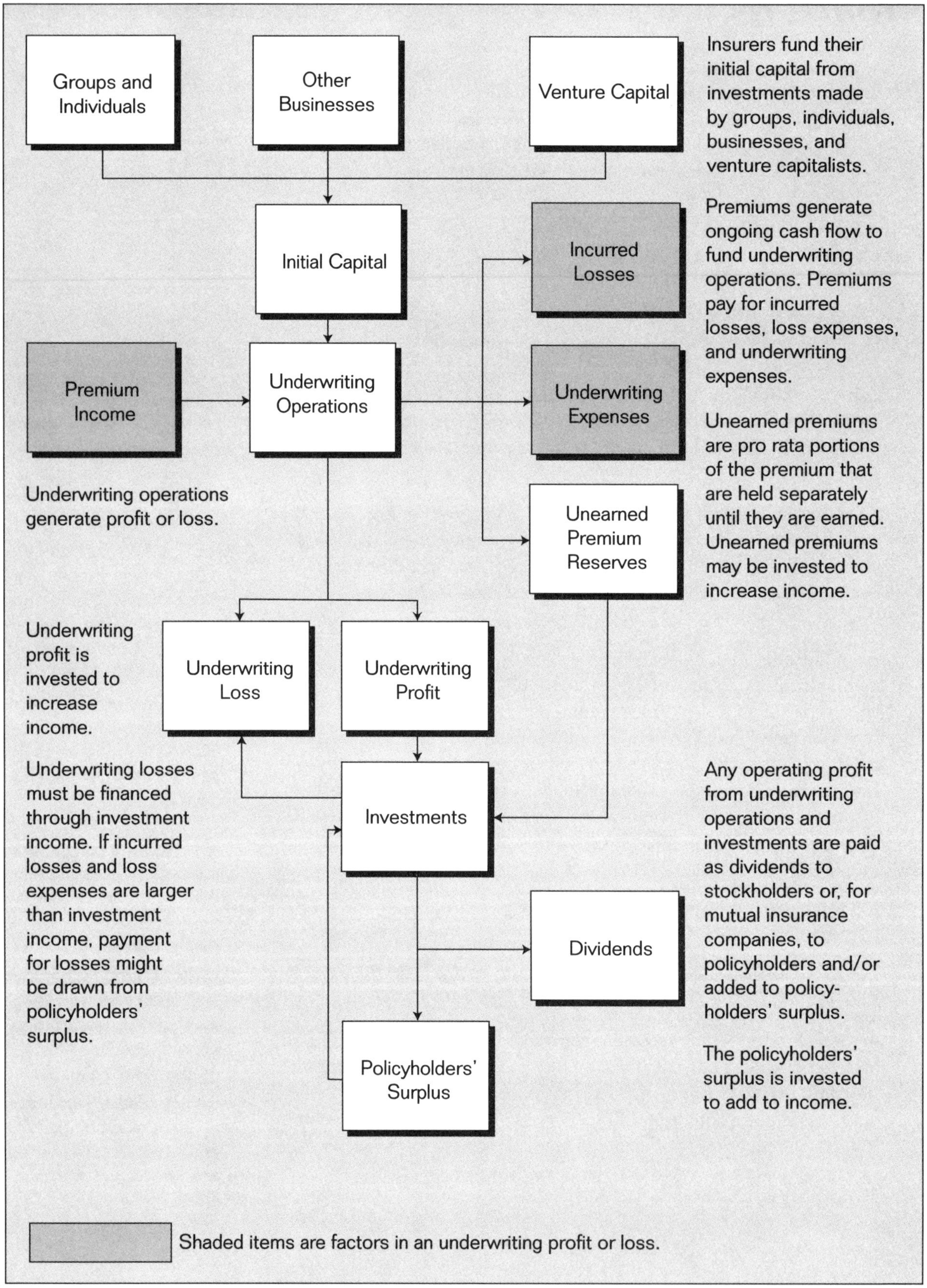

Educational Objective 2
Explain how the components of underwriting profit are measured, and describe factors that can increase or decrease each component.

Measuring Underwriting Profit

Insurers try to control underwriting profit by measuring components of underwriting profit, monitoring changes in the components and comparing changes with goals, and then taking action to control the components. Insurers have limited control over some of the factors affecting the three components of underwriting profit. Premium income, for example, reflects the effectiveness of the sales force, the rates that regulators approve for use by the insurer, the success of the competition in attracting policyholders away from the insurer, and cycles within the insurance industry as a whole. Incurred losses can be significantly affected by catastrophes, by changes in legislation, and by social changes. Although insurers have more control over underwriting expenses, pressure to compete often influences spending decisions.

Measuring Premium Results

Premiums are the major, on-going source of income for insurers. The amount of insurance a company writes, reflected in its premium income, depends on a variety of factors including the following:

- The lines of business it writes
- The number of producers and the cost of commissions
- The regions and territories in which it writes
- Its underwriting philosophy
- The competitiveness of its pricing
- The comprehensiveness of the coverage it offers
- Its reputation for claim service

Adjustments to any of these factors will increase or decrease an insurer's ability to write business and generate premium income.

In addition to reflecting an insurer's sales, premiums can also influence other components of underwriting profit, including the following:

- The volume of potential claims, which increases as the number of in-force policies increases
- Projected changes in the insurer's operating expenses, which tend to rise and fall with increases and decreases in the volume of insurance written

As a result, insurers examine premium results closely and calculate premiums in two different ways—as earned premiums and written premiums.

Earned Premium

Insurance is not a product like a book that can be purchased and delivered in a single, brief transaction. The insurer agrees to provide insurance protection for the duration of the policy period, and the earned premiums reflect this idea. The concept is similar to a magazine subscription. If a $24 annual subscription represents 12 magazines, each costing $2, each month in which the subscriber receives a magazine $2 of the annual fee is used up. If the subscriber cancels after receiving only eight issues, the publisher returns the unused portion of the annual subscription fee ($8).

Similarly, if an annual policy is issued at a premium of $1,200, the insurer earns that premium at a rate of $100 each month. If the policyholder cancels after eight months, the insurer returns $400 to the policyholder, representing the unearned portion of the premium paid. As a result, insurers include only earned premiums in income calculations and maintain an unearned premium reserve as a part of their balance sheet.

Written Premium

An annual subscription fee is the cost of a year's worth of magazines. Similarly, written premiums reflect the price of insurance protection for an entire policy period. To calculate written premiums for any calendar year, an insurer totals the price it charged for all policies that have effective dates between January 1 and December 31 of that year.

Written premiums are not considered part of underwriting profit until they have been earned. However, written premiums provide valuable information. For example, since losses can occur at any time during a policy period, written premiums represent the amount of risk an insurer has assumed. An insurer's staff members might review the low earned premium for a portfolio and inaccurately estimate that the assumed risk is also low; however, only the written premium provides the measurement of the entire portfolio. Whether a policy remains in force or cancels mid-term, the cost of underwriting and issuing the policy remains the same. Written premiums can therefore provide an indication of underwriting expenses.

Exhibit 5-3 provides an illustration of the relationship between earned and written premiums. A hypothetical insurer offers only annual policies. Depending on the coverage purchased, annual premiums are either $600 or $1,200. During the year, the insurer writes four policies (one in February, one in March, one in June, and one in September) for a total written premium of $3,600. However, at year-end the earned premium for these four policies is only $2,450. The difference of $1,150 is the unearned premium.

A comparison of written premiums and earned premiums can also reflect the activities of an insurer. For example, during a period of rapid growth, written premiums can exceed earned premiums by far more than usual. Conversely, if an insurer is retiring from a territory or a line of business, earned premium can potentially exceed written premium as business runs off the books.

Exhibit 5-3
Comparison of Earned Premium to Written Premium

Written	Jan	Feb	Mar	Apr	May	Jun	Jul	Aug	Sept	Oct	Nov	Dec	Earned
$600		$50	$50	$50	$50	$50	$50	$50	$50	$50	$50	$50	$550
$1,200			$100	$100	$100	$100	$100	$100	$100	$100	$100	$100	$1,000
$1,200						$100	$100	$100	$100	$100	$100	$100	$700
$600									$50	$50	$50	$50	$200
$3,600 Written Premium												**Earned Premium**	**$2,450**

Measuring Loss Results

Payments for incurred losses often consume from 65 to 100 percent of a company's premium income and sometimes exceed it. As a result, an insurer's loss results are always the focus of scrutiny. As illustrated in Exhibit 5-4, three elements combine to make up an insurer's incurred losses: (1) paid losses, for which the insurer has indemnified the claimant, (2) changes in loss reserves, and (3) loss expenses.

Exhibit 5-4
Calculation of Incurred Losses

Incurred losses = Paid losses + Changes in loss reserves + Loss expenses

Paid Losses

Tracking paid losses is a weekly, monthly, quarterly, and annual function for insurers and underwriters who manage portfolios of policies, because trends in paid losses might indicate problems. Also, by tracking paid losses, the underwriter can determine whether the losses paid represent many small losses or a few large losses. For example, an increase in losses paid for physical damage automobile claims in one territory over a period of time might indicate (1) many small losses due to an event such as a hailstorm or (2) a few large losses due to theft.

Loss Reserves

Because society sees prompt and full indemnification of claimants as essential, laws and regulations have been developed to help ensure the financial strength of insurers. For example, when a policyholder reports a loss, the insurer is required to quickly estimate the value of the claim and then set a loss reserve to acknowledge its obligation to pay the loss. As the insurer receives more information about each claim, reserves can be increased or decreased to more accurately reflect the claim's anticipated final cost to the company.

Insurers are also required to maintain reserves for claims that have been incurred but not yet reported (IBNR). For example, windstorm damage to a summer home that occurred in December might not be discovered and reported by the policyholder until the following January. Even for routine claims, a few days typically elapse between a loss and report of the loss to the insurer.

An insurer's accuracy in establishing reserves is important. When reserves are too high, capital is tied up unnecessarily. When reserves are too low, the company exposes itself to both financial strain and regulatory censure.

In addition, reserves can alter the measurements of incurred losses. For example, a $500,000 reserve that is established for a bodily injury loss will count in the loss results as an incurred loss of $500,000. If the insured is later found to be only partially responsible for the loss, the reserve for the loss should be reduced appropriately. If the reserve is not reduced, the automobile losses would appear to be larger than they actually are. Consider what could happen if this over-reserving occurred for many losses in one territory. Insurance company managers and underwriters might decide to tighten underwriting guidelines or restrict policy writings based on the false assumption that the territory experienced excessive losses.

For losses occurring in a given year, reserves are zero at the beginning of the year and any posted reserves are "changes in reserves." In subsequent years, only the new changes to those reserves are counted in calculating incurred losses. A large reduction in a reserve can make a territory or a product appear more profitable than it actually is. A substantial reduction in a reserve in the current year for a loss that was originally reserved in a prior year can cause the current loss results to appear low. If this occurs, it could mask other loss frequency or severity problems. For this reason, underwriters monitor reserve changes and their effects on a portfolio for which the underwriters are responsible. Part of the problem is that the "incurred losses" element of the usual formula for underwriting profit/loss includes new claim payments and reserve changes for losses that occurred at any time up to the present, including losses from past years. Accounting methods can compare the current year's earned premiums to only the current year's losses to determine how current business is performing. Nevertheless, the usual formula for underwriting profit/loss includes incurred losses from past years.

Loss Expenses

Loss expenses, sometimes called loss adjustment expenses (LAE), are the expenses necessitated by the process of investigating and settling insurance claims according to the terms specified in the insurance policy.

When a policyholder reports a loss, a claim representative investigates to determine whether the loss is covered, establishes the value of the claim, and settles the claim. This process is called claim handling. Losses can be handled by insurance company staff or by independent adjusting firms contracted by the insurer. This investigation and settlement of a claim can involve a variety of **loss expenses** payable by the insurer. Examples of loss expenses include the cost of salaries or fees for claim representatives, legal opinions, medical examinations, and site investigations. While simple property losses may be inexpensive to handle, the cost of handling complex liability claims can be significant. But all losses require some expense for the claim representative's time.

Thorough investigation can save an insurer money. It prevents the payment of claims for which there is no coverage and helps to establish a fair and realistic value for covered losses, avoiding over-payment. However, a detailed investigation can be costly, and loss expenses might exceed any resulting savings in paid losses. Insurers are under both competitive and regulatory pressure to settle claims promptly and fairly. Extended investigations can hamper their ability to do so. As a result, insurers attempt to strike a balance, completing sufficient investigation to reasonably protect their own interests while controlling loss expenses. By comparing trends in the relationship between loss expenses and paid losses, an insurer can develop information regarding the efficiency and cost-effectiveness with which it handles claims.

Measuring Expense Results

Along with earned premiums and incurred losses, the third component in the calculation of underwriting profit is an insurer's operating expenses, commonly referred to as underwriting expenses. Underwriting expenses include costs directly related to marketing, underwriting, application processing, and policy issuance as well as salaries and employee benefits, computer systems, building rent and maintenance, and office supplies and equipment.

As much as possible, an insurer tries to match expenses with the income those expenses generate. For example, both income and expenses are usually tracked within each of the following categories:

- Line of business (such as personal automobile)
- Coverage (such as personal automobile bodily injury liability)
- Producer or distribution system (such as a specific agent or policies sold over the Internet)
- Geographic territory or region
- Branch or regional office
- Company (such as a provider of preferred homeowners insurance within a group of companies)

This allows an insurer to develop a clear picture of where its profit is generated. With data presenting a comparison of its areas of profitability, an insurer can identify and correct unprofitable products, lines of business, or territory results.

Measuring Overall Underwriting Profit or Loss

Underwriting profit or loss is the amount of money an insurance company gains or loses through its insurance operations excluding investment earnings and federal income taxes. While the amount of a company's underwriting profit or loss is important, the dollar value alone is not a good indicator of the overall performance of the company. For example, while an underwriting profit of $100,000 may be considered excellent for a small company, it could be disappointing for a larger organization. In order to evaluate premium, loss, and expense results in a meaningful way, insurers and regulators use a variety of ratios, or comparisons, often expressed as percentages.

Exhibit 5-5 illustrates three of the commonly used ratios: the loss ratio, the expense ratio, and the combined ratio. Reviewed together, these three ratios present a comprehensive picture of an insurer's underwriting profitability and overall performance.

Exhibit 5-5
Underwriting Profitability Ratios

Ratio	Calculation	Comments
Loss ratio	$= \frac{\text{Incurred losses}}{\text{Earned premiums}} \times 100$	This ratio compares incurred losses with earned premiums for a specific time period, such as a year. It illustrates what percentage of an insurer's earned income is "used up" by reserves and claim payments. For example, a loss ratio of 70 percent indicates that for every $1.00 the insurer earns in premium income it pays $0.70 in incurred losses.
Expense ratio	$= \frac{\text{Underwriting expenses}}{\text{Written premiums}} \times 100$	This ratio compares underwriting expenses with written premiums for a specific time period. It illustrates what percentage of an insurer's income goes to pay underwriting expenses. For example, an expense ratio of 28 percent indicates that for every $1.00 of insurance a company writes, it pays $0.28 in underwriting expenses.
Combined ratio	= Loss ratio + Expense ratio	This combination of the loss and expense ratios presents a clear picture of the insurer's overall underwriting performance and compares the inflow and outflow of money from insurance operations. A combined ratio above 100 percent indicates an underwriting loss. A combined ratio below 100 percent indicates an underwriting profit.

Exhibit 5-6 illustrates the application of these ratios. A hypothetical insurance company has incurred losses of $10 million with earned premiums of $15 million. That results in a loss ratio of 67 percent. The same company has $7.5 million in underwriting expenses, and $20 million in total written premiums, resulting in an expense ratio of 38 percent. When the loss ratio and expense ratio are added together, they generate a combined ratio of 105 percent. This indicates that for every premium dollar the organization collects, it pays $1.05 in claims and expenses. Based solely on the combined ratio, the company is losing money.

Exhibit 5-6
Underwriting Profitability Example

Loss Ratio		Expense Ratio		Combined Ratio
[$10,000 incurred losses × 100] / $15,000 earned premium	+	[$7,500,000 underwriting expenses × 100] / $20,000,000 written premiums	=	
67 percent	+	38 percent	=	105 percent

The combined ratio has two limitations, however. The first is that incurred losses include loss reserves, which represent expected payments that might be made in the future for losses that have already occurred. Thus, reserves are an estimate that can be inaccurate. The second limitation is that the combined ratio illustrates underwriting profit only, and ignores the contribution of investment income to an insurer's overall profitability, illustrated earlier in Exhibit 5-2.

Educational Objective 3
Explain how an insurer establishes goals for overall underwriting profitability, and explain how it separates those goals to establish individual goals for product segments, product lines, and territories.

Establishing Goals for Underwriting Profitability

Successful businesses adhere to the adage "Plan your work and work your plan." Establishing and communicating goals, or objectives, and measuring actual performance against those goals helps an insurer succeed in the following ways:

- A clear understanding of what is expected helps departments and individuals focus their efforts on achieving the desired results.
- Measuring actual performance against established goals provides on-going feedback and encouragement and identifies shortfalls before they become significant.
- Coordinating and communicating organizational goals ensures that all departments are working cooperatively to achieve a common objective, rather than working at cross-purposes.

Generally, objectives are established during a formal, annual planning process that includes input and participation from all functional areas within a company. Insurers set goals for the following year and may also create a broad strategy for the next three to five years.

Goals are usually described in terms of strategy and **tactics**. Tactics may be further broken down into **activities** and **tasks**. Different groups

Reminder

Strategies are large-scale action plans for interacting with the business environment in order to achieve long-term goals.

Tactics are the specific actions required by the organization to implement its strategy.

Activities are actions required by organizational units or departments for completing a tactic.

Tasks are defined limited assignments with target completion dates.

and individuals throughout the organization assume responsibility for different portions of the plan. Senior executives are usually responsible for the achievement of broad strategies. Middle managers implement the supporting tactical plans. Supervisors and line staff members contribute to the achievement of overall corporate goals by completing the activities and tasks that support the tactical plans. Tactics, activities, and tasks are often fine-tuned to meet the unique circumstances in a region or territory or to reflect the specific performance or potential of a line of business.

Exhibit 5-7 provides a simple illustration of how a corporate goal cascades through an organization, soliciting involvement and commitment at all levels and encouraging the coordination of efforts and cross-functional cooperation. In this example, tactics, activities, and tasks are uniquely defined for each territory and line of business.

Establishing Projected Premiums, Losses, and Expenses

To establish realistic goals, an insurer reviews earned premium, incurred losses, and underwriting expenses over the previous several years. The insurer then uses that information to project the next year's results. The next step is to trends in industry trends, individual company trends, and other factors affecting the insurance marketplace as well as the insurer's need to control expenses.

Once an insurer has projected its performance, it can establish goals that are challenging but achievable. This process often involves discussion and negotiation among all departments and levels within the organization. For example, a region with a projected annual growth rate of 8 percent might establish a goal of 10 percent growth. The manager of a product line with a projected loss ratio of 74 percent might negotiate a goal of reducing the loss ratio to 68 percent.

Industry Trends

The insurance industry is highly competitive. Insurers regularly introduce new products and services, lower prices, and imaginative distribution systems. Consumers' needs, preferences, and demands change over time. In addition, technology has significantly altered the way in which many insurers interact with consumers.

Industry trends can have a significant effect on an insurer's future underwriting profits by changing its competitive position relative to other insurers, increasing or decreasing its exposure to claims, or necessitating significant increases in its underwriting expenses. The most successful companies identify industry trends early and incorporate the effect of those trends during the goal-setting process.

Some examples of industry trends and their potential effect include the following:

- The industry's performance has traditionally followed an insurance cycle. Individual insurers consider the current phase of the insur-

Exhibit 5-7
Planning and Goal Setting

Goal			Example	Responsibility
Strategy			We will increase overall written premiums by 10 percent	Sr. vice president, sales
Tactic			Region A will increase written premiums by 8 percent.	Regional manager
	Activity		Each territory will appoint at least 15 new sales agents per quarter.	Territory managers
		Task	Each field representative will identify and recommend three new sales agents for appointment each quarter.	Marketing representatives
	Activity		Each territory will increase homeowners written premiums by 8 percent over the year.	Territory managers
		Task	Each territory will plan and implement a homeowner sales incentive contest within the first quarter.	Territory managers
		Task	Each territory will plan and deliver an "account selling" seminar for sales agents by March.	Territory managers
Tactic			Region B will increase written premiums by 15 percent.	Regional manager
	Activity		The region will reduce automobile rates by 5 percent effective January 1 for new business and renewals.	Regional manager
		Task	Updated rates will be programmed into the system by December 15.	Information services manager
	Activity		The region will provide sales agents with training on underwriting guidelines to facilitate placing business with us.	Underwriting manager
		Task	Underwriters will spend one week each month visiting sales agents and providing training.	Underwriters
	Activity		The region will launch the new Pleasure Craft Policy in March.	Regional marketing manager
		Task	Seminars reviewing the Pleasure Craft Policy coverage, underwriting, and rating for sales agents will be delivered in each territory by February 28.	Territory managers

ance cycle when setting premium, loss, and expense goals so as to maintain their competitive positions.

- An industry move to broader coverage, enhanced policies, and new products may allow insurers to increase written premiums but may also expose them to more claims.
- Increased use of automation and technology (such as producer interface, automated quotations via telephone, or insurance sales via the Internet) can reduce expenses over the long term; however, each new venture into technology requires a large initial investment.

- Telephone claim handling can result in expense reductions through increased efficiency. However, it can also result in decreased written premiums if policyholders who prefer personal contact place their business with another insurer.
- The appearance of alternative marketing and underwriting channels (such as affinity groups targeting only members of the teaching profession or alumni of a college) can present a real competitive challenge, particularly when these alternatives focus primarily on pricing as their marketing tool. Lowering rates may help an insurer gain or retain business, but it also exposes the company to reduced premiums and resulting higher loss ratios.

Individual Company Trends

Improving an insurer's underwriting profitability is like piloting an ocean liner—the process requires constant monitoring and small corrections to stay on course. Constant small corrections can keep the liner on course; however, correcting the direction for a liner that has drifted drastically off course requires significant effort and time. Similarly, an insurer is careful to track and monitor its performance monthly, quarterly, and annually by region, territory, department, line, product, and coverage. This allows the insurer to identify any negative trends early and respond quickly with a small correction rather than having to make a significant adjustment later. These corrections are incorporated in the organization's premium, loss, and expense goals.

Some examples of internal trends to which an insurer will respond quickly by establishing appropriate goals include the following:

- Slowing growth or a net decrease in policy count in a region or territory
- Increasing loss ratios for a particular line or coverage
- Increasing loss expenses
- Increasing underwriting expenses not matched by increasing written premiums

Other Trends

In addition to industry-wide trends and a company's own internal trends, an insurer considers other factors in establishing premium, loss, and expense goals. These include new companies in the marketplace, changes in regulation, catastrophe experience, and changes in reinsurance arrangements.

New Companies in the Market

New insurers can enter the market in a variety of ways. Mergers and acquisitions can create new entities. Insurers can start independently or break away from existing larger organizations. Companies from other industries can expand their operations to include the sale and servicing of insurance. For example, banks are increasingly interested in selling property and liability insurance.

The entry of new players into the marketplace affects how insurers establish goals in several ways. First, new insurers increase competition, particularly when they offer lower prices in an effort to establish themselves quickly. Also, some new insurers target particular territories, groups, or lines of business. This specialization can make them extremely attractive to consumers, as in the case of insurers that target consumers over age 55 by offering special low rates or other benefits.

On the other hand, the entry of new insurers can reduce pressure on existing companies in situations where state regulation mandates each insurer to underwrite its proportionate share of certain high-risk business. For example, regulators may require insurers to provide automobile insurance for poor drivers or homeowners insurance in storm-prone areas. As new players enter the field, the proportionate share of each insurer in the marketplace decreases.

In addition to directly creating increased competition, new entrants often bring additional or alternative strengths that existing insurers have not yet developed and to which they are forced to respond. For example, because of their existing technological capabilities, both banks and securities brokerages that sell insurance are currently embracing the Internet as a distribution channel far more rapidly than are traditional insurers.

Changes in Regulation

Insurance is a highly regulated industry, and regulatory changes can significantly affect insurers, particularly in the area of underwriting profit. Some examples of significant regulatory changes include the following:

- Changes in the criteria that may be used for underwriting and rating risks
- Changes in the way rate increases or decreases are approved and implemented
- Changes to the state-mandated benefits payable for some types of claims
- Changes to the financial stability and reporting requirements for insurers
- Changes to regulations controlling insurers' ability to enter or withdraw from a line or territory

Insurance regulation changes for a variety of reasons; however, changes are frequently a response to political pressure by consumers or consumer advocates. Generally, regulatory changes occur to protect policyholders and claimants and discourage unfair trade practices. These changes, however, can significantly affect insurers' underwriting profits. They can sometimes inadvertently have a negative effect on consumers as well. Exhibit 5-8 presents two examples of regulatory changes.

Exhibit 5-8
Examples of Regulatory Changes

- In 1998, Texas enacted reforms to its civil justice system including caps on exemplary damages, stricter standards for joint and several liability, and stronger deterrences against frivolous lawsuits. Because regulators expected these changes to reduce liability claim costs, the state mandated insurance rate reductions effective January 1, 1999.
- California voters passed Proposition 213, which was implemented by the insurance department in 1998. The proposition restricted the eligibility of uninsured drivers to recover certain damages from insured drivers. Regulators required rate **rollbacks** to reflect the reduction in liability exposures.

Rollbacks are reductions in prices to a previous level. Rollbacks are often taken on a state or national level.

Catastrophe Experience

Catastrophes are usually the result of extreme weather events such as hurricanes, windstorms, hailstorms, snowstorms, floods, droughts, or earthquakes. They are devastating, not only to their victims and the communities in which they live but also to insurers. While each individual claim an insurer receives as a result of an extreme event may not be large, they can add up to a staggering total. For example, during the 1990s, the United States suffered at least eight natural disasters including Hurricane Andrew and the Northridge earthquake, with insured losses greater than $1 billion for each disaster. Total catastrophe losses for all lines of insurance in 1994 and 1995 totaled $17 billion and $8.3 billion, respectively. In 1992, the industry suffered $22.9 billion in catastrophe losses.[1]

Catastrophic events often cannot be accurately predicted, and the frequency of catastrophes reflects global climatic changes and seismic activity. However, historical data can help identify catastrophe-prone areas, and insurers take this into account when setting premium, loss, and expense goals or deciding whether to offer coverage in those areas. For example, an insurer's marketing strategy might vary geographically to limit the company's sales and resulting loss exposure in catastrophe-prone areas. An insurer could plan to introduce policy changes to limit coverage in catastrophe-prone areas, thereby reducing potential losses. Alternatively, a company may choose to sell coverage (for example, flood or earthquake insurance) designed and priced specifically for high-risk areas. Finally, an insurer might plan to control its catastrophic loss exposure by purchasing appropriate reinsurance coverage.

The **ceding company** is the insurer that cedes, or transfers, premiums and loss exposures to the reinsurer.

Changes in Reinsurance

The relationship between an insurer and its reinsurer is similar to the relationship between a policyholder and his or her insurer. The **ceding company** pays premiums to the reinsurer and in turn the reinsurer indemnifies the ceding company for all or part of the losses it sustains.

Reinsurance agreements vary based on the needs of the ceding company. Exhibit 5-9 illustrates some of the purposes that reinsurance serves.

Exhibit 5-9
Functions of Reinsurance

Capacity	To ensure companies' financial strength, regulations stipulate that insurers must maintain policyholders' surplus at or above a specific percentage of written premiums. An insurer with limited policyholders' surplus is therefore unable to grow. Ceding written premium to a reinsurer allows an insurer to reduce its ratio of written premiums to policyholders' surplus and therefore write more business.
Catastrophe	Reinsurance protects the ceding company against a single, catastrophic loss or multiple large losses.
Stabilization	Reinsurance helps smooth the ceding company's overall underwriting results from year to year.
Withdrawal	Transferring premiums and loss exposure to a reinsurer is one way for a ceding company to withdraw from a line of business or geographic area.
Market entrance	Reinsurance allows a ceding company to share the risk on new lines of business until premium volume has grown to a level that can reasonably meet projected losses.

With proper notice, either the ceding company or the reinsurer can change the terms and conditions of the reinsurance agreement. When establishing premium and loss goals, an insurer reviews its current reinsurance arrangements and might adjust them. Conversely, if a reinsurer changes a ceding company's reinsurance, the insurer will need to adjust its goals to reflect the changes.

Establishing Goals for New Product Lines

In addition to enhancing coverage on existing products, insurers offer new products in an effort to increase sales potential. For example, an insurer that writes homeowners and automobile insurance could decide to provide coverage for watercraft or seasonal residences as well. An insurer can enter a new product line through acquisition of another company's book of business or by launching a new product of its own. Both of these options have significant implications for underwriting profit, and insurers are careful to establish premium, loss, and expense goals for any new product they offer.

The Effect of Growth on Profitability

Whether an insurer enters a new product line from scratch or by acquisition, underwriting expenses immediately increase. This increase arises from such activities as hiring and training staff, advertising, reprogramming computer systems, and printing forms and manuals. In addition, insurance accounting rules require insurers to recognize policy acquisition costs immediately, even though the premium from each policy is earned only gradually over the life of the policy. Therefore, when growth is rapid, underwriting expenses increase at a rate disproportionately higher than the increase in premiums. Insurers project these increases as part of the planning process and monitor expenses closely.

Each new policy an insurer writes or acquires exposes the company to loss, and claims can occur at any point during the policy period. Large losses are always a risk. If an insurer enters a new product line from scratch, its exposure to loss grows as policies are written. However, when an insurer enters a new product line by acquiring a book of business, it assumes the loss exposure of the entire line before any premiums are earned.

Regardless of the method an insurer chooses to enter a new product line, it takes time to earn sufficient premiums to cover the increased expenses and potential incurred losses. As a result, new products often produce an initial underwriting loss. Provided that the product is properly rated and underwritten, eventually sufficient premium should be earned to improve the product's profitability. In the interim, an insurer plans to manage expenses as effectively as possible and may elect to protect itself through the purchase of reinsurance until earned premiums reach an acceptable level.

Assuming New Problem Accounts

One of the risks involved in acquiring a book of business is that an insurer might assume problem accounts as part of the portfolio, including any of the following:

- Accounts with poor loss history (such as a homeowners policy with several theft claims)
- Accounts with poor payment history (such as direct debits from bank accounts that might not have sufficient funds)
- Accounts with an uncooperative policyholder (such as a policyholder who does not provide information or cooperate in settling claims)
- A disproportionate share of policies in a catastrophe-prone area

Problem accounts can have a negative effect on premiums, losses, and expenses. When assuming problem accounts, an insurer has three options:

1. Retain the account with no modification
2. Attempt to modify the account to resolve the problem (examples include increasing the deductibles, reducing coverage, insisting on full payment up front, and transferring the policies to different rate levels or tiers)
3. Terminate the policy

Changing policy terms and conditions or terminating a policy for underwriting reasons can usually only be done at renewal. As a result, it takes a full year to work through a portfolio and deal with all the problem accounts, and the effect of the changes might not be apparent for another year.

Establishing Goals for Retiring Product Lines

Insurers retire from product lines for a variety of reasons, including the following:

- An insurer might acquire another insurer that offers a product incompatible with the corporate philosophy of the purchaser.
- Changes in legislation or regulation could make a product line unattractive.
- Competitive or regulatory forces might make it impossible for an insurer to charge sufficient premium to make a line profitable.
- Competitive forces could make it impossible for an insurer to write enough business in the line to generate the premium levels required for profitability.
- A line of business might be prone to higher-than-anticipated losses, either due to broadness of coverage or vulnerability to catastrophe.

Most frequently, insurers retire from product lines because they are unprofitable. Unfortunately, the process of retiring a line decreases premiums, increases expenses, and does little to protect the insurer from losses until all business in the line nonrenews or cancels. As a result, insurers plan carefully to minimize the potentially negative effect on overall profitability as they retire a product.

The Effect of Account Reduction on Profitability

If a product has an annual policy term, it can take a full year to retire from the line if policies are nonrenewed. During that year, the insurer continues to incur expenses and to be exposed to losses while premiums diminish.

Withdrawing from a line often temporarily increases expenses associated with that line. Examples of the reasons for this increase include the following:

- An insurer might print and mail brochures explaining its position and outlining policyholder options.
- Verbal communication with producers and policyholders increases, resulting in higher long-distance telephone expenses.
- To speed the process, an insurer might offer incentives to policyholders who replace coverage before renewal.
- To speed the process, an insurer may take increased advantage of opportunities to cancel policies mid-term (where such cancellations are allowed and warranted) by registered notice, increasing postage expenses.

Jargon Alert!

When an insurer retires a product line, or nonrenews any group of policies, the process usually takes a year to complete. During this time, insurers use the expression "the *policies run off the books*" or "*business runs off the books.*" This simply refers to the nonrenewal process during the retirement.

Jargon Alert!

A *frequency problem* refers to a problem with a product line that incurs more losses than are contemplated by the rates.

A *severity problem* refers to a problem with a product line that incurs losses that are larger than those contemplated by the rates.

Reallocating resources as the *business runs off the books* can offset these increased expenses. For example, claim representatives and underwriters can be retrained and transferred to other product lines. Insurers withdrawing from a line establish expense goals and monitor expenses closely.

An insurer continues to receive and settle claims during and after the period required to run the business off the books. Liability claims might not be reported and settled for years. If the line's poor performance is a result of a *frequency problem*, that frequency of losses and associated loss expenses will continue. If the line suffers from a *severity problem*, the insurer remains exposed to large losses.

As expenses potentially increase and losses continue, earned premiums diminish, both directly and indirectly as a result of the insurer's decision to retire from the line. As the insurer nonrenews policies that are not replaced with new sales, the insurer's written premiums decrease, directly resulting in lower earned premiums. Additionally, insurers often lose related business in other lines by retiring a line, resulting in indirect loss of earned premium. For example, an insurer retiring from the yacht market often will lose the automobile and homeowners policies of those clients as well.

Exhibit 5-10 illustrates the effect of diminishing earned premium on the loss and expense ratios.

Even though companies lose money during the runoff period, they will accept that short-term loss because it will be less than the long-term loss associated with that book of business.

Exhibit 5-10
Effect of Decreasing Earned Premium

Elements	Ratio	Comments
Incurred losses→ / Earned premiums↓	= Loss ratio↑	As incurred losses continue and earned premiums diminish, the loss ratio increases.
Underwriting expenses↑ / Written premiums↓	= Expense ratio↑	As underwriting expenses increase or remain constant and written premiums decrease, the expense ratio increases.

The Effect of Large Losses

During the process of retiring from a line of business, an insurer continues to be exposed to the potential of large losses. As premiums diminish, the effect of large losses becomes progressively more significant. Exhibit 5-11 illustrates the effect of a single large loss at various earned premium levels, assuming that the loss and expense ratios remain constant.

Exhibit 5-11
Effect of Large Losses During Product Retirement

Earned premium	$1,000,000	$250,000	$8,000	As the earned premium drops...
Incurred losses	$750,000	$187,500	$6,000	
Loss ratio	75%	75%	75%	
Large loss	$250,000	$250,000	$250,000	...a single severe loss...
Adjusted loss ratio (includiung large loss)	125%	200%	3,225%	...dramatically increases the loss ratio.

Educational Objective 4
Explain how insurers increase underwriting profit.

Improving Underwriting Profitability

An insurer can improve underwriting profitability by adjusting any or all of the three elements that comprise it. Increasing premiums, decreasing losses, or reducing expenses, individually or in combination, will improve a company's underwriting results. However, any adjustments to improve an element of profitability can negatively affect the other elements. For example, an underwriting change to decrease losses can also decrease premiums through the reduced number of new policies accepted. Any change is made with careful consideration of the interrelationship of the elements. Adjustments to improve underwriting profitability are difficult to accomplish while maintaining a balance among the elements of profitability.

Increasing Premium

Insurers can manage expenses and underwrite carefully to control losses, but the primary source of increased underwriting profits is growth. Insurers can increase premiums in the following three ways:

- By the sale of more policies or the acquisition of business by purchasing other companies
- By increasing the average premium per policy
- By raising rates

Insurers wishing to sell more policies or to sell policies with higher average premiums have several options including selective growth, growth in niche markets, and point-of-sale marketing.

Financial Limits on Growth

Insurers manage growth carefully because it is possible to grow too quickly and expose the company to so much risk that it becomes insolvent. Regulators monitor insurers' financial results closely to protect consumers from insurer insolvency. One of the key financial ratios that regulators evaluate is the written premium to policyholders' surplus ratio. This ratio can signify an insurer's vulnerability to pricing errors, above-average losses, and declines in the value of its investments. This ratio compares the cushion provided by policyholders' surplus to the risk represented by written premiums. It can also indicate an insurer's capacity to underwrite additional insurance. Ratios of greater than $3 written premium to $1 policyholders' surplus are a cause for concern.

Selective Growth

Premium growth is not automatically profitable. If increased premiums cause losses and expenses to grow disproportionately more, the strategy of premium growth will be counter-productive. Growth may be desirable in some lines but not in others. For example, Exhibit 5-12 shows the three-year performance for a hypothetical insurer that sells homeowner and automobile policies.

Exhibit 5-12
Auto and Homeowners Results

(in millions	Premiums			Losses			Expenses			Underwriting		
of dollars)	YR1	YR2	YR3	YR1	YR2	YR3	YR1	YR2	YR3	Profit (Loss)		
Auto liability	21	24	28	16	19	23	5	6	7	0	(1)	(2)
Homeowners	30	30	30	20	19	19	7	7	7	3	4	4
Total	51	54	58	36	38	42	12	13	14	3	3	2

The insurer's personal automobile liability line showed no profit in Year 1 and posted losses of $1 million and $2 million in Years 2 and 3. Fortunately the homeowners book of business is performing better, showing an underwriting profit in each of the last three years. In this case, the insurer will plan to grow selectively by increasing sales of its profitable homeowners policies.

Selective growth can also be used to increase the average premium per policy. For example, Exhibit 5-13 compares two portfolios of homeowners insurance.

The additional coverage purchased may increase underwriting expenses for Portfolio B because of additional physical inspections to verify replacement cost values, additional underwriting time to review scheduled fine arts, and so forth. Also, Portfolio B has a potentially higher loss exposure due to the increased values. Nevertheless, Portfolio B generates over $1 million more written premium than does Portfolio A. An insurer could increase its average premium per policy by increasing sales of high-valued policies.

Exhibit 5-13
Homeowners Portfolio Comparison

	Portfolio A	Portfolio B
Number of policies	5,000	5,000
Average value of homes	$92,000	$165,000
Average base premium	$450	$600
Number of policies with additional coverage	652	2,468
Average additional premium	$60	$156
Total written premium	$2,289,120	$3,385,008

Growth in Niche Markets

Another approach insurers use to increase premiums is to target niche or specialty markets. Niche market insurers serve risks that standard insurers are not willing to cover, such as mobile homes, customers with highly valuable collections of antiques, or customers with a history of large or frequent claims. Insurers that sell to niche markets believe that these markets offer the following advantages:

- Less competition
- Less price-sensitivity due to the reduced competition and the nature of the customers represented in the markets
- The ability to set underwriting standards more consistent with exposures
- The opportunity for large profits if underwriting and rating expertise is developed
- The opportunity to offer value-added services, such as storage of video tapes or digital images of collections scheduled on personal articles floaters
- More effective advertising due to a smaller market
- More referrals from current policyholders
- The insurer is recognized as an expert

While niche marketing has advantages, it also has the following risks and uncertainties:

- Because of the relatively smaller volumes, loss frequency and severity are less predictable than with more common products.
- Underwriting and pricing may be inadequate for the loss exposure assumed.
- Customer and regulatory response to new specialized products is unknown.
- Once begun, it might be difficult or impossible to withdraw from the market.

Insurers carefully evaluate the pros and cons of introducing specialty products or entering niche markets. Because of the risks involved and the potential effect on profits, specialty insurers evaluate many potential products and markets, selecting only the few with a relatively high probability of producing an underwriting profit.

Point-of-Sale Marketing

Personal insurance is marketed and distributed through a variety of channels. Insurers might hire staff to sell directly to individual consumers through direct marketing. Alternatively, insurers might distribute their products through independent insurance agents who represent several insurers. Finally, insurers might market to groups and associations, either directly or through an agent. Individual members of the group receive value-added services, specialized coverage, or reduced premiums if they purchase their insurance through the group plan. Insurers may select one or more of these product distribution channels. Exhibit 5-14 illustrates the various marketing channels for insurance products.

Exhibit 5-14
Insurance Marketing and Distribution

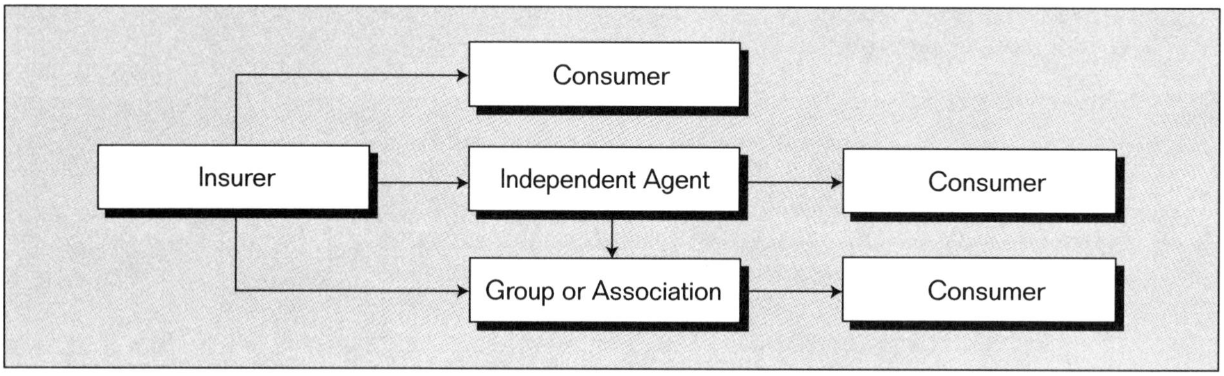

Point-of-sale marketing strategies change over time as insurers develop new ways to target potential purchasers. Traditionally, insurance was sold in a producer's office or perhaps at the purchaser's home. The sale was a face-to-face transaction and the producer recommended the appropriate levels and types of coverage for the purchaser. However insurers have developed new ways to reach consumers and increase premium growth. Examples of these new strategies include the following:

- Opening insurance offices in shopping malls or other public places
- Establishing toll-free services where consumers can purchase insurance by telephone
- Providing insurance quotations or selling insurance over the Internet

In addition to implementing new marketing strategies, insurers can increase premium growth by using their current distribution channels more effectively. Techniques insurers use to manage point-of-sale marketing activities include the following:

- Appointing producers in well-defined and potentially profitable territories

- Increasing the number of producers
- Increasing producer commission rates
- Creating additional sales incentives
- Reevaluating and modifying direct marketing programs
- Implementing alternative distribution strategies, such as direct or group marketing
- Increasing customer awareness of products through advertising, news bulletins, Web sites, or public service activities

Adjusting Rates

An insurer can grow by adjusting rates in either of the following ways:

- Raising rates to generate additional income from existing policies
- Lowering rates to make prices more attractive and sell more insurance

While each of these options can increase premiums, each also has a potential down side. For example, a small rate increase is unlikely to result in much customer dissatisfaction. However, larger increases often cause policyholders to shop around, particularly those who have the fewest losses. If this occurs on a large scale it has the following unfortunate results:

- Overall premiums decrease due to the loss of business.
- Loss ratios increase because the portfolio is disproportionately heavy in policyholders with poor loss experience who were unable to place their coverage elsewhere.

Some insurers only request rate increases that are in single-digit percentages. For example, an insurer would only request a 9 percent increase in homeowners rates, even though a 12 percent rate increase would have been acceptable to regulators. The insurer would then plan to obtain another rate increase the following year. Multiple small rate increases have less negative consumer effect than one large increase. In addition, small rate increases have a better chance of regulatory approval. Many regulators impose caps on the rate level increase that will be allowed when an insurer requests a change in rates.

Alternatively, an insurer can reduce rates in an effort to be more competitive. The risk here is that rates might be too low to cover losses and expenses. In this case, growth leads to unprofitability. In other words, as the insurer writes more policies, the more unprofitable the insurer becomes. As a result, when targeting growth, insurers adjust rates carefully and only as part of a broader sales strategy.

Decreasing Losses

Decreasing the frequency or severity of losses usually requires underwriting action. An insurer will determine whether producers and underwriters are complying with the company's underwriting guidelines. An insurer might find that its underwriting guidelines are ineffective and adjust them. Finally, an insurer will find ways to manage its catastrophe exposure.

Responding to Poor Loss Experience

Detailed examination of paid losses, loss reserves, and loss expenses can provide an insurer with indications as to the cause of poor loss experience and can suggest appropriate responses. Unfortunately, while an insurer's loss experience can deteriorate quickly as a result of catastrophes or large liability claims, for example, remedial underwriting measures can be slow to take effect, and results might not be apparent for some time. This is both a source of frustration for insurers and a cause for vigilance. The sooner deteriorating loss experience is identified and remedial action taken, the less the effect on the insurer's profitability. Exhibit 5-15 illustrates some of the factors that can adversely affect an insurer's loss experience, suggests remedial action, and presents some of the considerations associated with each remedy.

Checking Compliance With Underwriting Guidelines

To match premiums with loss exposures, insurers develop underwriting guidelines that specify which risks they will accept and how accepted risks are to be rated. Underwriting guidelines are applied by one or more of the following:

- The producer
- The insurer's underwriting staff
- The insurer's computer system

If the underwriting guidelines are not applied or are applied incorrectly, the premiums an insurer collects might be insufficient to cover its loss exposures. As a result, one response to unacceptable loss ratios is to check for compliance with underwriting guidelines. This process is called an underwriting review or underwriting audit.

Underwriting reviews can be completed by a permanent team of auditors, usually based at an insurer's head office or by an ad hoc team raised from outside the unit or region being audited. Auditors review a sampling of files to determine the quality of the underwriting and provide a report outlining any shortfalls or deviations from the guidelines. This information can be used as the basis for producer or underwriter training, system reprogramming, censure, or other remedial action. If an underwriting audit identifies significant deviation from an insurer's guidelines, a complete reunderwriting of the portfolio could be required to correct the situation.

Adjusting Underwriting Guidelines

An insurer might determine that its underwriting guidelines are ineffective in matching rates to exposures. For example, an insurer that offers a discount to young drivers with driver training could find that the loss experience this group generates is no different from the loss experience of young drivers without driver training, making the discount inappropriate. This happens most frequently when an insurer has entered a new line of business in which it is inexperienced; but it can also result from changes in society, the regulatory environment, or demographics.

Exhibit 5-15
Factors Adversely Affecting Losses and Possible Remedial Actions

Area	Factor	Remedial Actions and Considerations
Rating	Premiums are too low to cover loss exposures.	*Increase premiums.* Unfortunately, because premiums must be earned during the year, rate increases are slow to take effect. Also, regulatory and competitive pressures can limit an insurer's ability to increase rates.
Underwriting	Underwriting guidelines are ineffective or are not being correctly applied.	*Adjust/enforce underwriting guidelines.* This generally involves reunderwriting the portfolio and changing to coverage or rating at each policy's renewal. Therefore, changing it requires a full year to complete plus additional time for rating changes to be reflected in earned premium.
Policy wording	The insurer's policy language is open to broader interpretation than was intended, and this was not contemplated by the rates.	*Rewrite policy language.* Changes can strengthen the policy language. However, a complete reissue of new policies containing the new language requires a full year to implement, increased printing and mailing costs, plus additional time for the changes to be reflected in a reduction in paid losses. In addition, there is no guarantee that the new language will be free from misinterpretation or that it will receive regulatory approval.
Reserving	Loss reserves are inaccurate.	*Adjust loss reserves and train staff.* Insurers must be sure their reserves are wrong before adjusting them on a blanket basis. Manipulating reserves to achieve certain financial results is a form of fraud. Blanket reserve adjustments or changes in IBNR can be made relatively quickly. However, adjustments affect underwriting profits, policyholders' surplus, and the company's financial position. They are also subject to regulatory control. Training staff to improve reserve setting can be effective, but the effect on incurred losses is slow.
Claim handling	Loss expenses are too high or claim representatives are inefficient or are over-paying claims.	*Train staff.* Training staff to improve claim handling skills can be effective, but the effect on incurred losses is slow and the training itself generates additional expenses.

If an insurer determines its underwriting guidelines are ineffective, the insurer will make appropriate changes to its underwriting guidelines, follow up with producer and underwriter training, or initiate system changes. As its portfolio renews, the new guidelines will be applied to the insurer's existing policies.

Managing Catastrophe Exposures

While insurers cannot accurately predict catastrophes, they can anticipate them and work to minimize their exposure to them. Insurers mitigate or manage their catastrophe exposures by doing a variety of things including the following:

- Increasing deductibles or introducing deductibles that are a percentage of the insured loss
- Introducing policy exclusions and sublimits for windstorm or earthquake coverages
- Promoting safety programs and building code improvement programs by offering lower deductibles and premium discounts to policyholders who meet certain criteria
- Taking advantage of reinsurance to limit the effect of catastrophe losses on the insurer
- Joining with other insurers to form risk-sharing pools to underwrite significant exposures such as earthquakes
- Offsetting anticipated catastrophe losses by increasing lower-risk premium income from areas not prone to catastrophes
- Monitoring the geographic distribution of insured risks and limiting, as much as possible, the concentration of policy writing in catastrophe-prone areas

Jargon Alert!

Redlining is the practice of refusing to accept any business in a particular area, for example, a beachfront community susceptible to wind damage.

Insurers implement this last option carefully. While tracking loss exposures and premium writings by area or even by zip code helps insurers to develop detailed pictures of catastrophe-prone areas, regulation does not allow insurers to practice *redlining*. In fact, an insurer may even be required to accept its proportionate share of risks in a catastrophe-prone area.

However, regulation does allow an insurer to offset exposures. For example, an insurer offering windstorm coverage in Florida may choose to maintain a one-to-ten ratio of coastal properties to those located more than five miles inland.

Controlling Expenses

Insurers often respond to poor underwriting results by introducing expense control measures. Controlling expenses has two potentially positive effects on underwriting profits. First, reducing expenses lowers an insurer's combined ratio. In addition, reduced expenses can be passed along to policyholders in the form of lower rates, resulting in increased sales and higher premium income.

Insurers often respond to excessive expenses by introducing cost-cutting measures. Unfortunately, although expenses can be adjusted quickly, this approach is not always the most effective or profitable in the long term. For example, a minimum expense level is required to provide acceptable service to customers.

Aside from the direct effect that high expenses have on profitability, insurers have an additional motivation to control costs. To adjust rates, insurers must first receive approval from state regulators. Before approving any adjustment, regulators review the insurer's financial performance. An insurer with inflated expenses will be less successful in receiving approval than will an insurer that operates more cost effectively.

An insurer can control expenses in the following two ways:

- By maximizing the caliber, efficiency, and productivity of its employees
- By controlling or reducing the amount of money it spends

An approach to establishing a target budget for underwriting expenses, illustrated in Exhibit 5-16, involves estimating earned premiums, subtracting estimated losses, and then allocating the remainder as the budget for underwriting expenses. The application of this general approach has reduced expense ratios throughout the industry in past years and has encouraged the development of new, creative, and more cost-effective approaches to sales and customer service.

Exhibit 5-16
Establishing Underwriting Expense Targets

Target underwriting budget = Projected earned premiums – Estimated incurred losses

Maximizing Human Resources

An insurer's largest underwriting expenses are those related to its human resources. Salaries, benefits, training, and related costs make up a significant portion of every insurer's underwriting expenses. However, as a service business, insurance is necessarily a "people-heavy" industry. As a result, insurers try to maximize their use of human resources. Some examples include the following:

- Training employees thoroughly to improve productivity and reduce errors
- Equipping employees to be most efficient (such as with computers, calculators, and e-mail)
- Paying competitive salaries and benefits to attract and retain good employees
- Offering career development and advancement opportunities to attract and retain good employees

Another way in which an insurer can maximize its use of personnel is to automate where appropriate. Personal lines lends itself to automation because products are standardized and rating methods are consistent. Traditionally, personal lines staff complete many repetitive, manual calculations or processes daily. However, this is the kind of activity at which computers excel, in terms of both speed and accuracy. Automating these tasks has freed up staff to do those things at which computers are less skilled than are people (for example, identifying and meeting the needs of policyholders, offering advice, or building policyholder relationships). In addition, the increased efficiency with which computers can handle tasks such as rating, policy issuance, statistical analysis, and information management provides support to employees that allows each individual to accomplish more.

However, automation requires a significant initial investment. Before embracing computerization, insurers weigh the costs against potential savings in human resources, projected sales increases due to improved efficiency, and the degree to which the competition is already automated.

Fixed costs are expenses that remain the same, in the short term, regardless of the amount of business an insurer writes. **Variable costs** are expenses that change relative to premium volume increases or decreases.

Managing Underwriting Expenses

An insurer's underwriting expenses fall into two general categories: **fixed costs** and **variable costs**. An insurer's fixed underwriting expenses remain the same, in the short term, regardless of increases or decreases in premium volume. Fixed expenses include such costs as the lease of premises or computer systems, salaries and employee benefits, and the cost of maintaining a fleet of company cars. Variable underwriting expenses are those that are directly related to premium volume. Variable costs increase or decrease with changes in written premium. Variable underwriting expenses include expenses such as producers' sales commissions and premium taxes paid to the state.

There are two ways that an insurer can control its expenses or costs. The first is to spend less. For example, negotiating lower leasing costs for premises is an effective way of increasing profits by reducing a fixed cost. Obtaining property inspection reports at reduced costs is an effective way of increasing profits by reducing a variable cost. Other examples of methods insurers use to reduce fixed and variable expenses include the following:

- Reduce premises costs by consolidating branch offices into one central office
- Discontinue providing and maintaining company cars
- Avoid the hiring of additional staff by consolidating job functions.
- Outsource services such as systems support or marketing

The second way that an insurer can control underwriting expenses is to increase the productivity of the resources it has. For example, training can help an insurer's staff to work more efficiently. This can generate increased production without increasing expenses, resulting in higher underwriting profits. Other examples of efforts to improve productivity include the following:

- Reorganize an office layout to add work space for more employees
- Run two work shifts to double the use of office resources
- Allocate unused computer capacity to the automation of additional functions
- Sublet unused office space to generate income

Exhibit 5-17 illustrates the effect of changes in fixed and variable underwriting expenses on an insurer's expense ratio. The illustration in Exhibit 5-17 demonstrates the changes in the expense ratio with changes in fixed and variable expenses. However, reductions in expenses do not create easy corrections. For example, a reduction in commissions will probably result in a reduction in new applications submitted by producers. This is especially true if an insurer reduces commission below that of its competitors. The insurer should consider the consequences of any changes on overall profitability.

Exhibit 5-17
Fixed and Variable Underwriting Expenses

	Written Premium	Lease Payments (Fixed Cost)	Salaries and Benefits (Fixed Cost)	15% Sales Commissions (Variable Cost)	Total Expenses	Expense Ratio
The company posts $40 million in written premium. The company has fixed costs including lease payments and employee salaries and benefits, as well as variable costs including the 15 percent commission it pays producers.	$40 million	$900,000	$1 million	$6 million	$7.9 million	19.75%
Written premiums increase to $50 million and fixed costs remain the same. Commissions (variable cost) rise with increased sales. The increased written premium causes the expense ratio to decrease.	$50 million (increased sales)	$900,000	$1 million	$7.5 million	$9.4 million	18.8% (reduced expense ration)
Written premiums remain the same; however, the insurer has sublet a portion of its building and laid off some staff. This reduction in fixed costs results in a further decrease in the expense ratio.	$50 million	$700,000 (sublet space)	$900.000 (staff layoffs)	$7.5 million	$9.1 million	18.2% (reduced expense ratio)
The insurer reduces the commission rate it pays from 15 percent to 10 percent. This results in a significant reduction in overall costs and the expense ratio drops by 5 percent.	$50 million	$700,000	$900,000	$5 million (reduced to 10%)	$6.6 million	13.2% (reduced expense ratio)

Educational Objectives 5

Given a case study, describe actions an insurer might take to improve underwriting profitability.

Improving Profitability—Case Study

At the end of Year 1, Homesaver General Insurance Company, a hypothetical insurer writing only personal auto and homeowners policies, posted a $13 million underwriting loss. Concerned about this poor performance, the company's management team examined the results for the year. They quickly identified the personal automobile insurance portfolio as the source of the problem.

Almost 70 percent of Homesaver's written premium was generated by the sale of personal automobile insurance. Unfortunately, the line showed a loss ratio of 90 percent and a combined ratio of 119 percent. The results in the homeowners portfolio were much better, with a combined ratio of 89 percent and an underwriting profit of $3 million. Unfortunately, the relatively smaller size of the homeowners portfolio meant that this excellent performance had little effect on the insurer's overall results.

Review of the company's incurred losses for the automobile portfolio showed that reserving was adequate and that claim representatives were working very efficiently to keep loss expenses down. The high loss ratio was partially due to high paid losses. Further analysis indicated a frequency problem. Policyholders were making significantly more low-valued claims than projected, and the rates the insurer was charging were insufficient to cover the losses.

Homesaver's competitive position in the marketplace precluded it from increasing rates. The company already charged premiums higher than many other insurers, and the vice president of Marketing was concerned that a rate increase would make it extremely difficult to meet growth targets and to retain existing business.

The company distributes its products through independent agents. Many of these agents had long-term, loyal relationships with the company and continued to support it despite its uncompetitive rates. As a result, the insurer had been hesitant to follow an industry trend towards lower commissions and had not taken the 5 percent reduction that many other insurers had already implemented.

After discussions and negotiation among all departments and levels within the organization, as well as with many of its long-term agents, Homesaver established a strategic goal and tactical plans to support that goal. Exhibit 5-18 presents an overview of the plan. Exhibit 5-19 shows the company's year-end results for Year 1 and Year 2.

Exhibit 5-18
Homesaver's Strategy, Tactics, and Activity

- **Strategy** We will reduce the combined ratio to 103 percent.
  - **Tactic** Reduce the automobile loss ratio to 75 percent.
    - **Activity** Identify and reunderwrite all policies with more than 3 losses in the past 5 years.
    - **Activity** Increase physical damage deductibles on 60 percent of all automobile policies.
  - **Tactic** Improve the ratio of automobile to homeowners policies in force by increasing homeowners written premiums by 10 percent.
    - **Activity** Launch a homeowners sales incentive program.
    - **Activity** Decrease homeowners rates by 10 percent.
  - **Tactic** Reduce the overall expense ratio to 25 percent.
    - **Activity** Reduce commission rates paid to producers by 3 percent.

Exhibit 5-19
Homesaver General Insurance Company Year-End Results

Overall		**Year 1**	**Year 2**
	Written premiums	$119 million	$119 million
	Earned premiums	$113 million	$114 million
	Incurred losses	$92 million	$81 million
	Underwriting expenses	$34 million	$29.7 million
	Underwriting profit	($13 million)	$3.3 million
	Loss ratio	81%	71%
	Expense ratio	28.5%	25%
	Combined ratio	109.5%	96%
Automobile			
	Written premiums	$83 million	$80 million
	Earned premiums	$80 million	$78 million
	Incurred losses	$72 million	$59 million
	Underwriting expenses	$24 million	$20 million
	Underwriting profit	($16 million)	($1 million)
	Loss ratio	90%	75.6%
	Expense ratio	29%	25%
	Combined ratio	119%	100.6%
Homeowners			
	Written premiums	$36 million	$39 million
	Earned premiums	$33 million	$36 million
	Incurred losses	$20 million	$22 million
	Underwriting expenses	$10 million	$9.7 million
	Underwriting profit	$3 million	$4.3 million
	Loss ratio	61%	61%
	Expense ratio	28%	25%
	Combined ratio	89%	86%

* Numbers in parentheses indicate losses.

During Year 2, the management and staff at Homesaver's worked together to achieve their goals. Each month, the Management Information Group circulated reports to all staff comparing the company's performance to its goals. This helped to focus the organization and ensured all levels and departments worked cooperatively.

The reunderwriting of the automobile portfolio required more staff and caused some initial increases in expenses. A total of $2.2 million in written automobile premium was nonrenewed at the election of the insurer. In addition, sales in automobile insurance were very slow due to the uncompetitiveness of Homesaver's rates and an additional half million in written premiums was lost as policyholders replaced their coverage with more competitive insurers.

The increased deductibles were also responsible for a reduction in written premium. However, the Marketing Department convinced policyholders to increase deductibles to save money, and the company lost very few customers as a result of the change.

The combined effect of nonrenewing loss-prone drivers and increasing deductibles had a very positive effect on the company's claim frequency, and the loss ratio dropped to 73 percent.

The actions taken in the automobile portfolio reduced the total written premiums by $3 million over the year. In contrast, the sales incentive for producers and rate decrease in the homeowners line resulted in significant growth, and the company met its target of increasing homeowners written premiums by 10 percent.

Reducing the sales commission rate by 3 percent resulted in significant savings as well, and although Homesaver's sales agents were not enthusiastic about the change, the company compensated by increasing the producers' front-line underwriting authority. This change made writing business with the company faster and easier for producers and allowed them to provide better service to their customers. Increasing producers' underwriting authority also reduced some of the underwriting expenses incurred by the insurer. The combined result of these changes was an overall drop of 3.5 percent in Homesaver's expense ratio.

At the end of Year 2, the management and staff of Homesaver General had managed to exceed their goals and show a small underwriting profit.

Summary

An insurer raises capital from individuals, groups, other business, or venture capitalists to establish underwriting operations. Subsequently, policyholder premiums are the insurer's major source of income. Written premiums represent both an insurer's total sales and the amount of risk that the insurer has assumed. However, the insurer cannot count premiums as income until they are earned. After deducting incurred losses and underwriting expenses from earned premiums, the insurer may post an underwriting profit or loss. In the case of an underwriting profit, the funds can be invested to generate additional income for the insurer. Any remaining profits are added to policyholders' surplus, which in turn is reinvested. If the company posts an underwriting loss, current investment income is used to make up the shortfall.

An insurer's profitability can be affected by many things, including the adequacy of the premiums it charges, the efficiency of its operations, its loss experience, the competitive environment in which it operates, and other external forces such as catastrophes, changes in regulation, and changes in its reinsurance arrangements. As a result, insurers establish goals and monitor performance in each of the three components of underwriting profit: earned premiums, incurred losses, and underwriting expenses. If a company is not on target with its goals, there are a variety of actions it can take to improve its results including the following:

- Grow selectively
- Grow in niche markets
- Adjust point-of-sale marketing strategy
- Respond to poor loss experience
- Adjust rates
- Ensure compliance with underwriting guidelines
- Adjust underwriting guidelines
- Manage catastrophe exposures
- Maximize human resources
- Manage underwriting expenses

Chapter Note

1. Insurance Information Institute, *The Fact Book 1999: Property/Casualty Insurance Facts* (New York: Insurance Information Institute, 1998), pp. 73-74.

Pricing Personal Insurance Products

Chapter 6

Educational Objectives

1. Describe the pricing components used in personal lines insurance, and explain how the relativity factors are applied in personal lines insurance. (pp. 6-3 to 6-11)
2. Explain how insurers analyze loss data and forecast trends to determine rate levels. (pp. 6-11 to 6-15)
3. a. Describe the methods used by insurers to determine changes in rate levels.
   b. Given a case study, select the appropriate methods required to create a rate change. (pp. 6-16 to 6-19)
4. Describe methods actuaries use in ratemaking. (pp. 6-19 to 6-21)
5. Describe the role of investment income in ratemaking. (pp. 6-21 to 6-22)
6. Explain how insurers price new insurance products. (pp. 6-22 to 6-25)
7. Describe the regulatory objectives used in evaluating insurance rates. (pp. 6-25 to 6-28)
8. Describe the social objectives used in evaluating insurance rates. (pp. 6-28 to 6-31)
9. Given a situation in which an insurance product is experiencing a lack of profitability, explain how the insurer might use the following to restore profitability: (pp. 6-31 to 6-36)
   - Premium and loss analysis
   - Premium and loss forecasting
   - Rate relativities

Outline

I. Pricing Components
  A. Pure Premium, Base Rates, and Base Premiums
  B. Loss Costs
  C. Rate Relativity Factors
  D. Distributing Rate Relativity Factors Among Classifications

II. Analyzing Loss Data and Forecasting Trends
  A. Analyzing and Forecasting Loss Frequency Trends
  B. Analyzing and Forecasting Loss Severity Trends
  C. Comparing Loss Frequency and Severity Among Groups

III. Methods of Determining Rate Levels
  A. Frequency and Severity Analysis Method
  B. Loss Cost Analysis Method

IV. Ratemaking Methods
  A. Judgment Method
  B. Loss Ratio Method
  C. Pure Premium Method

V. Investment Income in Ratemaking

VI. Pricing New Insurance Products
  A. Potential for Profit
  B. Confidence in Estimates
  C. Projected Expenses

VII. Regulatory Objectives in Rate Evaluation
  A. Rate Adequacy
  B. Rate Equity
  C. Rate Moderacy

VIII. Social Objectives in Rate Evaluation
  A. Insurance Affordability
  B. Insurance Availability
  C. Loss Control Incentives
  D. Responsiveness to Change
  E. Rate Stability
  F. Controllable Rating Factors

IX. ABC Insurance Case Study
  A. Premium and Loss Analysis for ABC
  B. Premium and Loss Forecasting for ABC
  C. Rate Relativities Application for ABC

X. Summary

Chapter 6

Pricing Personal Insurance Products

Pricing personal insurance products is as much an art as a science. The manufacturer of a tangible object, such as a chair, can calculate the exact cost of producing and marketing that product and set its prices by adding operating expenses and a profit margin to its manufacturing and marketing costs. Insurers, on the other hand, sell promises and do not know which ones they will be called upon to fulfill, or when. Therefore, individuals responsible for pricing insurance products attempt to predict what an insurer's loss experience will be and base pricing on those predictions. Over time, they adjust pricing in response to the insurer's actual results. This process often involves input from several areas within an insurance organization, including the actuarial department, underwriting department, marketing department, and sales force.

This chapter presents the following aspects of personal insurance pricing:

- An introduction to actuarial terms, concepts, tools, and techniques
- An analysis of how an insurer uses information to establish and adjust pricing
- A presentation of the various internal and external factors that influence an insurer's pricing decisions
- A case study to review and consolidate the information contained in the earlier sections

Educational Objective 1

Describe the pricing components used in personal lines insurance, and explain how the relativity factors are applied in personal lines insurance.

Pricing Components

Actuaries use a variety of mathematical tools and techniques in pricing insurance products. While the calculations can be complex, the basic underlying concepts are relatively straightforward. The components of insurance pricing include the following:

- Pure premiums, base rates, and base premiums
- Loss costs
- Rate relativity factors

Pure Premium, Base Rates, and Base Premiums

To establish rates and premiums for a line of business and to calculate premiums for individual policies, an insurer's staff members complete the following steps:

1. Derive the **pure premium** per **exposure unit** by estimating the value of projected losses associated with that line of business based on past claim data and current trends.
2. Derive the **base rate** that the insurer must charge per **unit of coverage** to cover losses and expenses and to ensure that the line is profitable.
3. Calculate the **base premium** for each individual policy based on the total amount of coverage afforded by that policy.

Pure premium is charged per exposure unit because exposure units measure loss potential and pure premium is based solely on an insured's projected value of losses (disregarding other expenses and profits). Because the length of coverage affects the potential for loss, exposure units are often expressed in terms of time. For example, one house insured for twelve months constitutes one house-year. Two cars each insured for six months together make up one car-year. This approach allows actuaries to eliminate the effects of, or *factor out*, varying policy inception dates and policy periods from their calculations.

In contrast to pure premium, a base rate includes a charge for expenses and profits as well as a charge for potential loss. To develop a base rate, an insurer adds a standard charge for expenses and profits to the pure premium. This charge might be a percentage of the pure premium. By adding this standard charge, insurers facilitate the process of calculating premiums for individual policies. Base rates are expressed relative to a specific unit of coverage, such as $1,000 of Coverage A on a homeowners policy.

Pure premium is the average amount of money an insurer must charge *per exposure unit* in order to be able to cover the total anticipated losses for that line of business.

Exposure units (or **units of exposure**) are measures of loss potential.

The **base rate** is the amount of money per unit of coverage required to cover the insurer's losses, expenses, and profit for a line of business.

A **unit of coverage** (or **coverage unit**) is a standard block of insurance protection used in rating a line of business.

Base premiums reflect the basic cost of specific individual insurance policies.

Jargon Alert!

The term *factor out* refers to the elimination of an element in an analysis. The element eliminated is unnecessary and cumbersome to deal with, has a negligible effect on the calculation, or represents an uncharacteristic event that is unlikely to recur.

After developing the base rate, the insurer can multiply it by the number of coverage units to derive the base premium. The base premium represents the cost for basic coverage.

Exhibit 6-1 presents a simple illustration of the relationships among pure premiums, base rates, and base premiums for a homeowners insurance product.

Exhibit 6-1
Pure Premiums, Base Rates, and Base Premiums—Homeowners

Item	Value	Explanation
Exposure units	3,000 house-years	The exposure unit value used represents 3,000 houses insured for one year each. Each house is valued at $100,000.
Anticipated loss	$975,000	The insurer's actuaries establish this value based on industry-wide data, the insurer's own historical loss data, and an analysis of current trends.
Pure premium per exposure unit	$325	Pure premium is calculated as follows: Anticipated losses ÷ Exposure units = Pure premium $975,000 ÷ 3,000 = $325; average pure premium per house
Coverage unit	$1,000 of Coverage A	A standard block of insurance protection is established for rating purposes.
Base rate per $1,000 of Coverage A	$4.26	Base rate is calculated as follows: Pure premium per exposure unit ÷ number of coverage units $325 ÷ 100 = $3.25; 100 coverage units in a $100,000 house Pure premium per unit of coverage + expenses + profit $3.25 + $0.82 + $0.19 = $4.26
Base premium for $100,000 of Coverage A	$426	The calculation of the base premium for a single policy with $100,000 Coverage A limit is as follows: Coverage A limit ÷ Units of coverage × Base rate $100,000 ÷ 1,000 × $4.26 = $426

A **loss cost** is the average incurred loss per exposure unit for a line of business, risk classification, or coverage.

Loss development describes payment-related changes, such as increases and decreases in reserve amounts, over the life of a claim.

Loss Costs

An alternative method for establishing rates is by applying **loss costs.** The loss cost for a line of business, risk classification, or coverage is the average amount per exposure unit paid in claims for each category. To ensure that loss costs are accurate and representative, they are usually developed using data from several previous years.

Currently, pooled loss cost data, adjusted to reflect **loss development** and current trends, is available to insurers from advisory organizations such as Insurance Services Office (ISO) and the American Association of Insurance Services (AAIS). Unlike individual insurers, advisory organizations have access to industry-wide data. This wealth of data allows these organizations to better predict future loss costs. Pooled loss cost data help insurers develop rates that are statistically more credible than those based solely on their own individual loss experience.

Historically, advisory organizations developed actual base rates that included factors for losses, expenses, and even profits. Some insurers, particularly smaller companies, simply adopted these advisory rates. Others used advisory rates as the starting point from which they developed their own rates based on their own loss experience.

During the late 1980s, consumers and regulators became concerned that the use of advisory rates resembled price fixing. Consequently, in 1990 states began moving to a system in which advisory organizations developed and published projected loss costs only. The intent was to promote independence and increased competition among insurers while continuing to provide a statistically credible basis for ratemaking. Individual insurers were encouraged to base rates as much as possible on their own loss experience. However, if that experience was insufficient to develop statistically credible rates, they could still use an advisory organization's loss costs, adding factors for expenses and profits. Insurers using loss costs must file rates with the state but may do so by referencing the advisory organization's loss costs and filing their own expense and profit factors.

Rate Relativity Factors

When an insurer first establishes the base rate for an insurance product, it makes certain assumptions to help simplify the calculation. These assumptions include the following:

- The potential loss frequency, or number of losses, is uniform throughout the portfolio.
- The potential loss severity, or dollar value of individual losses, is uniform throughout the portfolio.
- The cost of settling claims is uniform throughout the portfolio.

In reality, however, the frequency and severity of losses within a portfolio and the cost of settling those claims can vary significantly. For example, the potential severity of a fire loss is greater if a home is located in a remote area. It takes firefighters longer to reach the site and a lack of hydrant protection means that the only water available to fight the blaze might be that which firefighters are able to transport. In addition, the cost of settling the claim may be greater because building materials and tradespeople will need to be brought in from a distance.

Insurers adjust pricing to respond to the different levels of risk within a line of business in the following way:

1. First, they subdivide the line into smaller, homogeneous groups for the purpose of adjusting rates for each group. This process is called **risk classification**. The groups formed through this process are also called risk classifications or **rate classes**.
2. Then they analyze the unique loss experience for each rate class.
3. Finally they adjust rates to reflect the relatively higher or lower loss exposure of each rate class by applying **rate relativity factors**.

Risk classification is the formation of different premiums for the same coverage based on a homogeneous group's characteristics. The group formed for this purpose is also referred to as a risk classification or a rate class.

A **rate relativity factor** is a number by which a base rate may be multiplied to reflect the relatively higher or lower loss exposure of one homogeneous group compared to that of another.

Rate classes are formed when there is not sufficient information to estimate a rate for an individual risk. To derive a rate, individuals who are expected to have the same loss experience are grouped together.

The development of appropriate rate relativity factors is an important step in ensuring adequate pricing. Insurers analyze claim data and then use this information as the basis for establishing or adjusting risk classifications. Throughout the insurance industry, standard rate classes are used to develop rate relativity factors in residential property and personal auto insurance. In many states, each insurer develops its own rate relativity factors for these rate classes based on its own loss experience. Some states, however, limit the range of variation in relativity factors, and others actually specify the factors that insurers must use. Regulations also stipulate those characteristics insurers may and may not use as rating factors.

To develop rate relativity factors, actuaries complete the following steps:

1. Select one rate class.
2. Establish an appropriate base rate for that rate class.
3. Assign this rate class a relativity factor of 1.0 and name it the **unity classification**.
4. Compare the loss experience of other rate classes with that of the unity classification.
5. Calculate the relative level of risk for each rate class.
6. Assign a rate relativity factor to each rate class based on its relative level of risk.

The **unity classification** is one rate class, selected as a baseline, to which all other rate classes are compared.

Exhibit 6-2 illustrates the basic calculation of rate relativity factors. Rate class A is the unity classification. By comparing the loss experience for rate classes B and C with that of rate class A, actuaries can establish the relative degree of risk for rate classes B and C and assign appropriate rate relativity factors.

Jargon Alert!

An insurer might wish to discourage applicants and policyholders with specific types of loss exposures from placing their coverage with the insurer. This generally occurs when the insurer has had excessive losses with similar exposures. Examples include houses with wooden roofs in fire-prone areas, high-value vehicles parked on the street, or valuable jewelry that is not kept in a vault. The insurer will raise the rate relativity for those risk classifications so that the insurer is not offering a competitive premium. The insurer has *priced itself out* of the competitive market for those rate classes.

Exhibit 6-2

Calculation and Application of Rate Relativity Factors

Group	Loss Experience	Rate Relativity Factor
Rate Class A (unity classification)	used as baseline	1.0 (unity)
Rate Class B	20% higher than unity classification	1.20 (20% greater than unity)
Rate Class C	5% lower than unity classification	0.95 (5% less than unity)

Insurers also use rate relativity factors as a marketing and portfolio management tool, increasing rates for undesirable rate classes and decreasing rates in more attractive classes. This allows the insurer to be competitive in the rate classes it wishes to write and to *price itself out* of rate classes in which it prefers to limit its exposure.

Residential Property Rate Relativities

In residential property rating, insurers classify risks according to a variety of characteristics including the following:

- Type of building construction (such as frame or masonry)
- Coverage A limits purchased
- Type of coverage purchased (such as named perils or "all-risks" coverage)
- Level of public coverage available (such as the distance to hydrants or number of units between fire walls in multifamily dwellings)

For each of these rate classes, insurers develop rate relativity factors based on industry-wide loss data, current trends, and their own past and projected loss experience.

Construction Class Rate Relativity Factors

Analysis of claim data confirms what common sense suggests: frame homes catch fire more frequently and burn more severely than do homes made of brick or stone. This information helps insurers classify residential risks based on construction types (such as frame, masonry veneer, or solid masonry). Each risk classification is assigned a rate relativity factor based on the loss experience it generates. Exhibit 6-3 illustrates the calculation of two construction class relativity factors and a comparison of the resulting adjusted base rates. In this case, the insurer has selected the masonry classification as unity and assigned a base rate of $3.45.

Exhibit 6-3
Residential Construction Class Rate Relativity Factors

Risk Classification (Construction Class)	Loss Experience	Rate Relativity Factor	Calculation (Base Rate × Rate Relativity Factor)	Adjusted Base Rate per $1,000 of Coverage A
Masonry (unity classification)	Baseline	1.0 (unity)	$3.45 × 1.0	$3.45
Frame	25% higher than masonry homes	1.25 (25% > unity)	$3.45 × 1.25	$4.31

Coverage A Rate Relativity Factors

Analysis of residential property losses indicates that the majority of claims are relatively small. As the severity of losses increases, the frequency of those losses decreases, and large losses are rare. Consequently, insurers match rates to exposures by charging relatively more for lower Coverage A limits than for higher limits. They do this by subdividing Coverage A limits into ranges and then developing a rate relativity factor for each range. Exhibit 6-4 presents an example of Coverage A rate relativity factors. The insurer has selected the lowest range as unity and has assigned a base rate of $4.00.

Exhibit 6-4
Coverage A Rate Relativity Factors

Risk Classification (Coverage A Range)	Base Rate	Rate Relativity Factor	Adjusted Base Rate per $1,000 of Coverage A
$1 – $100,000	$4.00	1.0 (unity)	$4.00
$100,001 – $150,000	$4.00	0.965	$3.86
$150,001 – $200,000	$4.00	0.91	$3.64
$200,001 +	$4.00	0.885	$3.54

Alternatively, an insurer may develop its rate relativity factors from a marketing perspective. For example, an insurer wishing to increase its writings of homes over $200,000 might reduce the rate relativity factor for that range to make its premiums for these homes competitive and more attractive to consumers.

Policy Form Rate Relativity Factors

Insurers sell a variety of residential property policies. Some policies, such as the Homeowners 2 Broad Form (HO-2), provide a basic range of perils. Some, such as the Homeowners 3 Special Form (HO-3), offer "all-risks" coverage with certain exclusions. In addition, some policy wording is tailored for tenants or condominium owners whose loss exposures are more limited than are those of homeowners. The broader the coverage provided by a policy, the wider the range of the losses to which it will respond. This results in a relatively higher number of incurred losses on forms providing broader coverage. Insurers analyze claim data by policy form to develop rate relativity factors that reflect the higher loss exposure associated with broader coverage. Exhibit 6-5 illustrates the basic calculation and application of policy form rate relativity factors. In this example, the insurer has selected the HO-2 as unity and has assigned a base rate of $3.25.

Exhibit 6-5
Policy Form Rate Relativity Factors

Risk Classification (Policy Form)	Loss Experience	Rate Relativity Factor	Adjusted Base Rate per $1,000 of Coverage A
HO-2 (unity classification)	baseline	1.0 (unity)	$3.25
HO-3	16% higher than unity classification	1.16 (16% > unity)	$3.77
HO-4 (Contents Broad Form)	30% lower than unity classification	0.70 (30% < unity)	$2.28

Public Protection Classification Rate Relativity Factors

The level of public fire protection available varies by community. Most urban areas have permanent, full-time fire departments, and homes are short distances from fire hydrants. Smaller communities may not have fire hydrants or may depend on a volunteer fire department. People in some rural areas may not have access to any conventional fire-fighting services.

The potential severity of any fire loss is directly related to the fire-fighting services available. ISO evaluates the fire-fighting factors of individual communities and assigns each a public protection classification (PPC) of from 1 to 10. The lower the grade, the better the fire-fighting services. This grading system is used for residential property rating by insurers in all states.

Actuaries develop rate relativity factors to reflect the anticipated risk of fire losses implied by each PPC. Exhibit 6-6 illustrates the use of PPCs in developing rate relativity factors and the effect of these rate relativity factors on base premiums in different communities. The insurer has selected a PPC of 5 as unity and has assigned a base rate of $3.75.

Exhibit 6-6
Public Protection Classification Rate Relativity Factors

City/Town	PPC	Rate Relativity Factor	Adjusted Base Rate per $1,000 of Coverage A	Base Premium by Community for $150,000 Coverage A
Adamston	5 (average)	1.0 (unity)	$3.75	$562.50 ($150,000 ÷ $1,000 × 3.75)
Bentonville	2 (excellent)	0.87 (13% < unity)	$3.26	$489.00 ($150,000 ÷ $1,000 × 3.26)
Carlisle	8 (limited)	1.18 (18% > unity)	$4.43	$664.50 ($150,000 ÷ $1,000 × 4.43)

Personal Auto Rate Relativity Factors

The calculation of premiums on personal automobile policies also involves the use of rate relativity factors. As with residential property rating, some states limit the amount of variation allowed in automobile rate relativity factors. Still, several reasonably standard automobile risk classifications relate to the driver, the vehicle, the coverage, and the territory in which the vehicle is garaged and used.

Auto Insurance Territory Rate Relativity Factors

Just as the potential severity of a fire can depend on the location of a home, an automobile's loss exposure depends on the environment in which it is garaged and operated. For example, vehicles regularly driven in heavy urban traffic are more exposed to collision losses than are vehicles driven in sparsely populated rural areas. Vehicles garaged in some locations may have an increased exposure to theft, vandalism, or weather-related losses.

Depending on the state, insurers, regulators, or rating organizations divide states geographically into rating territories used by all automobile insurers. Many states permit insurers to develop rate relativity factors that reflect their own incurred loss experience in each of these territories. However, other states have limitations and guidelines restricting the territory rate relativity factors for personal auto insurance. This is done to provide affordable rates in politically sensitive urban areas.

Other Auto Insurance Rate Relativity Factors

Depending upon state regulation, a variety of details relating to the driver, the vehicle and the coverage purchased may form the basis for automobile risk classifications and rate relativity factors. These include, among others, the following:

- Age and sex of operator
- Driving record of operator
- Years of driving experience of operator
- Use of vehicle (such as pleasure use or commuting use)
- Liability limits selected
- Physical damage deductibles selected
- Age, value, and repair costs of vehicle

Advisory organizations, regulators, and insurers analyze incurred losses for each of these risk classifications to determine the relatively higher or lower loss exposure of each and to develop appropriate rate relativity factors.

Distributing Rate Relativity Factors Among Classifications

The application of rate relativity factors might differ among risk classifications. This occurs because the base rates for many insurance products are made up of several components, each linked to a specific coverage or peril. For example, if only 20 percent of an insurer's base rate for an HO-2 policy is associated with the fire peril, the insurer applies a PPC rate relativity factor to only that portion of the base rate. Similarly, while a home's construction may affect its susceptibility to fire losses, construction has little, if any, effect on a policyholder's exposure to theft of contents. As a result, the insurer does not apply the construction class rate relativity factor to the portion of the base rate associated with the peril theft.

For personal automobile rating, the same principle applies. For example, different rating territories can generate different kinds of loss experience. Exhibit 6-7 illustrates the point by comparing three hypothetical automobile rating territories, including one that is primarily rural and one that is predominately urban. In this example, an analysis of claim data indicates that the different environments in these two territories give rise to different types of losses. This information allows an insurer to apply multiple coverage-related rate relativity factors within a single territory.

Exhibit 6-7
Distribution of Automobile Territory Rate Relativity Factors

Territory	Description	Coverage	Losses Compared to Unity	Details	Rate Relativity Factors
5	Unity classification		Baseline		1.0
2	High-density urban area in a moderate climate	Liability	20% higher than unity	Higher liability losses because traffic density results in more multivehicle accidents	1.2 (applies to the liability portion of the rate)
		Collision	15% higher than unity	Increased frequency of collision losses due to traffic density	1.15 (applies to the collision portion of the rate)
7	Low-density rural area in a climate with extreme weather conditions	Collision	10% lower than unity	Reduced traffic density results in lower collision frequency	0.9 (applies to the collision portion of rate)
		Other than collision (comprehensive)	5% higher than unity	Hailstorms cause increased frequency of other-than-collision claims	1.05 (applies to the other-than-collision portion of the rate)

Educational Objective 2
Explain how insurers analyze loss data and forecast trends to determine rate levels.

Analyzing Loss Data and Forecasting Trends

Insurers analyze their loss and loss expense data, industry data, and current trends to predict future losses. Based on these predictions, insurers develop and adjust rates.

Analyzing and Forecasting Loss Frequency Trends

Understanding previous loss frequency helps actuaries forecast losses. Insurers define loss frequency as the number of losses incurred per a specific number of exposure units, such as losses per hundred car-years or losses per thousand house-years. This approach allows actuaries to meaningfully compare the number of losses for a line of business, risk classification, or coverage from year to year, despite changes in in-force policy count. Loss frequencies are often expressed as percentages and are usually calculated for a particular period, such as one year. Exhibit 6-8 illustrates a hypothetical insurer's fire loss frequency for its homeowners product.

Often, insurers review several years' worth of loss frequency information to identify trends. Loss frequency trend analysis helps actuaries project future loss experience. For example, in Exhibit 6-8, the insurer's fire loss frequency is trending upwards, with the number of losses per 100 house-years increasing every year. Unless the trend is expected to change, the insurer may project a slightly higher loss frequency, perhaps 4.95 percent, for the following year.

Exhibit 6-8
Homeowners Fire Loss Frequency per 100 House-Years

	House-Years	Fire Losses	Calculation	Loss Frequency per 100 House-Years
Year 1	10,000	401	401 ÷ 10,000 × 100	4.01%
Year 2	10,500	487	487 ÷ 10,500 × 100	4.64%
Year 3	11,000	529	529 ÷ 11,000 × 100	4.80%

When analyzing loss experience, insurers consider many factors and try to identify the cause of any significant change in frequency. For example, an earthquake that ruptures gas lines and downs electrical wires can cause a significant increase in an insurer's fire loss frequency for the year in which it occurs. However, the insurer may not anticipate another earthquake for twenty years, and actuaries may recalculate the actual fire loss frequency for that year to factor out the effect of the catastrophe on any subsequent rate adjustments.

Analyzing and Forecasting Loss Severity Trends

Loss severity refers to the dollar amount of an individual loss. Large losses are relatively rare in first-party personal auto and residential property insurance. Although an insurer's potential exposure can equal the limits of a policy, claims are usually much smaller. To set rates commensurate with its real exposure, an insurer averages its claim payments. Analyzing loss severity helps insurers identify trends and predict the cost of future losses. Exhibit 6-9 illustrates a hypothetical insurer's fire loss severity for its homeowner product.

Generally, loss severity is relatively low because the majority of losses are small. Exhibit 6-10 presents a breakdown of the insurer's fire loss claim payments in Year 1.

Exhibit 6-9
Homeowners Fire Loss Severity

	Fire Losses	Total Paid Losses	Calculation	Fire Loss Severity
Year 1	452	$1,478,040	$1,478,040 ÷ 452	$3,270
Year 2	517	$1,323,520	$1,323,520 ÷ 517	$2,560
Year 3	439	$1,360,900	$1,360,900 ÷ 439	$3,100
Year 4	425	$1,253,750	$1,253,750 ÷ 425	$2,950
Average Severity				$2,970

As with frequency, insurers try to identify the cause of any significant variance in loss severity and may choose to factor out any event that results in misleading severity data. For example, a large loss reserve posted in a previous year is reversed in a subsequent year. This is called a *reserve takedown*. Reserve takedowns can occur, for example, when a lawsuit is settled out of court or when investigation of a claim determines that no coverage applies. A large reserve takedown reduces the incurred losses for the year in which the reserve reduction occurs. This could artificially reduce loss severity for that year. As a result, actuaries exclude the effect of reserve takedowns from their severity calculations.

Jargon Alert!

A *reserve takedown* is the reduction or total elimination of a previously established claim reserve. Because reserve changes are reflected during the time period when they are changed, large reserve changes can inflate or deflate actual loss results incurred during the same period.

Exhibit 6-10
Claim Payment Breakdown—Year 1

Claim Payment Range	Losses	Average Claim Payment	Total
$1 – $2,500	300	$800	$240,000
$2,501 – $5,000	76	$2,607	$198,132
$5,001 – $10,000	50	$6,850	$342,500
$10,001 – $25,000	16	$12,250	$196,000
$25,001 – $50,000	6	$31,650	$189,900
$50,001 – $100,000	3	$61,500	$184,500
$100,001 +	1	$127,008	$127,008
Totals	452		$1,478,040

Insurers may also choose to factor out the effect of very large losses, called *shock losses*, because they occur so rarely. Actuaries may either exclude a shock loss or *cap* the dollar amount of that loss to be included in severity calculations. Otherwise, severity might be overstated and rates may be set too high, adversely affecting the insurer's competitive position. Capping the shock loss at $100,000, for example, allows for its inclusion in severity calculations but also recog-

Jargon Alert!

Shock losses are large, unusual losses that have a small potential of recurrence. To factor out shock losses, an actuary might *cap* all losses at a maximum dollar value.

nizes the relative rarity of losses of this size. Exhibit 6-11 illustrates the potential impact of reserve takedowns and shock losses on the insurer's severity calculations for Year 1. If not factored out, the reserve take-down would result in the artificial understatement of loss severity. The effect of including the shock loss would be to overstate severity.

Exhibit 6-11
Impact of Reserve Takedowns and Shock Losses on Severity

	Effect of Reserve Takedown on Severity			
	Fire Losses	**Total Paid Losses**	**Calculation**	**Fire Loss Severity**
Year 1 results	452	$478,040	$478,040 ÷ 452	$1,058
Plus reserve takedown		$1,000,000		
Year 1 adjusted results		$1,478,040	$1,478,040 ÷ 452	$3,270
	Effect of Shock Loss on Severity			
Year 1 results	452	$1,478,040	$1,478,040 ÷ 452	$3,270
Plus shock loss		$1,000,000		
Year 1 adjusted results		$2,478,040	$2,478,040 ÷ 452	$5,482
	Effect of Capped Shock Loss on Severity			
Year 1 results	452	$1,478,040	$1,478,040 ÷ 452	$3,270
Plus capped shock loss		$100,000		
Year 1 adjusted results		$1,578,040	$1,578,040 ÷ 452	$3,491

Comparing Loss Frequency and Severity Among Groups

Insurers analyze claim data by product, coverage, geographic area, risk classification, producer, branch or region, and year. Actuaries compare the frequency and severity of losses among these different groups and use the results as the basis for establishing rate relativity factors.

Exhibit 6-12 presents a hypothetical insurer's residential property fire loss experience for two different construction classes for three calendar years.

Frequency Analysis

Using the claim data presented in Exhibit 6-12, insurers compare the incidence of fire losses for frame homes with that of masonry homes. First, actuaries calculate the loss frequency for each construction class. Next, they compare the two frequencies. The difference between the two loss frequencies will form the basis for a rate relativity factor. The process is illustrated in Exhibit 6-13.

Severity Analysis

Actuaries also use severity analysis to compare two rate classes. Continuing with the claim data from Exhibit 6-12, actuaries calculate the relative severity of fire losses for masonry and frame homes. The difference between the two loss severities will form the basis for a rate relativity factor. The process is illustrated in Exhibit 6-14.

Exhibit 6-12
Fire Losses on Frame and Masonry Homes—Year-End

Masonry Homes	House-Years	Number of Losses	Total Paid Losses
Year 1	2,000	19	$34,992
Year 2	2,500	39	$69,774
Year 3	3,000	52	$93,618
Totals	7,500	110	$198,384
Frame Homes			
Year 1	2,700	41	$66,348
Year 2	3,200	59	$110,693
Year 3	3,750	63	$156,996
Totals	9,650	163	$334,037

Exhibit 6-13
Loss Frequency Analysis

Construction Class	House-Years	Number of Losses	Frequency per 100 House-Years (Number of losses ÷ Number of house-years × 100)	Relative Frequency (Higher frequency – Lower frequency ÷ Lower frequency)
Masonry	7,500	110	1.47% (110 ÷ 7,500 × 100)	
Frame	9,650	163	1.69% (163 ÷ 9,650 × 100)	15% higher than masonry (1.69% – 1.47% ÷ 1.5 × 100)

Exhibit 6-14
Loss Severity Analysis

Construction Class	Number of Losses	Total Paid Losses	Severity (Paid losses ÷ Number of losses)	Relative Severity (Higher severity – Lower severity ÷ Lower severity × 100)
Masonry	110	$198,384	$1,803 ($198,384 ÷ 110)	
Frame	163	$334,037	$2,049 ($334,037 ÷ 163)	14% higher than masonry ($2,049 – $1,803 ÷ $1,803 × 100)

Educational Objective 3

a. Describe the methods used by insurers to determine changes in rate levels.

b. Given a case study, select the appropriate methods required to create a rate change.

Methods of Determining Rate Levels

Once an insurer has analyzed its loss experience, it can express the relative performance of each risk classification as a rate relativity factor. By applying these rate relativity factors to existing base rates, it can adjust its pricing.

Insurers adjust base rates using one or both of the following methods:

- The frequency and severity analysis method
- The loss cost analysis method

Frequency and Severity Analysis Method

Actuaries adjust rate levels by applying both the frequency rate relativity factor and the severity rate relativity factor to the base rate. Depending on the product, the adjusted base rate can include several components, each related to a particular coverage or peril. In that case, frequency and severity relativity factors are calculated for and applied to each component individually. The total of these components represents the adjusted base rate for the product.

Considerations in using the frequency and severity analysis method in rate adjustment include the following:

- An insurer must have written enough exposure units and paid enough claims over a sufficient period of time for the data to be credible. When an insurer has a sufficient quantity of its own data to use this method, the resulting rates best reflect the underwriting policies, expertise, and marketing strategy of the insurer.
- This method is less convenient to use when adjusting the price of coverage sold on a *flat premium* basis, such as the coverage provided by some homeowners and personal auto endorsements.

Jargon Alert!

Flat premium refers to an established dollar amount, unmodified by other rating factors, that an insurer charges for coverage changes, or endorsements.

Exhibit 6-15 illustrates how the frequency and severity analysis method is used to adjust the base rate allocated to the peril of fire on a homeowners policy. The calculations are based on the loss data presented in Exhibit 6-13. In this example, the insurer has selected the masonry construction class as unity and assigned a base rate of $3.75, of which 20 percent, or $0.75, is allocated to the peril of fire. Actuaries calculate the frequency and severity rate relativity factors for frame construction and then apply those factors, in sequence, to the fire portion of the base rate.

Exhibit 6-15
Loss Frequency and Severity Method of Adjusting Base Rates

Construction Class	Severity	Severity	Frequency Rate Relativity Factor	Severity Rate Relativity Factor	Adjusted Base Rate
Masonry	1.5%	$1,803	1.0 (unity)	1.0 (unity)	$3.75
Frame	1.69%	$2,049	1.13	1.14	$3.97 $0.75 × 1.13 = $0.85 $0.85 × 1.14 = $0.97 $3.75 – $0.75 + $0.97 = $3.97

The adjusted fire rate for frame construction is calculated using the following steps:

1. The fire portion of the unity classification is determined to be 20 percent of the base rate, or $0.75 (0.2 × 3.75 = 0.75).
2. The fire portion of the base rate for the unity classification is multiplied by the frequency rate relativity factor for frame houses (0.75 × 1.13 = 0.85).
3. Then this portion of the adjusted rate is multiplied by the severity relativity factor for frame houses (0.85 × 1.14 = 0.97).
4. The original fire portion of the rate ($0.75) is subtracted from the original base rate ($3.75), and the new fire portion ($0.97) is added to the original base rate (3.75 – 0.75 + 0.97 = 3.97).

Loss Cost Analysis Method

Insurers can also adjust rates based on the loss cost, or average claim payment per exposure unit. Considerations in electing to use the loss cost analysis method to adjust pricing include the following:

- If an insurer has credible data of its own, the loss cost analysis method can help actuaries verify or adjust the results of the frequency and severity analysis method.
- If an insurer has insufficient data of its own to complete a credible loss frequency and severity analysis, it can use pooled loss cost data from advisory organizations like the ISO or AAIS. However, when pooled loss costs from an advisory organization are used, the resulting rates may not be compatible with the underwriting policies, expertise, and marketing strategy of the insurer.
- Loss cost analysis is a convenient method to use when adjusting the price of coverage sold on a flat premium basis because the exposure units and the total paid losses used in the calculation are readily available, and because data may be too limited to perform a frequency and severity analysis.

When using the loss cost analysis method to adjust base rates, the relative difference between the loss costs for two lines, risk classifications, or coverages becomes the rate relativity factor. Exhibit 6-16 illustrates the calculation and comparison of loss cost relativity for masonry and frame homes and how the difference in loss costs translates into an adjusted base rate.

Exhibit 6-16
Loss Cost Method of Adjusting Base Rates

Construction Class	House-Years	Total Paid Losses	Loss Cost	Loss Cost Rate Relativity Factor	Adjusted Base Rate
Masonry	7,500	$198,384	$26.45	1.0 unity	$3.75
Frame	9,650	$334,037	$34.61	1.31 $34.61 ÷ $26.45	$3.98 $0.75 × 1.31 = $0.98 $3.75 – $0.75 + $0.98 = $3.98

The adjusted fire rate for frame construction is calculated using the following steps:

1. The fire portion of the base rate for the unity classification ($0.75) is multiplied by the loss cost rate relativity factor for frame houses (1.31).
2. The original fire portion of the rate is subtracted from the original base rate, and the new fire portion ($0.98) is added to it.

In this case, the $3.98 adjusted base rate for frame homes generated by the loss cost method is close to the $3.97 rate generated by the frequency and severity method. This is often the case. Actuaries compare the results of frequency and severity analysis with those of loss cost analysis before recommending rate adjustments.

Putting Rate Level Changes Into Context

The following case study provides an example of the application of rate level changes placed into context with an insurer's overall decision-making process.

Two years ago, ABC Insurance Company's research identified that approximately 23 percent of consumers operate small businesses from their homes. As a result, the company began offering home business coverage to policyholders last year. The coverage is provided by endorsement to the homeowners policy at a flat premium of $100. Unfortunately, sales have been disappointing. At the end of the first year, the company has sold only 156 home business endorsements. The reason appears to be that the coverage is not competitively priced. The sales manager recommends a price reduction.

Because this is a relatively new product, the insurer has not yet generated sufficient loss data to use the frequency and severity analysis method of price adjustment. However, since other insurers already offer similar products, credible loss cost data are available through an advisory organization. As a result, the actuaries opt to use the loss cost method to adjust the base premium for the coverage.

Based on the pooled loss cost data available, the actuaries are confident in reducing the flat premium for the endorsement by 31 percent. After factoring in expenses and profits, the resulting new premium for the coverage is $75. This reduction in premium is expected to help increase sales of the endorsement. Once sales have generated sufficient loss history, the insurer will fine-tune its pricing based on a frequency and severity analysis of its own actual results.

Educational Objective 4

Describe methods actuaries use in ratemaking.

Ratemaking Methods

So far, this chapter has introduced some of the tools and techniques actuaries use and has presented various ways in which an insurer's loss experience can be incorporated into its pricing. However, rates are based on more than just an insurer's loss experience. Underwriting expenses for such expenses as salaries, premises, and computer systems comprise a portion of the premiums charged to policyholders. In addition, insurers include a profit factor in their pricing.

Ratemaking is the art of incorporating the cost of losses and expenses and the need for profits into a pricing strategy that is fair, competitive, and acceptable to insurance regulators. The remainder of this chapter will review the approaches, constraints, and influences involved in ratemaking.

Three basic methods used in ratemaking are as follows:

- Judgment method
- Loss ratio method
- Pure premium method

Judgment Method

In the judgment method of ratemaking, the underwriter selects a rate based on his or her experience and judgment, using little or no statistical information. When rating new risks, underwriters who use the judgment method determine what rates they previously charged for similar risks and adjust those rates based on the relative loss exposure represented by the new risks.

The judgment method of ratemaking is the oldest of the three methods and is still used for some commercial lines such as ocean marine, aviation, inland marine, and some products liability coverages. In personal insurance, the judgment method is used by only a few insurers to rate unusual types of inland marine risks, such as rare guns, gold bullion, one-of-a-kind fine art of extremely high value, and collections in transit internationally or on exhibit. International insurers use the judgment method for some non-U.S. personal lines insurance coverages, such as personal property coverage for individuals who travel extensively.

Because the judgment method does not depend on accumulated statistical information, it can be used for new lines of insurance as well as for established lines.

Loss Ratio Method

In the loss ratio method of ratemaking, an existing rate is increased or decreased in response to loss experience that differs from that which was expected when the rates were developed. The rate change is calculated as follows:

1. The expected loss ratio is subtracted from the actual loss ratio.
2. The difference is then divided by the expected loss ratio.
3. The resulting percentage difference becomes the recommended rate change. A positive number indicates a rate increase, while a negative number indicates a rate decrease.

Exhibit 6-17 illustrates the loss ratio method of calculating the required change in rate. This calculation deals only with the loss portion of the rate. Factors for expenses and profits might also require adjustment in order to establish the final base rate.

Exhibit 6-17
Loss Ratio Method

Expected Loss Ratio 70%

Actual Loss Ratio 80%

$$\frac{(80\% - 70\%)}{70\%} = 14\%$$

A negative answer indicates a percentage rate reduction. A positive answer indicates a percentage rate increase.

The loss ratio method cannot be used to calculate rates for a new line of insurance since a new line would have no actual loss ratio for use in the calculation and no existing rate to adjust. For a new line of insurance, either the judgment method or the pure premium method is used.

Pure Premium Method

The pure premium method of ratemaking uses the average amount of money needed per exposure unit to pay incurred losses to determine the needed rate. Pure premium can be established based on loss costs. Once pure premium is calculated, the insurer adds the estimated cost of underwriting expenses per exposure unit plus the average profit per exposure unit to determine the total rate. Exhibit 6-18 illustrates the calculation used in the pure premium method.

Exhibit 6-18
Pure Premium Method

Pure Premium	$26.73	Pure premium can be calculated based on the insurer's own claim experience or developed from loss costs available from an insurance advisory organization for new lines of business.
Estimated Expenses per Exposure Unit	$9.72	For existing lines, insurers use actual data. For new lines, expenses per exposure unit may be estimated based on actual underwriting expenses for other lines the insurer currently offers.
Profit Factor	$4.05	The insurer has an initial profit goal of 10% of all base premiums. $26.73 + $9.72 = $36.45 ÷ 0.9 = $40.50 × 0.1 = $4.05)
Base Premium	$40.50	The base premium is total of the pure premiums, expenses, and profit per exposure unit.

Because pooled loss cost information is available to insurers through advisory organizations, this approach can be used to calculate the appropriate rate for a new line of insurance.

Educational Objective 5
Describe the role of investment income in ratemaking.

Investment Income in Ratemaking

The two sources of income for a property and liability insurer are its insurance operation and its investment operation. Because insurers typically collect premiums first and pay claims later, they have an advantageous cash flow. The insurance operation writes policies, collects premiums, and pays losses. The investment operation uses the cash flow generated by the insurance operation to buy bonds, stocks, and other investments to earn an investment profit. Investment profit is derived from three sources: investment income, **realized capital gains**, and **unrealized capital gains**.

Traditionally, property and liability insurers did not consider their investment income when setting rates, except perhaps indirectly when factoring in profits and contingencies. However, when an insurer posted an underwriting loss, investment income was often used to make up the shortfall.

Reminder

Investment income is interest, dividends, and net realized capital gains received by an insurer from the insurer's financial assets minus its investment expenses.

A **realized capital gain** is the profit earned by an insurer when an asset, such as a bond or stock, is sold for more than its cost.

An **unrealized capital gain** exists when the market price of an asset exceeds its cost and the insurer continues to hold the asset. It is a profit that is not yet earned.

Recently it has become more common to consider investment income in ratemaking. While regulators accept that insurers are entitled to earn reasonable profits, and in fact must do so in order to remain financially viable, the affordability of personal insurance products has become increasingly political. This has focused regulatory attention on ratemaking practices and has resulted in changes, particularly in the way in which investment income is factored into pricing. For example, many states now require insurers to include investment income when formulating rates. However, few states require the inclusion of capital gains, and those states that do usually consider only *realized* capital gains.

One method for reflecting investment income in rates is to estimate the amount of expected investment income on a line of insurance and deduct that amount from the expenses added to the rates. The pure premium rate calculation presented in Exhibit 6-18 is modified in Exhibit 6-19 to reflect investment income.

The effect of investment income on rates differs among lines of business because the profit earned depends partially on the duration of an investment. For example, liability claims take longer to settle than property claims; thus the insurer has more time to earn investment income before paying claims.

Exhibit 6-19
Investment Income in Ratemaking

Pure Premium	$26.73	Based on loss costs
Estimated Expenses per Exposure Unit	$9.72	Includes such costs as salaries, benefits, premises, and computer systems
Investment Income per Exposure Unit	$4.87	Estimated income from investment divided by total number of exposure units
Adjusted Expenses per Exposure Unit	$4.85	Expenses – Investment Income ($9.72 – $4.87 = $4.85)
Profit Factor	$3.51	Insurer has an initial profit goal of 10% of all base premiums ($26.73 + $4.85 = $31.58 ÷ .90 = $35.09 × 0.1 = $3.51)
Base Premium	$35.09	Total pure premiums, expenses, and profit per exposure unit

Educational Objective 6
Explain how insurers price new insurance products.

Pricing New Insurance Products

Understanding past loss frequency and severity helps actuaries price existing policies, but new products have no statistical history from which insurers can forecast results. Instead, actuaries make comparisons with similar products already offered and make reasonable estimates of the new product's probable loss and expense performance. The degree of confidence insurers have in their estimates influences how competitively a new product will be priced.

The three primary factors that influence new product pricing are as follows:

- The product's potential for profit
- The confidence actuaries have in their estimates
- The projected expenses for the product

Potential for Profit

An insurer's management staff ranks product proposals according to profit potential. Given similar implementation costs, those products with the highest projected profit will be priced more competitively than products with less profit potential. This occurs because greater profitability provides the insurer with a larger profit margin, sometimes called a cushion, to absorb unanticipated losses and expenses.

Confidence in Estimates

Although potential profit is a major factor in setting prices for new products, confidence in profit projections is also important. If an insurer is the first to offer a particular type of coverage, no historical information for that type of product exists. As a result, confidence in loss, expense, and profit projections for such a product would be low and the insurer might set initial rates relatively high as a result. Once sufficient loss experience has been developed, the rates can be adjusted.

An insurer's confidence in projected profits is influenced by a variety of factors, including the following:

- The availability of competitor's data
- The credibility of available data

Competitors' Data

Insurers must file product information and financial results with state insurance departments. As a result, insurers can often obtain and analyze competitors' premium and loss data. In addition, pooled loss costs are available through advisory organizations like the ISO or AAIS.

To increase its confidence in projected losses, expenses, and profit for a new product, an insurer analyzes the competitive data available for similar products. Data that provide five or more years' history can be particularly helpful in establishing rates. The value of competitor information is greater if it includes large numbers of similar risks that have a consistent number of small losses each year.

Insurers with too few years of competitors' data, inconsistent competitor results, or no competitor results to evaluate must assess their confidence in their own estimates of a new product's likely success. In those situations, insurers set rates high enough to justify offering a product.

Credibility refers to the level of confidence placed on the predictive value of loss data.

Credibility of Data

An insurer's confidence in its projections is based on the **credibility** of the data it uses. Credibility depends on the consistency of the loss results and the size of the portfolio used as the basis for projections.

Consistent loss results over many years improve the accuracy of forecasted results. Loss data for portfolios with consistent loss ratios over many years have higher credibility than do data generated by portfolios with loss ratios that fluctuate significantly by year.

The size of a portfolio also influences credibility. For example, a consistent loss ratio over five years would be highly credible only if large numbers of risks are insured and enough claims occur each year to establish a predictable average frequency and severity of losses. On a small portfolio with few losses, the loss ratio would be less credible.

Exhibit 6-20 presents three years' worth of data for two different insurance portfolios. In this example, the data generated by portfolio A are more credible because of the larger number of exposure units and the consistency of the losses. In contrast, portfolio B does not include sufficient exposure units, and the loss frequency is too low to generate statistically credible data.

Exhibit 6-20
Credibility Based on Portfolio Size and Consistent Loss Results

	Portfolio A	Portfolio B	Comments
Exposure Units	10,000	1,000	Credibility improves as exposure units increase.
Loss Ratio Range	52% – 58%	58% – 65%	Consistent loss ratios are only credible given a large enough portfolio and sufficient incurred losses.
Loss Frequency	22% – 27%	2% – 6%	Lines with low loss frequency (such as personal umbrella portfolios) produce less credible data than lines with higher frequency.
Loss Severity	$2,763	$9,037	Lines with low loss frequency (such as personal umbrella portfolios) often have higher severity.
Credibility	Good	Poor	Portfolio A has sufficient exposure units and claim experience to provide credible data.

Projected Expenses

The price of new products is also influenced by expense estimates. An insurer's initial expenses when launching a new line or coverage can be significant and include the costs of the following:

- Researching and analyzing statistics
- Setting rates
- Developing contract language
- Preparing underwriting guidelines
- Training staff
- Advertising
- Regulatory filing and approval

An insurer considers these initial costs as well as the expenses common to all insurance products, such as sales commissions, underwriting and policy issuance costs, administrative overhead, taxes, and regulator assessments, when determining rates for new products.

Because of the higher initial expenses associated with launching a new product, they generally have a higher expense ratio than established products until these initial expenses are offset by premium income.

Educational Objective 7

Describe the regulatory objectives used in evaluating insurance rates.

Regulatory Objectives in Rate Evaluation

Although actuaries propose rates based on statistical analysis and projections, an insurer's actual flexibility in setting rates is limited by regulation. These regulatory requirements are introduced in INS 21 and API 28. However, analysis of regulatory objectives is also required in any examination of insurance pricing. This section provides a perspective of regulation as it affects insurance pricing.

The regulatory environment within which insurers operate provides a legal framework for ratemaking. Although regulatory systems vary by state, rates in all states are required to meet the following criteria:

- They must be adequate.
- They must be equitable.
- They must be moderately priced.

Rate Adequacy

Adequacy implies that the rate charged for a particular rating class is sufficient to cover all anticipated losses and expenses associated with that class. Incurred losses represent the largest component of insurance rates and are used by actuaries to establish pure premiums as the basis for pricing. However, pure premiums do not include the costs of underwriting expenses, nor do they anticipate the effect of investment income as an offset to underwriting expenses and losses. As a result, insurers factor in net expenses separately to establish adequate rates. Once the adequacy of a rate is established, an acceptable profit level is factored into the final pricing.

Quantifying Pure Premium Amounts

Since incurred losses form the largest component of rates, calculation of pure premiums is the first step in determining rate adequacy. Provided an insurer has a sufficient volume of exposure units and loss experience to generate credible results, the insurer may use its own data as a basis for quantifying pure premiums. Exhibit 6-21 illustrates the process of calculating pure premiums for homeowners risks and illustrates how this forms the basis for devising an adequate rate.

Considering Industry Results

In determining rate adequacy, most insurers consider industry results in addition to their own experience in order to enhance the credibility of the data and increase confidence. However, caution is required when evaluating statewide information as it includes losses from all insurers, some of which may have posted results that are not typical, such as results due to a particularly severe windstorm season. Also, statewide information includes premium and loss data for both profitable and unprofitable insurers. Actuaries attempt to identify and factor out anomalous and unprofitable results from industry data prior to using it as the basis for establishing rate adequacy.

Rate Equity

The second regulatory criterion for insurance rates is that they must be equitable. In other words, they must not be unfairly discriminatory. Each insured should pay his or her fair share of the insurer's losses and expenses. Theoretically this would require each risk to be rated individually, based on its own unique loss and expense attributes; however, this is impractical. As a result, each insured's fair share is generally determined based on a proportional distribution of the insurer's estimated future losses and expenses among homogeneous groups of insureds. As long as risks in a particular risk classification are homogeneous, rate equity is presumed.

One important point about rate equity is that rating laws do not prohibit discrimination; they prohibit *unfair* discrimination. Fair and justified rate discrimination based on loss potential is not only allowed, it is encouraged. Discrimination forms the basis for both the establishment of risk classifications and the development of rate relativity factors. For example, individuals with poor driving records are statistically more likely to be involved in accidents, and as a result reasonable discrimination in rating allows insurers to charge more premium for drivers with poor experience. On the other hand, automobile liability rating based on sex is considered to be unacceptable in some states.

Exhibit 6-21
Devising Adequate Rates—Homeowners

Item	Value	Explanation
Exposure Units	3,000	Measured in house-years
Average Coverage A Limits per Risk	$150,000	Used to calculate total units of coverage. Pure premium is translated into a rate based on the insurer's total units of coverage.
Anticipated Losses	$975,000	Established based on industry data, the insurer's own loss data and an analysis of current trends
Pure Premium	$325	Calculated by dividing the insurer's anticipated losses by the total exposure units: $975,000 ÷ 3,000
Net Expenses	$525,000	Calculated by subtracting investment income from total allowable underwriting expenses as stipulated in regulations
Units of Coverage	450,000	Standard unit of coverage is $1,000 worth of Coverage A. The insurer calculates its total units of coverage as follows: Average Coverage A limits × Number of house-years insured ÷ Standard unit of coverage $150,000 × 3,000 ÷ $1,000
Adequate Rate (Note: This does not yet include a factor for profit.)	$3.33	Adequate rate per unit of coverage is calculated as follows: Anticipated losses + Net expenses ÷ Units of coverage $975,000 + $525,000 ÷ 450,000

Rate Moderacy

The third regulatory criterion is that rates should be moderate; in other words, they should not be excessive. Both regulatory and competitive pressures help to ensure that consumers are generally charged a fair price for their home and automobile insurance coverage. First, insurers are required to file rates with state insurance departments, and regulatory authorities typically prevent insurers from charging unreasonably high rates. In some states, proposed rate changes are not approved without statistical evidence that incurred losses and expenses warrant the requested change. In other states, regulators may limit rate increases and restrict total rate levels, regardless of an insurer's evidence of need. Finally, regulators have the authority to roll back rates if necessary.

Competitive forces also help to ensure that rates are not excessive. Policyholders tend to view their personal insurance coverage as a commodity and to change insurers for relatively small savings in premiums. This is particularly true for an insurer's best customers, who are those with the fewest losses. Significant rate increases prompt an insurer's best customers to shop around. This results in a loss of business, and the remaining portfolio becomes disproportionately weighted with poorer risks, which are those with the most losses. The potential effect of such changes on an insurer's profits is sufficient to encourage most insurers to keep rates competitive.

Further, both regulatory and competitive pressures prevent rate changes from being excessive and insurers are sometimes precluded from making indicated adjustments to their rates. If, for example, actuarial analysis indicates that a 50 percent increase in base rate is required, it is probable that neither state regulators nor policyholders will approve. As a result, insurers are sometimes required to phase in indicated rate increases over a period of years.

Educational Objective 8
Describe the social objectives used in evaluating insurance rates.

Social Objectives in Rate Evaluation

In addition to regulatory control, the insurance marketplace is becoming increasingly subject to social pressures, particularly in the areas of personal automobile and residential property insurance. Insurers are being called upon to offer products that:

- Are affordable
- Are available
- Encourage loss control
- Respond to change
- Provide rate stability
- Have controllable rating factors

Insurance Affordability

Affordability has become an important social objective in determining proper rates. For example, in many cities the cost of property insurance has risen despite a decline in property values. Rates that are statistically adequate to cover the increased exposures of crime, arson, and unoccupany found in inner-city areas can cause insurance to be beyond the financial resources of many urban residents.

Strategies to ensure affordability include the following:

- Capping insurance rates

- Setting rates so as to transfer some of the costs of high-risk policyholders to the remaining policyholders
- Subsidizing unaffordable rates through sources outside the standard insurance marketplace

Insurance Availability

The availability of insurance coverage is another social issue insurers consider in ratemaking. It is, in part, related to affordability. Insurers often retire from a line, risk classification, or coverage because the rate required to offset expected losses is so high that regulators will not approve it. For example, many insurers have rejected higher-risk urban properties in favor of newer, better-protected homes in suburban communities. Consequently, some urban residents may be prevented from purchasing a home because lenders do not offer mortgages on uninsured properties.

Catastrophes also adversely affect insurance availability. For example, many companies stopped writing homeowners insurance in Atlantic coastal areas after hurricanes Hugo and Andrew.

Insurance regulators are concerned about the social problems of affordability and availability. One solution has been to establish risk-sharing pools in which all insurers participate. Rates are controlled, and each insurer's exposure is limited.

Loss Control Incentives

Insurers are able, to some extent, to influence the behavior of policyholders, and pricing is one of the tools with which they do so. Premium discounts for safe drivers or loss-free homeowners not only reward policyholders but also encourage them to drive carefully and to maintain their home, reducing the chance of accidental loss. Discounts for policyholders who install burglar alarms or fire extinguishers encourage the use of devices that can help control the severity of losses. The reduced potential frequency and severity of losses that result from insurers' pricing strategies not only benefit insurers in terms of increased profits but also benefit society.

Responsiveness to Change

Another social objective in insurance pricing is to structure rates in such a way that pricing responds quickly and effectively to changes in underlying loss exposures. Responsiveness helps ensure that rates are adequate without being excessive. For example, accident and violation surcharges on automobile policies adjust rates to more accurately reflect the increased exposure. On the other hand, improvement in a community's PPC can be promptly reflected in a change in a home's risk classification, resulting in reduced premiums.

Rate Stability

Rate stability requires that rates not vary dramatically by year. Policyholders expect a certain degree of stability in their rates. To some extent, the affordability of insurance depends on a policyholder's ability to reasonably estimate the cost of insurance each year.

Jargon Alert!

Spread-of-risk is the disbursion of loss exposures in a portfolio of policies. An adequate disbursion is achieved when single loss events cannot create claims for a significant number of individuals or properties insured within the portfolio.

The basic *spread-of-risk* concept of insurance involves the sharing of potential losses among many individuals. This forms the basis of insurance pricing. However, spread of risk can also relate to time. For example, the incidence of hurricanes on the east coast of the United States can vary widely by year. If windstorm insurance rates mirrored this variation in loss exposure, policyholders would face significant changes in homeowners premiums almost annually. Insurers try to maintain rate stability by basing rates on loss experience over a long period of time and by tempering the statistics of years with unusually high loss experience with long-term averages.

Controllable Rating Factors

In recent years, some consumer advocates have proposed that insurers should be allowed to use only those rating factors that insureds can control, rejecting age, gender, and territory as the basis for insurance pricing. For automobile insurance, some propose limiting rating factors to driving record, mileage, and vehicle.

Legislators and regulators in some states have responded to this concern by modifying the basis for risk classification, for example, by changing age to years of driving experience. However, the costs to settle losses and pay operating expenses are not affected by changes in rating criteria. Changes to rating criteria simply serve to redistribute the cost of insurance among different customers. While that benefits those customers who receive a lower rate from such a change, those who receive a rate increase pay the difference.

Exhibit 6-22 summarizes the regulatory and social objectives that guide the ratemaking process.

Exhibit 6-22
Regulatory and Social Objectives in Ratemaking

Regulatory Objectives	
• Adequacy	Rates are known to be sufficient to cover losses and expenses.
• Equity	Rates are based on a proportional distribution of estimated future losses and expenses among homogeneous groups. Fair discrimination, based on statistically sound criteria, is encouraged (e.g., higher rates for poor drivers).
• Moderacy	Competitive and regulatory pressures generally keep rates from being excessive. Regulators can change rating criteria, roll back rates, or refuse to approve increases if necessary.

Social Objectives

• Affordability	Rates that are statistically adequate to cover some high-risk exposures are often beyond the financial resources of some policyholders. Rate affordability strategies include rate capping, transferring costs to lower-risk policyholders, or subsidizing unaffordable rates.
• Availability	Insurers often retire from a line, risk classification, or coverage if the rate required to offset expected losses is so high that regulators will not approve it. One strategy to ensure availability involves risk pooling, where all insurers take a proportionate share of higher-risk business.
• Loss control incentives	Insurers use premium discounts to affect the behavior of policyholders. The resulting reduction in losses not only benefits insurers in terms of increased profits but also benefits society.
• Responsiveness to change	Insurers structure rates in such a way that pricing responds quickly and effectively to changes in underlying loss exposures (e.g., accident surcharges). Rate responsiveness helps insurers meet regulatory objectives that rates be adequate but not excessive.
• Rate stability	Insurers try to maintain rate stability by basing rates on loss experience over a long period of time and by tempering statistics generated in years with unusually high loss experience by using long-term average loss data.
• Controllable rating factors	Consumer advocates have proposed that insurers should be allowed to use only those rating factors that insureds can control. Some states have responded by modifying the basis for risk classification. However, loss costs and expenses are not reduced by changes in rating criteria. This approach simply serves to redistribute the costs of insurance.

Educational Objective 9

Given a situation in which an insurance product is experiencing a lack of profitability, explain how the insurer might use the following to restore profitability:

- Premium and loss analysis
- Premium and loss forecasting
- Rate relativities

ABC Insurance Case Study

ABC Insurance Company is a medium-sized insurer that has offered personal auto and residential property insurance for over twenty-five years. Unfortunately, over the past three years, the company's traditionally profitable Tenant's Choice product, a tenant homeowners policy, has performed poorly. The deterioration in the product results has been reasonably consistent in all territories in which ABC writes the coverage.

Exhibit 6-23 presents the insurer's Tenant's Choice year-end results for each of the past three years. As the portfolio has grown and the average amount of coverage per policy has increased, the loss ratio has climbed. While the company has been able to maintain a stable expense ratio of 25 percent over the three-year period, the increasing loss ratio has resulted in an underwriting loss in each of the past three years.

Exhibit 6-23
ABC Insurance Company—Tenant's Choice Three-Year Results

	Two Years Prior	Prior Year	Current Year
Exposure Units	20,000	22,000	25,000
Average Contents Limit per Risk	$15,000	$17,500	$19,000
Earned Premiums	$4,980,000	$6,391,000	$7,885,000
Written Premiums	$4,920,000	$6,301,000	$7,767,000
Incurred Losses	$3,984,000	$5,687,990	$7,648,450
Losses	3,200	4,180	5,250
Underwriting Expenses	$1,245,000	$1,597,750	$1,971,250
Loss Ratio	80%	89%	97%
Expense Ratio	25%	25%	25%
Combined Ratio	105%	114%	122%
Current Base Rate	$16.60	$16.60	$16.60

As a result of this declining performance, ABC's general manager requested that the actuarial team analyze the product's results and recommend pricing adjustments if required. As a first step, the team completed a premium and loss analysis.

Premium and Loss Analysis for ABC

The actuarial staff began by calculating the average loss costs for the product over the past three years. Exhibit 6-24 illustrates the calculations.

Once ABC's loss costs had been calculated for the period, actuaries compared the company's own results in each year with pooled data for the territories in which ABC writes tenants insurance. This pooled data was available through an insurance advisory organization. Exhibit 6-25 presents the results of the comparison.

Because ABC's own loss costs tracked reasonably closely with the pooled data available, ABC's results were seen as credible. As a result, the actuaries' confidence in the company's own data increased.

After reviewing loss costs, actuaries completed a frequency and severity analysis of the Tenant's Choice product results. Exhibit 6-26 illustrates the results.

Exhibit 6-24
Calculation of Tenant's Choice Average Loss Costs

Year	Exposure Units	Incurred Losses	Calculation	Loss Costs
Two years prior	20,000	$3,984,000	$3,984,000 ÷ 20,000	$199
Prior year	22,000	$5,687,990	$5,687,990 ÷ 22,000	$259
Current year	25,000	$7,648,450	$7,648,450 ÷ 25,000	$306
Totals	67,000	$17,320,440	$17,320,440 ÷ 67,000	$259

Exhibit 6-25
ABC's Loss Costs Compared With Industry Data

Year	ABC's Loss Costs	Pooled Loss Costs	Relative Performance
Two years prior	$199	$207	ABC's loss cost is 96% of pooled loss costs.
Prior year	$259	$251	ABC's loss cost is 103% of pooled loss costs.
Current year	$306	$315	ABC's loss cost is 97% of pooled loss costs.

Exhibit 6-26
Tenant's Choice Loss Frequency and Severity

Year	Exposure Units	Losses	Incurred Losses	Loss Frequency	Loss Severity
Two years prior	20,000	3,200	$3,984,000	16%	$1,245
Prior year	22,000	4,180	$5,687,990	19%	$1,361
Current year	25,000	5,250	$7,648,450	21%	$1,457

Next, the actuarial staff checked whether these results might have been skewed by any event such as an increase or decrease in reserves, a natural disaster, or a shock loss. They confirmed that no such event had occurred and that the frequency and severity data were accurate and credible. The next step was to forecast the following year's results based on past experience.

Premium and Loss Forecasting for ABC

Both ABC's loss costs and the loss costs generated from pooled data had steadily increased over the previous three years. Actuaries calculated the percentage increase for each year and then determined the average increase for the period. The results from both sets of data were consistent, further enhancing the credibility of the data.

After examining the trends in both ABC's data and the pooled data, actuaries projected that loss costs would continue to increase, estimating that ABC's average loss cost for the Tenant's Choice product would be 24 percent higher, or $379, in the following year. Exhibit 6-27 illustrates the calculations.

Exhibit 6-27
Projected Loss Costs

Year	ABC's Loss Costs	Change From Prior Year	Pooled Loss Costs	Change From Prior Year
Two years prior	$199		$207	
Prior year	$259	$199 + 30%	$251	$207 + 22%
Current year	$306	$259 + 18%	$315	$315 + 26%
Average % increase		24% (30% + 18%) ÷ 2		24% (22% + 26%) ÷ 2
Projection	$379	24% increase		

After consideration of ABC's loss frequency and severity over the past three years as well as industry results and current trends, actuaries projected the company's loss frequency and severity for the following year. They anticipated a 2.5 percent increase in frequency and an 8 percent increase in severity. Exhibit 6-28 illustrates the calculations.

Exhibit 6-28
Projected Loss Frequency and Severity

Year	Loss Frequency	Change From Prior Year	Loss Severity	Change From Prior Year
Two years prior	16%		$1,245	
Prior year	19%	16% + 3%	$1,361	$1,245 + 9%
Current year	21%	19% + 2%	$1,457	$1,361 + 7%
Average % increase		2.5%		8%
Projection		2.5% increase		8% increase

The final step was to translate these projected results into indicated rate relativity factors and make appropriate adjustments to ABC's existing rates.

Rate Relativities Application for ABC

When using rate relativity factors to adjust pricing, one homogeneous group is selected as the unity classification and all other risk classifications are priced relative to it. As a result, it is essential that the base rate for the unity classification be adequate. If the base rate for the unity classification is inadequate, any other rates developed from it will also be inadequate.

ABC knew that its current rates for its Tenant's Choice product were not adequate. If actuaries simply calculated how much greater losses will be next year, and then increased current rates by that percentage, the Tenant's Choice rates would continue to be inadequate. As a result, actuaries took the following approach:

1. First, they estimated what the current year's rates should have been, using the loss cost method and basing calculations on the current year's data.
2. Then they used the next year's projected frequency and severity to develop rate relativity factors that reflected the company's anticipated results for the following year.
3. Finally, they applied these relativity factors to the rates developed in Step 1, which they knew were adequate, instead of to the actual rates, which they knew were inadequate.

By using this approach, actuaries could be confident in the rates charged the following year. Exhibit 6-29, 6-30, and 6-31 present the calculations.

Based on these calculations, the adjusted base rate for the following year was $23.60. However, this posed a problem in that the current rate was only $16.10. Correcting the current rate would require a 47 percent increase. State regulators would be unlikely to approve such an increase, and policyholders would not accept such a significant change in their premiums. After discussions with the underwriting manager, the sales manager, and the chief actuary, ABC's senior management ultimately decided to phase in the required rate adjustment over three years. This would result in further underwriting losses until the rate reached an adequate level, but the company felt that its regulatory, social, and competitive obligations would be better served by this approach.

Exhibit 6-29
Calculating an Adequate Base Rate Using Loss Costs

	Value	Details
Exposure Unit	25,000	
Incurred Losses	$7,648,450	
Loss Cost	$306	Incurred losses ÷ Exposure units $7,648,450 ÷ 25,000 = $306 Loss cost = Pure premium
Total Expenses	$1,971,250	
Total Units of Coverage	475,000	The standard unit of coverage for tenants insurance is $1,000 of Coverage C. (Average Coverage C limit × Exposure units) ÷ $1,000 ($19,000 × 25,000) ÷ $1,000 = 475,000 coverage units

Continued on next page.

	Value	Details
Rate Component for Losses	$16.10	The amount ABC needs to charge per unit of coverage in order to pay losses. Incurred losses ÷ Units of coverage $7,648,450 ÷ 475,000 = $16.10
Rate Component for Expenses	$4.15	The amount ABC needs to charge per unit of coverage in order to pay expenses. Expenses ÷ Units of coverage $1,971,250 ÷ 475,000 = $4.15
Rate Subtotal	$20.75	Component for losses + Component for expenses $16.10 + $4.15 = $20.25
Rate Component for Profit	$1.09	ABC's goal is to make a 5 percent underwriting profit. $20.25 ÷ 0.95 = $21.32
Adequate Base Rate	$21.32	Incurred loss + Expenses + Profits

Exhibit 6-30
Deriving Rate Relativities From Projected Frequency and Severity

Year	Change in Loss Frequency	Change in Loss Severity
Two years prior		
Prior year	3% increase	9% increase
Current year	2% increase	7% increase
Average percent increase	2.5% increase	8% increase
Projection	2.5% increase	8% increase
Rate relativity factor	1.025	1.08

Exhibit 6-30
Adjusting Adequate Base Rate

Frequency Rate Relativity Factor	Severity Rate Relativity Factor	Adjusted Base Rate
1.025	1.08	$23.60 ($21.32 × 1.025) = $21.85 ($21.85 × 1.08) = $23.60

Summary

Pricing personal insurance products is as much an art as a science. Actuaries use a variety of mathematical tools and techniques to adequately price insurance. Although the calculations can be complex, the underlying concepts are readily understandable. The basic components of insurance pricing include pure premiums, base rates, base premiums, loss costs, and rate relativity factors.

To establish rates, insurers can use the judgment method, the loss ratio method, or the pure premium method. In many cases, actuaries will use more than one approach and compare the results before making a pricing recommendation. Over time, they continue to adjust pricing in response to the insurer's actual results.

An insurer prices new products by comparing the products already offered and making reasonable estimates of the new product's probable losses and expenses. Confidence in the estimates can be increased by pooling data from other insurers.

Actuaries adjust prices based on predictions of future losses. To project future losses, actuaries review the frequency and severity of an insurer's past losses as well as the average amount the company pays in claims per exposure unit. They look for trends, analyze industry data, and compare the results generated by different risk classifications. This information helps actuaries project loss experience and identify which groups are relatively higher risks. This difference in risk inherent in each group forms the basis for the rate relativity factors insurers use to match rates to exposures.

Insurance premiums not only cover an insurer's projected losses but also must be sufficient to cover expenses and profit. In addition, the effect of an insurer's investment income is factored into any rate calculations.

Finally, ratemaking decisions are subject to both regulatory and social pressures. State regulators ensure that rates are adequate, not unfairly discriminatory, and not excessive. In addition, competitive pressures, consumer advocates, and society as a whole help to ensure that insurance is affordable and available; that it encourages responsibility and loss control among consumers; that it is responsive to change; and that the criteria upon which prices are based are stable and fair.

Reunderwriting Personal Insurance Portfolios

Chapter 7

Educational Objectives

1. Describe the purpose of portfolio reunderwriting. (pp. 7-3 to 7-5)
2. Explain the portfolio reunderwriting process, including the following steps: (pp. 7-5 to 7-19)
   a. Analyzing the portfolio
   b. Identifying problems
   c. Identifying possible corrective actions
   d. Selecting corrective actions
   e. Implementing corrective actions
   f. Monitoring the portfolio to determine the effectiveness of the corrective actions
3. Identify and describe the individuals who are responsible for performing portfolio reunderwriting and the types of situations when portfolio reunderwriting is performed. (pp. 7-19 to 7-25)
4. Explain how the reunderwriting process can improve the control of portfolio results and improve decision making regarding changes to the portfolio. (pp. 7-26 to 7-28)

Outline

I. The Purpose of Portfolio Reunderwriting

II. The Steps in the Reunderwriting Process
   A. Analyzing the Portfolio
   B. Identifying Problems
   C. Identifying Possible Corrective Actions
   D. Selecting Corrective Actions
   E. Implementing Corrective Actions
   F. Monitoring the Portfolio

III. Who Performs Portfolio Reunderwriting and When?
   A. Variations in Monthly Reports
   B. Quarterly Reports
   C. Underwriting Audits
   D. New Business Reviews
   E. Loss Reviews
   F. Special Event Reviews

IV. Improving Control and Decision Making
   A. Improvement Through Reunderwriting
   B. Improvement With Hypothetical Models

V. Summary

Chapter 7

Reunderwriting Personal Insurance Portfolios

Insurance company staff members constantly compare the results for a portfolio of policies to established goals for variances that might cause the insurer to fail to meet its overall profitability goals. An insurance company staff member identifying a variance will determine the reason for the difference and take corrective action, if it is required. Some of these types of variances and corrective actions are described in other chapters of this text:

- Chapter 4 examines variances in written premium or policy count that might indicate the need for a new product or a change to an existing product.
- Chapter 5 discusses the goals established for a portfolio. Goals establish the benchmarks for the annual results for a portfolio. In examining variations, insurers might determine that the goals require reexamination.
- Chapter 6 describes pricing adjustments, some of which might be made in response to variances in the profitability of a portfolio.

This chapter introduces reunderwriting, which is a process for correcting variances from established goals in portfolio results. As an insurer's staff members monitor the results during a calendar year, discrepancies in loss results can jeopardize the insurer's ability to reach its profitability goals for that year. Actions are often required to identify the cause for the losses and reduce or eliminate future losses from similar causes. Although pricing is an activity that is used to compensate for losses that are greater than expectation, an insurer can soon find that it has priced its products higher than its competitors. High prices can result in a loss of written premium, compounding the corrective actions that the insurer must take to regain profitability. Rather than addressing the problem through pricing, staff members must often determine the root causes for the losses and stop the pattern of similar losses in the future.

Educational Objective 1
Describe the purpose of portfolio reunderwriting.

The Purpose of Portfolio Reunderwriting

The management of the profitability of a personal lines portfolio by examining losses is generally referred to as reunderwriting. Although the term reunderwriting is used to describe many activities by insurers' staff members, for the purposes of this course, it will encompass all of the activities associated with the analysis, identification, and correction of loss-related variances in a portfolio. The reunderwriting process might also be used to address written premium variances, such as the examination of new policy growth that exceeds expectations, but this occurs less frequently than the examination of losses.

The purpose of portfolio reunderwriting is to correct results in a portfolio of policies that are not achieving the profitability goals established for those policies. Portfolio reunderwriting begins and ends with monitoring activity. Insurance company staff members, who are responsible for achieving portfolio goals, continually monitor the results against the planned goals to determine whether corrective action is necessary.

As an illustration of the purpose of reunderwriting, assume that the information provided in Exhibit 7-1 displays the results for a portfolio of homeowners policies written by the AmberRock Insurance Company. Insurance companies' reports used to compare results to goals vary according to the individual requirements of each company. The report shown in Exhibit 7-1 includes annual goals for premiums, policy count, and losses. Goals for the year are shown with monthly results. The percent of goal shown is a comparison of the results that should have been experienced year-to-date (YTD) and the actual results experienced. In addition, expenses and overall combined ratios might be displayed. Such reports are usually generated and reviewed monthly.

Reminder

Reunderwriting is the process of analyzing the characteristics of policies within a portfolio and the trends of those characteristics. Through this analysis, common loss exposures are identified that generate losses that were not anticipated at the time rates were established for the exposure units. Possible activity for correction is then identified and one or a combination of activities is selected for implementation. The portfolio is monitored to determine the effectiveness of the reunderwriting activity.

Exhibit 7-1
Six-Month Results for AmberRock's Homeowners Portfolio

	Premiums		Policies			Losses			
	Written percent of goal (000s)	Earned percent of goal (000s)	PIF	New policies	Retention	Incurred percent of goal (000s)	Loss count percent of goal	Average loss	Loss ratio
Annual Goals (Monthly goals are an even distribution of annual goals throughout the year.)									
	$7,000	$6,650	16,471	3,294	80%	$4,300	3909	$1,100	65%
YTD Results									
Jan.	$583 100%	$554 100%	15,976	275	80%	$394 110%	358 110%	$1,100	71%
Feb.	$1,167 100%	$1,086 98%	16,059	1,043	81%	$781 109%	710 109%	$1,100	72%
Mar.	$1,715 98%	$1,613 97%	16,108	1,290	80%	$1,161 108%	1,143 117%	$1,015	72%
Apr.	$2,263 97%	$2,150 97%	16,388	1,675	81%	$1,562 109%	1,642 126%	$952	73%
May	$2,858 98%	$2,715 98%	16,553	2,059	81%	$1,989 111%	2,248 138%	$885	73%
June	$3,465 99%	$3,292 99%	17,294	2,471	81%	$2,430 113%	2,834 145%	$857	74%
	Written and earned premiums are roughly on target for YTD results compared to the annual goals. The earned premium is about 95% of written premium because this is a line of business that is growing.		Retention is on target YTD. However, at six months, the new policy count has reached 75% of the annual goal. These new policies have been reviewed and are determined to meet underwriting guidelines.			Through six months, incurred losses are 13 percent above the YTD goals, and the number of losses is 45 percent above the YTD goals. The result is a loss ratio, which is substantially above goal and increasing.			

In the example shown, AmberRock's homeowners policy results are displayed for the first six months of the year along with the goals and the percent of the goals achieved. Assume that you are a staff member reviewing this report for trends, comparing results to plan, and beginning an examination for any results that are unlikely to reach the annual goals established if they follow the current trends. Based on the information shown, premiums are roughly on target, the policies in force (PIF) and new policy count is growing faster than the established annual goal, but the notation indicates that the growth has been examined, and the new policies meet underwriting guidelines. However, the losses incurred are far above plan. If you allow these trends to continue, it is likely that the loss ratio will continue to deteriorate, and the portfolio will be unprofitable. To meet the annual goals, you will have to take some type of action. The reunderwriting process will help you answer the following questions in order to address this problem:

- What is causing the increase in losses?
- What are the possible actions that I can take to address the cause of the losses to correct the problem?
- Of the possible ways that I can address the cause of the losses, which is the best action?
- How will I implement the action I have chosen?
- How can I determine whether the action was effective?

Portfolio reunderwriting is the process that will address these questions. After a variance from incurred loss goals is identified in a portfolio, the more quickly the steps in the reunderwriting process are implemented, the better the chances of correcting the problems and improving the results.

Reunderwriting can also identify loss exposures or hazards that exist before a problem manifests as an increase in losses. This might be an activity performed as an insurer assumes a portfolio from another insurer or if an insurer suspects an increase in loss exposure due to a change in the physical, social, or legal environment.

Educational Objective 2

Explain the portfolio reunderwriting process, including the following steps:

a. Analyzing the portfolio
b. Identifying problems
c. Identifying possible corrective actions
d. Selecting corrective actions
e. Implementing corrective actions
f. Monitoring the portfolio to determine the effectiveness of the corrective actions

The Steps in the Reunderwriting Process

To identify loss exposures in an insurance portfolio and take corrective action to improve results, an insurer's staff members will perform progressive steps to discover what problems are causing an increase in losses, loss exposures, or hazards. Staff members then work to resolve the problems as quickly and effectively as possible. Because of the limitations in the possible corrective actions that are available to resolve problems, analyzing and identifying the problems are crucial. If staff members make an error in identification and take corrective action based on that error, a significant amount of time may pass before the actual cause of the problem can be identified and effective action taken. By the time effective action can be taken, loss results may have deteriorated.

Analyzing the Portfolio

An insurer's staff members are working with a significant amount of data in a portfolio of insurance policies. To analyze the portfolio to identify a problem, the staff members must find some way of organizing the data to identify patterns. Data organization can be aided or hindered by the extent to which the data has been captured for the individual policies in the portfolio and the access the staff members have to that data. If all of the data on the policy applications as well as the history of the policies and the details of any losses have been captured in a computer database the analysis is simplified. Staff members can then order various reports comparing and sorting that data, making analysis more effective and efficient. In an even more ideal situation, staff members might be able to capture data from the portfolio and manipulate it on a personal computer. However, data collection and report ordering is often limited by the organizational demands placed on data collection systems and access. As a result, staff members performing an analysis must work flexibly with available resources. An analysis might require manual data collection through a physical review of policy files.

Information System Data Collection

Whatever data can be identified and collected from an information system database should be gathered first because it is usually the fastest and easiest method of performing an analysis. Standard reports might be available for an insurer's staff members, or staff members performing the analysis might establish the parameters of reports based on the circumstances.

Continuing in your role as a staff member for AmberRock and using the homeowners portfolio from Exhibit 7-1 as an illustration, you must begin an analysis to determine why the loss ratio is deteriorating. The portion of the report displaying loss results is copied in Exhibit 7-2.

Exhibit 7-2
Six-Month Results for AmberRock's Homeowners Portfolio: Loss Results

	Incurred (000s)	Percentage of goal	Loss count	Percentage of goal	Average loss	Loss ratio
Annual Goals - (Monthly goals are an even distribution of annual goals throughout the year.)						
	$4,300		3909		$1,100	65%
YTD Results						
January	$ 394	110%	358	110%	$1,100	71%
February	$ 781	109%	710	109%	$1,100	72%
March	$1,161	108%	1,143	117%	$1,015	72%
April	$1,562	109%	1,642	126%	$ 952	73%
May	$1,989	111%	2,248	138%	$ 885	73%
June	$2,430	113%	2,834	145%	$ 857	74%

Through six months, incurred losses are 13 percent above the YTD goals, and the number of losses is 45 percent above the YTD goals. The result is a loss ratio that is substantially above goal and increasing.

Because the incurred losses exceed the YTD goal of $2,150 ($4,300 ÷ 12 ∞ 6) and the loss trend is moving upward, you need to take action relatively quickly to change this trend. The loss count, or number of losses, is far above the planned goal, indicating a loss frequency problem. By dividing the loss count by the incurred losses for each month of the year, you find that the average loss is decreasing. Therefore, this does not appear to be a severity problem. Following an underwriting rule of thumb, you recognize that deteriorating results caused by a loss frequency problem can indicate a policy selection shortcoming while unprofitable results caused by a loss severity problem would indicate a pricing inadequacy. As a result, you decide to examine the losses that have occurred in the last six months and the associated loss exposures that are causing the losses. If you can find a pattern in the losses that have occurred, you might then be able to identify the associated loss exposures or hazards and take action.

The next step in your analysis will be to request a report from the claim database that will help you find a pattern in the losses. The categories of data requested might be for a basic profile of the claims and the property. Therefore, you order a report with the data categories:

1. Summary of all homeowners claims reported January 1 through June 30 of current year
2. Cause of loss
3. Territory

This report will provide a basic profile of the type of losses that have occurred this year and their location. The report that you receive as a result of your request appears in Exhibit 7-3.

Exhibit 7-3
AmberRock's Homeowners Portfolio—First Analysis Report Requested

Summary of All Homeowners Claims Reported
January 1 Through June 30 of Current Year

CAUSE OF LOSS			TERRITORY	
Code	**Description**	**Percentage of Losses**	**Territory Code**	**Percentage of Losses**
01	Windstorm	2.2	24	5.3
02	Hail	0.1	25	7.6
03	Earthquake	0.0	26	4.5
04	Fire—forest/wild fire	0.0	27	3.2
05	Fire—arson	**5.0**	29	**15.4**
06	Fire—other	**12.3**	30	**27.3**
07	Theft	**39.4**	31	**14.9**
08	Vandalism	4.7	32	4.7
09	Liability	5.2	33	7.2
10	Medical payments	4.0	34	3.9
11	Other property loss	27.1	35	3.7
			36	2.3
	Total	100.0	Total	100.0

From this basic report, you notice that there are some arson losses and other fire losses, a high percentage of theft losses, and a large percentage of losses that have been placed in an "other property loss" category. Three territories have a large concentration of losses. From a territory map, you determine that these territories border each other and that these territories are inland from any large body of water. Because the percentage of windstorm and hail losses is low, this concentration of losses cannot be caused by an isolated storm. In addition, the loss count appearing in Exhibit 7-2 is accelerating each month. For a windstorm or hail loss, a large number of losses is often reported during one or two months, with the number of losses tapering in subsequent months as other minor damage is discovered by property owners. Further, you compare the profile of the causes of loss and the losses by territory to prior years and discover that this is not a typical pattern.

From this information, you form an assumption that some type of activity is occurring in territories 29, 30, and 31 that might involve theft, fire, and other types of property losses. Although this report does not unquestionably support your assumption (the accumulation of losses from other causes might be concentrated in territories 29, 30, and 31, while the theft, fire and other type of property losses are spread throughout the state), you choose this as a point for beginning your investigation.

The next step in your analysis would be to learn more about this concentration of losses. You need to determine what is similar about the losses occurring in these territories so that you can identify any increased loss exposures or hazards. To identify additional patterns, you order a report on all of the theft, fire, and other property losses that have occurred in territories 29, 30, and 31. In this report, you request the ages of the dwellings, Coverage A values, number of prior losses, and the year that the policies were first written with AmberRock. However, the report identifies no particular patterns.

The details of the claims occurring in these territories could provide information that would be helpful in identifying a pattern. However, when you request a list of the policies with the identified causes of loss and territories, over 1,200 claims fall into this category. It is not feasible to review all of these claim files without help. To reduce the number, you select only those losses that have occurred in June reducing the claim files to review to about 250.

Manual Data Collection

Manual data collection can be performed with spreadsheet or database software on a personal computer. Manual data collection can also be performed without a computer or software by recording data on worksheets and identifying similarities.

Reviewing 250 claim files in the AmberRock portfolio is time consuming. However, observations from claim representatives might be included in the claim reports that cannot be captured from computer generated reports. In addition, claim reports include pictures and records of conversations with policyholders that could provide patterns of similarity. Rather than reviewing the entire set of claim files, a sampling of 50 or 100 files might be sufficient to identify a pattern.

In addition to reviewing the claim files, data recorded in the policy files and applications might provide patterns that reveal loss exposures that were not identified during the initial underwriting of the policies. If this data has not been recorded in an information system database, the only way to recover the data is to manually collect it.

Next, you determine and list the categories of data to be collected. For the AmberRock homeowners portfolio, you might choose the following data categories to review in the claim files:

- *Preventable?* Could the loss have been prevented by insured?
- *Carelessness?* Was carelessness a factor in the claim?
- *Maintenance issues?* Did poor maintenance contribute to the loss?
- *Additional living expense paid?* Was additional living expense coverage paid?
- *Economic pressures?* Are any indications of economic pressures present in the policyholders' comments?

After reviewing 100 claim files, you have developed the information shown in Exhibit 7-4 using database software on a personal computer.

Exhibit 7-4

AmberRock Homeowners Portfolio: Results of Claim Review for Sample Claims in Territories 29-31

Characteristics	**Percentage of "Yes" Occurrences**
The loss could have been prevented by the insured.	55%
The insured was careless, and carelessness was a factor in the claim.	10%
Poor maintenance contributed to the loss.	38%
Additional living expenses were paid in the claim.	12%
Economic pressures were found in the policyholders' comments.	78%
Other	
Policyholder was unemployed at the time of the loss.	59%
Claim has not been paid. File is marked for investigation for arson, fraud, or suspected policyholder involvement.	17%
Maintenance issues did not contribute to the loss; however, photographs reflect maintenance problems or morale issues.	48%

The additional observations included as *other* emerged as you reviewed the files. Although they were not questions originally asked, they appeared as significant factors during the review.

You might compare the results in the sample to another sample drawn from other territories if you were unsure whether the percentages found were higher than normal. However, the high percentage of unemployment identified and the economic pressures reflected in the policyholders' comments are probably sufficient to conclude the analysis. From the profile of the samples, you complete your analysis of the portfolio's increase in losses reported that are higher than goal. The losses have generated from three adjacent territories and can be associated with economic pressures: (1) decline in property maintenance because funds are unavailable for repairs, (2) increase in theft losses by others in the community or possibly from policyholder fraud, and (3) increase in suspected arson as policyholders attempt to relieve the burden of financial obligations.

Identifying Problems

Identifying the problem or multiple problems following an analysis can be difficult. Exhibit 7-5 is an advertisement offering a perspective.

An analysis of deteriorating loss results can be much more complicated than the one illustrated for the AmberRock portfolio. The deterioration can result from an increase in losses covering several states with multiple causes. Even after an analysis is completed, the underlying problem and the size of the problem can be difficult to identify with certainty.

Assuming that the analysis of the AmberRock homeowners portfolio losses is correct, the sudden economic decline in a community can result from the loss of one or more large employers in an area that has no other industry to offer employment and return economic stability to the community. This can occur when other possible employers are too far away for property owners to commute to other jobs while retaining their property. The price of real estate drops as property owners attempt to relocate. Property owners are unable or unwilling to perform maintenance on property when outcomes are unknown. When the market value of property drops too far below mortgages for owners to be able to absorb the losses, some property owners might resort to drastic measure, such as insurance fraud, to eliminate the financial burden the property creates.

An increase in theft losses is another symptom of a community with economic problems. Some individuals might break into homes to obtain property that can be converted to cash; property owners might feel justified in exaggerating the extent of a theft loss. Vacant homes, abandoned or waiting for sale, can become targets for thieves and vandals.

AmberRock's staff members must identify the size of the problem and the extent to which the portfolio might continue to decline. If AmberRock uses credit reports as an underwriting tool, a review of all of the credit reports for all policyholders submitting fire, theft, or other property loss claims in territories 29, 30, and 31 would be useful. If the percentage of unacceptable credit reports is significantly higher for those territories than the average number of unacceptable credit reports identified for new applicants or for renewals, the extent of the problem can be identified by ordering credit reports for the entire portfolio or for policies in selected territories. If AmberRock does not use credit reports, property inspections in the selected territories can be used to identify vacant houses or maintenance problems that might lead to further losses.

Exhibit 7-5
Advertisement Addressing Portfolio Problems

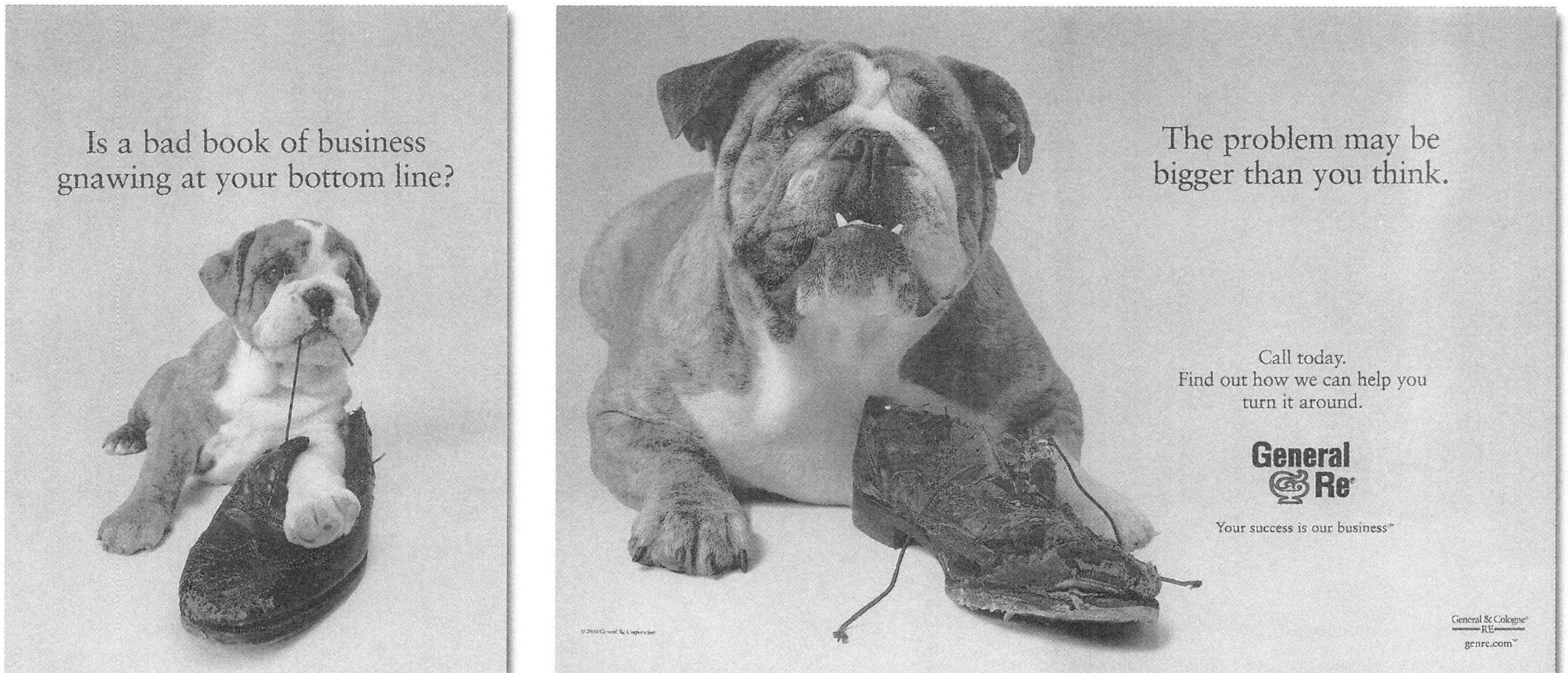

General Re, Advertisement appearing in *National Underwriter*, November 1999.

Identifying Possible Corrective Actions

Correcting a problem in a portfolio that is unprofitable because of losses that exceed expectations begins with identifying all of the possible corrective actions that might be applied. Some corrective actions might appear obvious considering the circumstances; however, restrictions in the policy language or state regulations might limit an insurer's ability to cancel or nonrenew personal insurance policies. The possible corrective actions that follow are listed in order of their complexity, from simple solutions that affect only some policies to complex solutions that affect all of the policies in the portfolio.

Nonrenew All Policies With an Identified Loss Exposure

The AmberRock homeowners portfolio illustration demonstrates moral and morale hazards that are causing significant losses in a community. One possible corrective action is relatively simple. If state regulations allow the use of credit reports for the nonrenewal of homeowners policies, AmberRock staff members can order credit reports for the identified problem territories, additional territories, or the entire portfolio to identify risks with similar hazards. Those policies with unsatisfactory credit ratings can then be nonrenewed. It takes little imagination to see how homeowners policy nonrenewals based on credit reports can generate anger toward insurance companies; a policyholder who's only failing is the inability to pay bills to creditors on a timely basis would appear to present no negative underwriting concern. However, significant evidence supports the relationship between a poor credit history and losses, just as a poor driving history is a predictor of future traffic accidents.

A **material misrepresentation** is a fact that has been misstated or omitted if it could reasonably be considered as affecting the insurer's decision to enter into the contract, the insurer's evaluation of the degree or character of the risk, or the calculation of the premium.[2]

An insurer electing to nonrenew a portion of its policies in a portfolio as a corrective measure will continue to experience losses until an entire annual cycle (or six-month cycle if allowed by state regulation) of the unacceptable policies have been nonrenewed. An insurer may reject new applications with unacceptable loss exposures or hazards, but only rare circumstances allow an insurer to cancel a policy in the middle of a policy term. The general rule is that a **material misrepresentation** made in an application by the applicant for insurance coverage will void the insurer's obligation under the policy.[1] A material misrepresentation can justify a midterm cancellation or declination of a claim. An intentional loss and nonpayment of premium can also justify a midterm cancellation.

Insurers might identify numerous criteria as the reasons for policy nonrenewal if the criteria are found to be the basis for loss exposures or hazards that threaten the profitability of a portfolio. For example, a deteriorating roof is a physical hazard that can lead to a loss. As a composition shingle roof ages, it deteriorates and loses its ability to protect the property from windstorm loss. An insurer might establish a maximum age limit of 25 or 30 years for composition shingle roofs. Any policy insuring a house with a roof older than the maximum age would be nonrenewed at the next anniversary. This activity could take place as a preventative measure before losses occur.

Modify Coverages

To reduce the losses or loss exposure for a portfolio of personal lines policies, modification of coverages might be an effective option. For example, an insurer might limit its exposure to earthquake losses by increasing the deductible for earthquake coverages. A similar deductible could be established for windstorm losses for property located within an established distance, such as ten miles from the ocean. An additional example is the elimination of theft coverage for compact discs (CDs) from automobiles, if the portfolio has been experiencing excessive losses from the theft of such property.

Any modification of coverage made in this way must be clearly communicated to policyholders. Insurers normally make such changes as policies renew. Notification is sent to the policyholders with the notification of the renewal. Insurers take great care to ensure that any change in coverage is explained in language that is easy to understand. In addition, any mailers containing the notification of such changes are labeled to draw the readers' attention to the information. To take less than this degree of care in communicating a change might result in an angry customer at the time of a claim. If a change and the reason for the change is not clearly communicated, a policyholder might deny having been notified. Ultimately a court could rule in the policyholder's favor, requiring the insurer to pay for the loss.

Modify Coverage Limits To Match Property Values

Portfolios of residential property policies can experience a loss in profitability if Coverage A property values fall significantly below the value for which the policies were designed. Because most property losses are partial losses, rates are developed with the expectation that total losses will be rare. If property insured in a portfolio is significantly undervalued, average losses will equal a larger percentage of the average Coverage A limits. The portfolio might also experience a greater number of losses equal to the total Coverage A limit. Overall, the profitability of the portfolio will decline. An alternative might be to increase the rates charged or to modify the Coverage A limits for each policy to more closely match the values of the properties they cover. Increasing the rates charged does not resolve the underlying problem of insuring property to its appropriate value.

There are some specific issues that make insurance to value difficult to evaluate:[3]

- During periods of economic growth, more money is available for customization of houses.
- Houses have become bigger in square footage and more elaborate than in the past.
- Even standard houses have upgrades and extra features.
- Remodeling and interior upgrades with custom finishes and woodwork has become more common and more expensive than in the past.

- According to the National Association of Realtors, many homeowners upgrade their houses within nine months of moving into them. These changes represent as much as a 5 percent addition to the original cost of the houses.
- The National Association of Homebuilders states that the money spent on modifications to houses is growing significantly. These modifications represent upgrades to kitchens, bathrooms, finished basements, and added living spaces. For example, in 1982, homeowners in the United States spent $43 billion on remodeling and repairs, while in 1994 that spending almost tripled to $120 billion. While some modifications are required to maintain the value of a house, other modifications increase the replacement cost of the property.
- It can cost up to 40 percent more to reconstruct a house than it cost to build the original. This is attributable to several factors: (1) contractors reduce costs of building materials when they can mass produce houses in a subdivision; (2) reconstruction requires contracting artisans for a single construction assignment, which is more expensive than contracting artisans to complete work on houses in a subdivision over a period of years; (3) reconstruction might require upgrading systems to comply with new zoning or building ordinances; and (4) older houses may contain features such as slate roofs and hardwood moldings, which are expensive to reproduce in the current market.

According to studies by Marshall & Swift through their valuation services, approximately 70 percent of homeowners are underinsured by 30 percent. A major reason for this is the improvements homeowners make to their property. Because insurers and producers do not ask evaluation questions frequently enough, these changes go unreported.[4]

Although most homeowners and dwelling fire policies include clauses providing penalties for insuring property below 80 percent of its replacement cost, insurers rarely invoke these penalties in personal lines contracts. Because of different valuation methods, adjuster time constraints, or an insurer's staff members' inability to conduct a physical inspection of the property, only those properties that are found to be significantly underinsured are identified for further review. Unless the insurer can verify that the home is grossly underinsured, the partial or total loss is usually paid at the time of a claim.[5]

Insurers correct insurance-to-value problems by instituting formal programs. Every year, inflation factors are applied to increase Coverage A limits. Inflation factors can be refined by state and zip code to more accurately increase coverage limits to match increasing replacement values. Insurers also communicate with policyholders to encourage them to increase their coverage limits so that they will not lose financially if a total loss occurs. Insurers provide questionnaires and work sheets that help policyholders calculate the replacement cost for their property. In addition, continual communication with policyholders encourages coverage increases following renovations and property improvements.

Modify the Risk Profile of the Overall Portfolio

Insurance rates are based on the risk characteristics of the policies that are written within a portfolio. These characteristics are roughly defined by the underwriting guidelines. However, there is latitude within the underwriting guidelines. For example, the Greenwood Insurance Company might develop a preferred personal automobile portfolio. The underwriting guidelines allow a maximum of two traffic violations in the last three years for any operator listed on a policy. Because this is the maximum allowable traffic violations, staff members at Greenwood expect that one traffic violation will be the average for all drivers in the portfolio when they examine the risk profile. However, the rates offered are attractive for drivers that have had two traffic violations. After one year, staff members at Greenwood review the risk profile for the portfolio to find that drivers have an average of 1.9 traffic violations. In other words, the maximum allowable number of violations has nearly become the average. Because traffic violation records are an indication of future driving habits and a valid predictor of future accidents, it is likely that the losses will be higher than the goals established for the portfolio.

To correct this problem, Greenwood's staff members might work to improve the risk profile by reducing the average number of traffic violations per driver insured in the portfolio. They might accomplish this by doing one or more of the following:

- Increase discounts for drivers with no violations to attract drivers with better driving histories.
- Increase rating factors for drivers with more than one violation to discourage drivers with traffic violations.
- *Jawbone* policyholder selection with producers.

Jargon Alert!

Some insurers call discussing or suggesting an improvement in policyholder selection by a producer *jawboning*. Although insurers do not provide an incentive or prohibit a continuation of current behavior, a strong appeal is made to producers to help in correcting a situation.

Modify the Underwriting Guidelines

Some loss exposure problems in a portfolio can be corrected by modifying the underwriting guidelines. Continuing the previous example for the Greenwood Insurance Company, staff members might be unable to alter the current discounts or increase the rating factors due to state regulations. If the discussions with producers encouraging the submission of applications including drivers with fewer driving violations are unsuccessful, Greenwood's staff members might modify the underwriting guidelines. The maximum allowable violations could be reduced from two to one per driver.

If this change is implemented, the new underwriting guidelines might require filing with state regulators. In addition to communicating the change to producers, underwriters, and customer service representatives, Greenwood's staff members must also decide about the policies that are currently in the portfolio that include drivers with more than one violation. If Greenwood's average is 1.9 violations per driver, this could be a significant enough problem to begin a nonrenewal process for all policies that exceed the new underwriting guidelines.

Insurers also alter underwriting guidelines for loss exposures that are anticipated but have not yet manifested as losses within a portfolio. For example, in the 1990s sport utility vehicle (SUV) sales climbed to over 20 percent of overall private passenger vehicle sales in the United States. SUVs' large size and weight provide protection for occupants; however, studies by the Insurance Institute for Highway Safety showed that occupants of sedan-style cars are 10 times more likely to die in a crash with an SUV than with another sedan-style car. In anticipation of the increase in the severity of liability losses involving SUVs, an insurer might change its underwriting guidelines to provide coverages for SUVs only if the drivers in the household have had no accidents or violations in the last three years.

Insurance executives and underwriting managers rely on external reports from research organizations, such as those by the Insurance Institute for Highway Safety, the Highway Loss Data Institute, and the Insurance Research Council, to identify trends and changes in loss exposures and hazards. Armed with this information, an insurer's staff members can take appropriate actions to protect the profitability of their insurance portfolios before these trends and changes manifest as losses.

Modify the Pricing Through Tiered Rates

Insurers work to maintain a balance among the rates charged, the losses incurred, and the written premiums for a portfolio. If losses increase, a rate increase might be warranted. However, if rates are increased above those of the competition, the written premiums will drop as policyholders seek better prices for their coverage. Often, the policyholders representing the lower chance of loss will leave for more attractive rates offered by another insurer. This can result in a decline in the risk profile for a portfolio.

To improve their competitive position in writing policies at the appropriate rates, some insurers have adopted a strategy of more closely relating rates to the loss exposures insured. By applying tiered rating, which is also called pricing on a sliding scale, insurers can more closely match rates to exposures. In tiered rating, policyholders are divided into segments within a portfolio according to underwriting guidelines established for each segment. Rates are applied according to the segment and risks represented by the policyholders within the segment. For example, a personal automobile portfolio might be divided into the following tiers:

- Segment A, which allows no moving traffic violations or accidents for any driver in the last three years
- Segment B, which allows one moving traffic violation or minor accident for any driver in the last three years
- Segment C, which allows a maximum of two moving traffic violations or minor accidents per driver in the last three years

Lower-than-average rates are offered to drivers in Segment A, average rates are offered in Segment B, and higher-than-average rates are offered to drivers in Segment C. Understandably, Segment C drivers will not be happy about paying higher rates, even though their driving records might merit higher rates. However, the insurers who have applied tiered rating will have a better opportunity to attract and retain Segment A drivers with lower rates. Overall, tiered rates can be used to improve the risk profile for a portfolio.

Discontinue the Portfolio

The most drastic corrective action an insurer might take is to discontinue a portfolio of policies. However, if all other possible corrective actions are ineffective in restoring the profitability of a portfolio or other options are not available due to regulatory restrictions, an insurer may elect to nonrenew all policies in a portfolio.

Selecting Corrective Actions

The corrective action or actions selected for implementation should clearly address the problems identified in the analysis and problem identification. Generally, the corrective actions that are the easiest to implement and that affect the smallest number of policies in the portfolio are chosen before any other alternatives. Modifications to correct problems in a portfolio can require expenses for (1) external reports, (2) coverage modifications and communication to policyholders, and (3) rate filings. Corrective actions that affect a small number of policies and address the problems in the portfolio minimize an insurer's expenses. In addition, any change to a policy can anger of confuse policyholders, even if the change is skillfully communicated. Therefore, changes affecting a large number of policies can decrease retention if policyholders shop for a new insurer as a result. However, when a choice among corrective actions is unclear, an insurer might implement several actions.

When existing losses exceed goals, insurance company staff members feel an urgency to implement corrections. In the AmberRock example shown in Exhibit 7-1, the incurred losses currently exceed the plan by $280,000 as of the end of June of the year shown ($2,430,000 in losses compared to a plan through June of $2,150,000 in losses). If the written premium exceeded the plan, there might be additional income to help to offset the losses. However, the written premium for this portfolio is roughly on target.

The urgency to correct a loss problem is compounded by the long time frame that is required to complete a corrective action. Any plans for nonrenewals or coverage modifications require time for the insurer's decision makers to reach an agreement, time for any state filing regarding coverage modifications, and a full year to implement the corrective action as the policies nonrenew (assuming policies are written for twelve months). Strategies to create tiered rates take a much longer period of time as the underwriting guidelines, rates, and communications are developed and as the new filings are submitted for approval.

Even with the urgency to implement corrective actions, an insurer's staff members must take care to ensure that the action selected is actually the best choice. Staff members might perform the following additional research to make certain that they have made the best possible selection given the available information:

Jargon Alert!

Redundancy describes the degree to which losses have been over-reserved compared to amounts for which they are actually settled. For example, if losses during a calendar year for a portfolio are reserved for $1,050,000 but are actually settled for $1,000,000, there is a 5 percent redundancy ($1,050,000 – $1,000,000 ÷ $1,000,000 = .05, or 5 percent).

- Review the claim reserves for the portfolio to determine whether any outstanding reserves might affect the incurred losses. Also, review the ratio of claim reserves to claim settlements to determine if any *redundancy* has occurred in the past that might also be present in the current incurred losses.
- Check for other patterns of losses within the portfolio by comparing loss results by producer, territory, property value, driver age, or any other major characteristic of the policies in the portfolio.

Some corrective action might not be permitted by state regulation, they might be actions that do not match the insurer's mission statement or strategies, or they might have consequences that are too severe to consider. For example, an insurer that markets policies through an independent agency system might be reluctant to discontinue a portfolio due to loss results. The effort required to build the necessary relationships with independent agents could be severely jeopardized or lost if the insurer withdraws from the market or from a line of insurance. Agents would be forced to write the nonrenewed policies with other insurance companies. This requires additional effort by the agency staff, and the agency might lose policyholders who take the opportunity to shop for coverage elsewhere. If the insurer creates such a situation, it might be difficult to regain the agents' trust. Reentering the market with a new product or encouraging the growth of PIF for other lines of coverage through the same agents would be difficult.

Implementing Corrective Actions

After one or more corrective actions are selected as appropriate activities to address the problems identified, an insurer's staff members put the processes in place that will ensure consistent implementation. If criteria are established for the nonrenewal of some policies, activity must take place far enough in advance of the current policy expirations to select the policies, order any necessary external reports, review the reports, and issue notice to the policyholder, mortgagees, and lienholders. The amount of time required for issuing a nonrenewal notice before the expiration of a policy is established in each policy contract; however, a 30-day notice is a standard requirement. Insurers often work 90 to 120 days in advance of the policy expiration dates to ensure that all policies that need to be discontinued are properly processed. Policies that are not processed in time for adequate notice to be issued must be renewed for another policy term.

Actions that require state filings for rate changes, underwriting changes, or the development of tiers are expedited as quickly as possible. Any delay can result in additional losses that further deteriorate the profitability of the portfolio.

Actions that involve increasing the Coverage A limits to more closely reflect the values of the dwellings might require a review of all policies within a portfolio. Insurers might obtain external reports and use vendors who specialize in calculating insurance to value in order to develop recommendations. Insurers can then recommend to policyholders to increase the coverage value in the middle of the policy term or at the next renewal. A project of this extent will generate additional expenses. However, the projected increase in premiums can justify the associated expenses.

Monitoring the Portfolio

The reunderwriting process began with problems identified as staff members monitored the results of a portfolio compared to the goals established, and the cycle begins again with monitoring the results to determine whether the actions taken have corrected the problems identified.

Changing the direction of the results in a portfolio is a long process. If policies are written on a twelve-month basis, twelve months must pass before a corrective action involving the nonrenewal of policies can be completed. Twenty-four months may pass from the time a problem is identified, corrective actions are selected, and the corrective actions are applied to the entire portfolio.

In the months following the implementation of a nonrenewal process, an insurer's staff members must cautiously evaluate the success of the actions. Another spike in losses could result from storms or winter-related losses that are not related to the original problem identified. To determine the success of an action, staff members must monitor the same type of losses originating from similar loss exposures or hazards to detect a reduction in loss frequency. Staff members monitoring the result of one set of actions often initiate activity addressing unrelated trends.

The entire reunderwriting process requires a thorough understanding of the characteristics of the policies within a portfolio and the ability to recognize the underlying problems that cause results to deviate from goals. Ultimately, staff members who can anticipate changes in loss exposures from external trends and changes or who can recognize an increase in loss exposures from changes in a portfolio's risk profile can take corrective action before losses occur.

Educational Objective 3

Identify and describe the individuals who are responsible for performing portfolio reunderwriting and the types of situations when portfolio reunderwriting is performed.

Who Performs Portfolio Reunderwriting and When?

Each insurer apportions the responsibility for meeting the profitability goals of the organization among various staff members based on the company's organizational structure, staff, skill level of staff members, and tradition. Some companies assign responsibility for the overall underwriting profitability jointly to underwriting and marketing executives to maintain checks and balances between growth and policy selection. Other organizations assign the goals for premiums to marketing executives and goals for losses to underwriting executives. However the responsibility is assigned, the job of managing and monitoring the individual portfolios is usually delegated to line underwriters, staff underwriters, underwriting managers, or underwriting staff members working in partnerships with marketing representatives. Individuals assigned responsibility for managing portions of an overall portfolio will have annual goals specifically portioned to that smaller portfolio. Individuals assigned to manage overall policy portfolios or portions of the portfolios seek to identify trends and deviations from annual goals in the same way. They identify trends in standard reports and seek answers to questions found in the trends through reunderwriting.

Insurance company staff members responsible for portfolio management usually receive standard reports showing results at the end of each month. The staff members compare these monthly results to the goals established for each portfolio, which are divided throughout the months of the year. For example, the goals for new policies to be written are apportioned throughout the twelve months. The apportionment might be an even division, as they are in Exhibit 7-1, or an uneven distribution with higher goals for some months that traditionally generate higher volumes for new business.

Variations in Monthly Reports

Depending on the events that have occurred in the portfolio, staff members might modify the reports they receive and the questions they ask in order to determine what trends are occurring. Each calendar year begins a new accumulation of premiums and losses; therefore, results experienced in the early months of the year can fluctuate widely. This occurs because the accumulated earned premium has not grown large enough to balance catastrophe or shock losses that also occur early in the year. A large catastrophe loss can change the results for the entire year, masking other problems occurring in a portfolio. For this reason, staff members might view the results and ask the question, "What is occurring that we cannot observe because the catastrophe losses have substantially changed the results?" To answer that question, staff members might modify a standard report to show actual results with the catastrophe losses as well as results excluding the catastrophe losses. Continuing the previous example for AmberRock's homeowners portfolio, the results of a catastrophe early in the year would appear in a monthly report as illustrated in Exhibit 7-6.

Exhibit 7-6
AmberRock's Homeowners Portfolio Illustrating a Catastrophe Loss Early in the Year

	Losses With Catastrophe						Losses Without Catastrophe			
	Incurred (000s)	Percentage of goal	Loss count	Percentage of goal	Average loss	Loss ratio	Incurred (000s)	Loss count	Average loss	Loss ratio
Annual										
	$4,300		3,909		$1,100	65%	$4,300	3,909	$1,100	65%
YTD										
Jan.	$921	257%	619	190%	$1,488	166%	$394	358	$1,100	71%
Feb.	$1,534	214%	1,192	183%	$1,286	141%	$781	710	$1,100	72%
Mar.	$2,161	201%	1,618	172%	$1,285	134%	$1,161	1,143	$1,015	72%
Apr.	$2,723	190%	2,124	163%	$1,282	127%	$1,562	1,642	$952	73%
May	$3,135	175%	2,525	155%	$1,242	115%	$1,989	2,248	$885	73%
June	$3,225	150%	2,971	152%	$1,086	98%	$2,430	2,834	$857	74%
	Through six months, incurred losses have exceeded goals because of an ice storm catastrophe experienced in January and reported through March. Losses excluding the catastrophe are on target for expected loss count.						Excluding the January ice storm catastrophe, the number of losses is 45 percent above the YTD goals. The result is a loss ratio that is substantially above goal and increasing.			

With the catastrophe losses, it might be impossible for staff members responsible for achieving the annual goals to reach the desired loss results for the portfolio. However, had they not determined the loss results without the catastrophe losses, an increasing loss trend might have gone undetected further deteriorating the results.

Quarterly Reports

The results experienced at the end of each quarter are given particularly thorough examination. If loss-related problems are identified at the end of the first quarter, most negative trends can be improved if not corrected by year-end. At the end of the second quarter, some corrections can still be made to improve the results by the end of the year. At the end of the third quarter, it might take drastic measures to improve that year's results.

Underwriting Audits

Insurance companies conduct periodic underwriting audits to determine whether the applications selected by underwriters meet the criteria established by the underwriting guidelines. Although guidelines might appear to control much of the acceptance or rejection of applications, a substantial amount of individual judgment exists in evaluating some underwriting factors, such as photographs or inspections of houses. The purpose of an underwriting audit is to provide feedback to an underwriter as well as instruction regarding changes in activity that might help an underwriter improve his or her decision-making process.

As part of the underwriting audit, the auditor might develop a report for the new policies accepted by an underwriter or written for a portfolio in the last six or twelve months. This report demonstrates trends in risk selection by an underwriter or automated risk selection that fails to identify underwriting criteria that can lead to an increased chance of loss. Exhibit 7-7 provides an example of an excerpt from an underwriting audit.

Exhibit 7-7
Sample Underwriting Audit Report

Underwriting Guidelines	Risk Profile for Portfolio	Underwriting Audit Notes	Auditor's Recommendations
Maximum of one driving violation or accident per driver	The average number of violations or accidents per driver is 0.85.	The average number of accidents is on the high end of acceptability. This can lead to a greater level of accidents, losses, and major violations, such as driving under the influence (DUI). Two policies have drivers who received DUIs after the inception of the policy.	Determine whether the high percentage of drivers with accidents and violations is coming from any one or several producers. Order new motor vehicle reports (MVRs) annually for all policies.
Credit reports reflect positive payment habits	10 percent of policies reviewed reflected payments in excess of 90 days past due.	Late payment histories have been linked to vehicle owners with an above average likelihood of comprehensive losses and accidents.	Meet with underwriting supervisor to establish more structured criteria for the selection of applications. Reunderwrite policies accepted in the last 24 months based on the new criteria.
No sports cars with primary operators under age 25	27 policies were identified with sports cars and drivers under age 25 in the household (although they were not listed as primary operators).	Although the drivers under age 25 are not primary, it is likely that they might be operating the sports cars at some time.	Discontinue accepting policies with drivers under age 25 where a sports car is in the household and the number of drivers exceed the number of vehicles.

An underwriting audit is based on a sample of policies drawn and examined individually. Based on the findings in the sample, staff members might decide to reunderwrite the portfolio or portions of the portfolio to determine whether the trends continue through all of the policies written.

New Business Reviews

If underwriters are reviewing each application individually, it is sometimes difficult to acquire a sense of the profile of risks that are being accepted over a period of time. An underwriter might notice an occasional application in one geographic area for homeowners policies written for the minimum limit of Coverage A allowed in the underwriting guidelines. Over time, the underwriter might sense a pattern emerging in the new policies written that does not allow for a geographic spread of risk and does not represent risks that meet more than the minimum underwriting requirements. To obtain a more complete image of the policies accepted, the underwriter might reunderwrite those homeowners policies accepted in the previous twelve months to determine whether a problem exists.

Loss Reviews

The occurrence of a series of losses or a trend in losses is a common reason for insurance staff members to reunderwrite a portfolio. Determining the reason for a deteriorating loss ratio that is not related to a catastrophe loss can be a frustrating process. Staff members recognize the need to act relatively quickly to change the trend and improve the profitability of the portfolio. However, the cause of the problem must be identified before corrective action can be initiated. A deteriorating loss ratio can be the result of multiple problems. Just as a doctor can have difficulty diagnosing an illness when the patient's symptoms are conflicting, conflicting trends in a portfolio can make problem detection difficult. For example, a homeowners portfolio with an increasing frequency of theft losses also has an improving risk profile. The profile of the houses insured within the portfolio reflect newer homes, more homes with alarm systems and deadbolt locks on windows and doors, and more homes in crime watch neighborhoods. The improving profile should result in a decrease in theft losses. A review of the claims can help detect other patterns and reasons for the losses.

Special Event Reviews

When one insurance organization merges with another or acquires a portfolio from another as a result of an acquisition or transfer of accounts, the insurer assuming responsibility for the portfolio will have concerns about the types of risks it has acquired. The acquiring insurer may reunderwrite the portfolio to determine the risk characteristics of policies compared to the risk profile expected. It is unlikely that the two organizations would be using identical underwriting guidelines or processes. The portfolio being assumed might include policies that are written below acceptable policy minimums or with loss exposures that have been reduced in the acquiring insurer's portfolio.

An insurer considering acquiring a portfolio will review the risk profile of the portfolio and compare it to (1) the profile that it would consider ideal, (2) the underwriting guidelines established for the portfolio to identify compliance with guidelines, and (3) the rates applied to the portfolio. Based on the outcome of the review, the insurer will determine what effort will be required, if any, to improve the profitability of the portfolio. If reunderwriting will be required, the insurer will consider the cost involved with that process as well as the drop in written premium for the policies that might be nonrenewed. Such a review can be complicated by the availability and credibility of data about the portfolio. The following is a case study illustrating how an insurer might reunderwrite in preparation for the acquisition of a portfolio and how the resulting information might be used.

Reminder

Economy of scale is a reduction in the average cost of a product or a process as the size of a company increases. In this case, AmberRock will gain economy of scale if it can increase the size of its portfolio while keeping its expenses constant.

AmberRock Insurance Company is considering the acquisition of a portfolio of personal automobile policies currently written by Singlewing Insurance. Singlewing, an aircraft insurer, ventured into automobile insurance five years ago. During those five years, the personal automobile portfolio that Singlewing developed has been marginally profitable but very small. By incorporating these policies into their existing personal automobile portfolio, AmberRock might be able to improve its overall profitability through economy of scale.

AmberRock's staff members have reviewed the underwriting guidelines used by Singlewing and the risk profile of Singlewing's portfolio compared to the underwriting guidelines and risk profile for AmberRock's own personal automobile portfolio. The rates charged by both companies for automobile insurance are the same. Exhibit 7-8 displays a chart with these comparisons.

Based on the comparison of the underwriting guidelines, AmberRock's staff has determined that Singlewing's personal automobile portfolio will contain:

- Some primary drivers under the age of 20
- Some primary drivers with less than one year of driving experience
- Some sports cars
- Some vehicles used in business to transport customers
- Some policies with drivers having more than one at-fault accident in the last three years
- Approximately two thirds of the policies have MVRs that are not current by AmberRock's standards
- No policies have been reviewed by use of credit report

If AmberRock's staff members plan to incorporate Singlewing's policies into their current personal automobile portfolio, they might be willing to accept the risk characteristics as they are currently written. However, they might determine that reunderwriting Singlewing's portfolio to the same underwriting guidelines applied by AmberRock would provide the best opportunity for profitable results. Assuming that the latter is the case, AmberRock's staff members must determine the cost of reunderwriting and the number of Singlewing's personal automobile policies that will be nonrenewed (assuming that such nonrenewals are allowed by the states in which they are written).

AmberRock's staff members might be able to obtain some information, such as the number of policies with sports cars or more than one at-fault accident in the last three years, from Singlewing's database. However, some information, such as the number of vehicles with business use that includes the transportation of customers, might only be

Exhibit 7-8
Personal Automobile Risk Profile and Underwriting Guideline Comparison

	Underwriting Guidelines	
	AmberRock	**Singlewing**
Age of drivers	No primary operators under age 20	No primary operators under age 18
Driver experience	Primary drivers must have at least one year of experience	<not addressed in guidelines>
Violations and accidents	No more than two violations or accidents in last three years	No more than two violations or accidents in last three years
Vehicle types	No sports cars	Vehicles must pass state safety inspections
Business use	No business use involving transportation of customers	<not addressed in guidelines>
Previous losses	No more than one at-fault accident in last three years	No more than two at-fault accidents in last three years
Motor vehicle reports	Ordered every year	Ordered for new applications and every third renewal
Credit report	Ordered for all new applications	<not addressed in guidelines>
	Risk Profile	
Average liability limit	$100,000/300,000/50,000	$50,000/25,000/10,000
Percentage of policies with drivers under age 20	19%	27%
Percentage of policies with one reported claim	20%	31%
Annual policy retention for previous year	70%	75%

available by reviewing individual policies and files and possibly contacting policyholders. Staff members might decide to review a sample of such policies with business use vehicles to estimate the total number. Finally, AmberRock's staff members will develop a recommendation that includes the following:

- The number of policies in the Singlewing portfolio that will be nonrenewed
- The increased loss exposure outside AmberRock's underwriting guidelines from any policies assumed that cannot be nonrenewed
- The increased cost of performing the activities required to nonrenew policies
- The increased cost of external reports that will be ordered and the review of the reports

This information will be used to determine the value of Singlewing's portfolio and the feasibility of purchasing the portfolio. In some situations, the costs associated with assuming the portfolio are greater than a company can assume profitably.

Educational Objective 4

Explain how the reunderwriting process can improve the control of portfolio results and improve decision making regarding changes to the portfolio.

Improving Control and Decision Making

During the reunderwriting process, an insurer's staff members perform an analysis to identify the cause of a problem. The reunderwriting process also requires the development of possible alternatives that might address the cause of the problem. Analysis and the development of alternatives help improve control and decision making.

Improvement Through Reunderwriting

One question that remains in the review of a portfolio is why adequately detailed and effectively implemented underwriting guidelines for a portfolio are not sufficient to achieve the planned results. When an insurer establishes its loss, premium, expense, and profit goals for a portfolio, it also identifies the types of risk characteristics it will write and the premium for those risks. The risk characteristics are defined in the underwriting guidelines. It would seem that appropriate underwriting guidelines that are effectively implemented should result in a profitable portfolio. If underwriting guidelines are not effective or appropriately implemented, these factors should be addressed to improve results. However, many events cannot be addressed by underwriting guidelines. The following are hypothetical examples of events that could change the profitability of a portfolio but cannot be addressed through underwriting guidelines:

- The number of fire losses increases for homeowners and dwelling policies in areas bordering some state parks. (An investigation reveals that state parks with easy coastal access by boat are being used as the drop-off point for drugs being brought into the United States from other countries. Forest fires are used to divert forest rangers while watercraft access the coast.)
- Theft and fire losses increase for large sport utility vehicles soon after a dramatic increase in the cost of gasoline. (An investigation reveals that owners of the vehicles have submitted fraudulent theft claims or committed arson to eliminate the burden of the unaffordable vehicles that have dropped in popularity and cannot be easily sold.)
- The average cost of windstorm losses increases in one coastal state for houses constructed in the last ten years compared to older homes. (An investigation reveals that the building codes in the

state were changed ten years ago allowing changes in construction that were thought to be esthetic but increased the risk of damage to the structure of the home in strong winds.)

In these examples, changes occurred that might not have been anticipated at the time the underwriting guidelines and rates were established. A change in the environment has occurred, and a change in the losses for the portfolio has also occurred. The connections between the changes are not always clear. A change in the portfolio might have several combined causes or causes that are never fully identified. To improve profitability, the underwriting guidelines can be changed, but that does not address the problems with existing policies. The premiums can be increased to include any increase in losses, but premium changes are a slow process. The remaining tool to reduce losses and improve the control over the profitability of the portfolio is reunderwriting.

Improvement With Hypothetical Models

One of the benefits of the reunderwriting process is developing a chart of the portfolio results, such as the charts shown in Exhibit 7-1 and Exhibit 7-6. By using spreadsheet software, an insurance company staff member can project the year-end results if the current trends continue. The staff members can then apply changes to a portfolio to create hypothetical models of the results based on proposed changes.

Continuing the AmberRock homeowners portfolio example including catastrophe losses, assume that an insurance company staff member has determined that the majority of the losses during the year have come from policies written by four producers. The staff member is trying to determine whether the problem might be caused by poor policy selection by these producers or whether another element might be the root cause of the problem. The staff member takes the following actions:

- The staff member projects the year-end results assuming that the current loss trend will continue through the year. The loss ratio at the end of the year is used to measure the outcome. If the current trend continues, the loss ratio will be 87 percent.
- The staff member then eliminates all of the premium, policy counts, and losses from the four producers to determine whether the results would improve. The loss ratio improves to 76 percent, however more than half of the premium and policies have been eliminated. A recommendation to nonrenew the policies written by these producers would have negative consequences for the portfolio with a loss ratio that has been only moderately improved.

The results of the staff member's actions are displayed in Exhibit 7-9.

Because many of the losses have been weather related, the staff member creates another projection for year-end results by eliminating all of the premium, policy counts, and losses for homes located within fifty miles

Exhibit 7-9
AmberRock's Homeowners Portfolio—Hypothetical Projections

	Premiums				Policies			Losses				
	Written (000s)	Percentage of goals	Earned (000s)	Percentage of goals	PIF	New policies	Retention	Incurred (000s)	Percentage of goal	Loss ratio	Percentage of goal	Loss ratio
Annual Goals												
	$7,000		$6,650		16,471	3,294	80%	$4,300		3,909		65%
YTD Results												
Jan.	$583	100%	$554	100%	15,976	275	80%	$394	110%	358	110%	71%
Feb.	$1,167	100%	$1,086	98%	16,059	1,043	81%	$781	109%	710	109%	72%
Mar.	$1,715	98%	$1,613	97%	16,108	1,290	80%	$1,161	108%	1,143	117%	72%
Apr.	$2,263	97%	$2,150	97%	16,388	1,675	81%	$1,562	109%	1,642	126%	73%
May	$2,858	98%	$2,715	98%	16,553	2,059	81%	$1,989	111%	2,248	138%	73%
June	$3,465	99%	$3,292	99%	17,294	2,471	81%	$2,430	113%	2,834	145%	74%
Year-End Projections Based on Current Trends												
	$6,930	99%	$6,650	100%	17,624	4,118	81%	$5,805	135%	6,450	165%	87%
Year-End Projections Eliminating Policies and Losses From Selected Producers												
	$3,150	45%	$3,126	47%	6,424	1,153	81%	$2,365	55%	2,228	57%	76%
Year-End Projections Eliminating Policies and Losses Within 50 Miles of Beach												
	$3,990	57%	$3,791	57%	9,388	2,668	81%	$1,935	45%	1,681	43%	51%

of the ocean. This drops the premium and policy count significantly, but it also reduces the loss ratio to 51 percent, which is an improvement of 36 percentage points.

From these hypothetical models, the property near the ocean seems to be sustaining a large portion of the losses. Without these models, the staff member might have recommended the elimination of producers writing profitable policies. The staff member can now refine the decision with models that reduce the distance to the ocean and models that combine the distance to the ocean with the age of the structure, the type of construction, and the type of construction materials.

Summary

Although reunderwriting has no universally accepted definition, it is used here to describe a systematic process for identifying a portfolio's variations in results compared to goals and taking corrective actions to improve results. The reunderwriting process includes the following steps:

1. Analyzing the portfolio results, including a review of reports from databases as well as the manual collection of data when necessary
2. Identifying the problems causing a deterioration of the results
3. Identifying possible corrective actions, including the nonrenewal of policies, modification of the coverages, coverage limits, the risk

profile, underwriting guidelines, or pricing strategies, and the discontinuation of portfolios

4. Selecting corrective actions that address the problems identified allowing sufficient time to order and process reports and to issue notices for nonrenewals
5. Implementing one or more corrective actions.
6. Monitoring the portfolio to ensure correction of the problem

Reunderwriting might be performed when an insurer's staff members review monthly or quarterly reports, as the result of an underwriting audit or new loss trends, for new business received, or for special events such as the acquisition of a portfolio.

The individuals responsible for ensuring that a portfolio achieves the goals established are usually the individuals who will perform any reunderwriting necessary. These individuals and their job functions vary depending on the responsibilities assigned within an insurance organization.

Reunderwriting processes can be used to improve the control over a portfolio and the decision making applied in changing a portfolio by initiating corrections that might not be addressed through underwriting guidelines or price adjustments. In addition, data collected during analysis can be used to project the results of hypothetical decisions. Staff members can create models to view the anticipated results from proposed activities.

Chapter Notes

1. See example: Christiania General Insurance Corporation v. Great American Insurance Company, 979 F.2d 268 (2d Cir. 1992). Numerous states, including New York, California, Florida, Delaware, and Massachusetts, have codified the common law with respect to material misrepresentations in insurance policy applications.
2. See examples: Nappier v. Allstate Insurance Company, 961 F.2d 168 (11th Cir. 1992); and American Home Assurance Company v. Fremont Indemnity Company, 745 F. Supp. 974 (S.D.N.Y., 1990).
3. CPCU Society's Chicago West Suburban Chapter, *The Valuation Industry: A Brief History of Insurance to Value* (Research Project, Chartered Property Casualty Underwriters, 1997), pp. 11-12.
4. CPCU Society's Chicago West Suburban Chapter, p. 12.
5. CPCU Society's Chicago West Suburban Chapter, p. 30.

Gaining Efficiencies in Personal Insurance Operations

Chapter 8

Educational Objectives

1. Describe the work flow used to process personal insurance applications, and illustrate the following: (pp. 8-3 to 8-11)
   a. How insurers gain efficiency in work flow
   b. How the work flow might further evolve
2. Given a case study involving an insurer's work flow for personal insurance applications and processing, suggest improvements and justify those suggestions. (pp. 8-11 to 8-17)
3. Describe the effect that catastrophes have on personal lines insurers and the insurance industry, and give examples of the following: (pp. 8-18 to 8-24)
   a. Insurance company response to catastrophes
   b. Contingency plans to maintain insurer operations after catastrophes
   c. The insurance industry's response to catastrophes

Outline

I. Personal Insurance Policy Processing Work Flow
   A. Gaining Underwriting Efficiency
   B. Gaining Insurer Support Staff Efficiency
   C. Gaining Producer and Marketing Efficiency
   D. Gaining Insurer Management Efficiency
   E. Improving Resource Utilization

II. Work Flow Case Study
   A. Documenting Current Work Flow
   B. Identifying Work Flow Bottlenecks
   C. Gaining Work Flow Efficiencies
   D. Implementing Efficiencies

III. The Effect of Catastrophes on Personal Lines Insurance
   A. Catastrophes and Personal Lines Insurers
   B. Catastrophes and the Insurance Industry

IV. Personal Insurers' Responses to Catastrophes
   A. Mitigating the Impact of Catastrophes
   B. Contingency Plans
   C. Managing Operations After a Catastrophe

V. Insurance Industry Response to Catastrophes

VI. Summary

Chapter 8

Gaining Efficiencies in Personal Insurance Operations

Reminder

Underwriting expenses are an insurer's operating costs including expenses directly related to marketing, application processing, policy issuance, salaries, employee benefits, computer systems, building rent and maintenance, and office supplies and equipment.

Underwriting expenses are a component in the calculation of underwriting profit or loss; therefore, controlling underwriting expenses is important in the management of an insurer's portfolio of policies. However, a complete discussion of controls that can be applied to underwriting expenses is beyond the scope of this text. Insurers' staff members who are responsible for portfolio management usually have little influence over underwriting expenses other than those expenses associated with work flow management and policy processing. Therefore, this chapter will concentrate on the work flow management portions of the overall underwriting expenses.

Effective management of insurance work flow requires the following fundamentally different competencies:

- The ability to run day-to-day operations as efficiently as possible
- The ability to respond immediately and effectively to infrequent yet catastrophic events

Over the past twenty years, the pace of change in the insurance industry has accelerated. Competitive pressures and improvements in technology have resulted in the appearance of new insurance products, services, and distribution systems. Computers are allowing insurers to communicate better with customers and to provide the services customers demand. Paradoxically, insurance is seen as a commodity by many consumers who make purchasing decisions based on price alone. Competition, the demand for services, and pricing issues pressure insurers to operate as efficiently as possible to keep underwriting expenses and premiums low.

Efficient organizations are those that are staffed, equipped, and resourced only to the extent required for day-to-day operations. However, when a catastrophe hits, such as an earthquake, hurricane, or other natural disaster, insurers are expected to respond to policyholder needs promptly. Two important aspects of insurance company management include understanding an insurer's catastrophe exposure and planning how best to deal with it.

Educational Objective 1

Describe the work flow used to process personal insurance applications, and illustrate the following:

a. How insurers gain efficiency in work flow
b. How the work flow might further evolve

Personal Insurance Policy Processing Work Flow

In personal insurance, the policy processing **work flow** includes the following steps:

A **work flow** is the series of steps or actions that must be completed, in sequence, to accomplish a particular task.

1. Collecting and evaluating data
2. Deciding on risk acceptability
3. Issuing policies or endorsements
4. Billing policyholders and collecting premiums
5. Recording statistical and management information

An insurer that is able to increase the efficiency with which it processes policies can improve service to policyholders and reduce operating expenses. Reduced underwriting expenses can be passed along to policyholders in the form of lower premiums. As a result, both regulatory and competitive pressures have encouraged insurers to strive for improvements in the following areas:

- Underwriting efficiency
- Insurer support staff efficiency
- Producer and marketing efficiency
- Insurer management efficiency
- Improved resource utilization

Gaining Underwriting Efficiency

Personal lines underwriting is the process of analyzing and classifying individual risks, agreeing or declining to provide coverage, and determining an appropriate premium for the coverage provided. Traditionally, the underwriting of personal insurance was a labor-intensive process often involving several individuals and much duplication of effort. Support staff often screened applications before sending them to underwriters, and underwriters were often required to refer some decisions to supervisors or managers for approval. Policyholder information was kept in paper files, rating and accounting were manual processes, policy documents were typed, and statistical data and management information were manually generated . As a result, delivery of documents to policyholders regularly took from thirty to forty-five days. Underwriting expenses were relatively high, and the availability of current detailed management information was extremely limited.

Reminder

Expert systems, sometimes called artificial intelligence systems, are software programs that duplicate the decision-making process. In insurance, expert systems complete the same steps that an underwriter takes in assessing a risk.

Beginning in the 1960s, the integration of computer systems into insurance processing allowed for increased speed, accuracy, and efficiency. Through the 1970s and 1980s, broad standardization and enhanced computer technology supported changes in underwriting relationships, roles, and responsibilities, which further increased the efficiency of the industry as a whole. During the 1990s, the development of expert systems improved electronic communication, and more sophisticated data management systems led to enhanced customer service, reduced underwriting expenses, and significant improvement in the quality and availability of statistical data. In addition, the Internet offers significant opportunities for achieving further underwriting efficiencies.

Underwriting Technology

With advances in technology, more and more of the underwriting process has been computerized. Many underwriters today review application data on screen and accept risk submissions with a password rather than a signature. Risk classification and premium calculation can be done automatically by an insurer's computer system once application data has been entered. One of the most significant developments in underwriting technology has been the evolution of expert systems.

Since the 1980s, computers have underwritten an increasingly larger percentage of applications. Currently, insurance company software can compare application data to underwriting guidelines and then order and review additional information, such as motor vehicle reports (MVRs) and credit reports. The system can automatically process applications that meet established selection criteria and issue a policy almost immediately. Only those risk submissions that fail to meet the system's selection guidelines are rejected or referred to an underwriter.

Jargon Alert!

A *prior carrier* is an insurance company that previously wrote an insurance policy for an applicant. *Prior carrier experience* refers to the claim history experienced by an insurance company that previously wrote the insurance policy.

Even where this level of sophistication is not currently in use, underwriters benefit from technology in other ways. For example, underwriting reports, such as MVRs and *prior carrier experience*, can be ordered and delivered electronically, significantly reducing delays in the underwriting process. System rating and premium calculation have reduced the time required to process applications and endorsements and have eliminated calculation errors. Some insurer systems allow underwriters access to information about producers' loss ratios and production levels from the computer on their desk.

Changing Underwriting Roles

One of the significant implications inherent in the increased use of technology and expert systems is that the underwriting process can be distributed. Today, a producer can enter application data directly into an insurer's system via a personal computer and modem. The insurer's expert system can provide almost immediate feedback regarding the completeness of the application, and the acceptability and the pricing of the risk. This not only results in faster service to the customer, but also serves to transfer some traditional underwriting responsibilities from the underwriter to the producer. Some insurers that have transferred the data input function from their internal processing departments to producers continue to perform **document maintenance**, receiving and reviewing the original paper documents. However, other insurers have shifted the responsibility for document maintenance to producers. In this case, the producer stores the underwriting documents, and the insurer merely conducts spot audits to verify the accuracy of the producer's data entry.

Document maintenance includes filing, maintaining, storing, and retrieving applications, photographs, inspection reports, policyholder correspondence, and all other underwriting documents.

As computers have become better able to evaluate risks, process policies, and generate meaningful management information, the underwriter's job has changed. Using personal computers linked to the insurer's policyholder database and sophisticated data analysis tools, underwriters can now examine premium, loss, and expense results for different combinations of risks, territories, producers, or customers. This ability has lead to enhanced underwriting authority and increased responsibility for managing the profitability of entire portfolios.

Gaining Insurer Support Staff Efficiency

Prior to the integration of computers into insurance processing, companies maintained large numbers of support staff. Even after insurers began to automate during the 1970s, policy processing continued to be labor-intensive and insurers continued to support large departments of clerical and data entry staff. The cost of salaries and benefits is a significant portion of an insurer's underwriting expenses. In addition, processing that is largely manual tends to be slow and prone to errors. To reduce underwriting expenses and improve the speed and accuracy of insurance processing, companies looked for ways of enhancing the efficiency of insurer support staff. The two strategies insurers typically use are as follows:

- Improving processing efficiency through automation
- Improving work flows with new technological capabilities

Improving Processing Efficiency

Computers complete standard, repetitive tasks far more quickly and consistently than do people. Also, computers can provide a much more efficient method of managing large amounts of information. Paper files, once essential to underwriting, verifying coverage, and settling claims are now merely backup documentation, used only to verify the accuracy of computer records. Computer systems that calculate premiums, assemble and print policy documents, store policyholder data, digitize and store paper documents, and generate reporting and management statistics have reduced or eliminated the need for many support positions, including rating clerks, policy typists, file clerks, and data coding clerks. This has helped insurers reduce underwriting expenses by allowing them to manage with fewer staff members. Transferring data entry functions to the producer or potentially to policyholders themselves will further reduce the need for data entry staff. In addition, automation of manual tasks has helped insurers improve the quality, consistency, and accuracy of insurance processing, and this reduction in errors also results in increased efficiency.

Improving Work Flows

Technology has helped insurers improve work flows in the following ways:

- The process of automating a task requires in-depth analysis of that task. In-depth analysis often helps insurers identify and eliminate previously unrecognized inefficiency and redundancy.
- Manual processes sometimes serve no other purpose than to facilitate information retrieval. These processes may be eliminated when an insurer automates since computers manage information so effectively.

Transactional filing is a filing system in which all paper documents for all clients are filed by the date on which they were processed. To retrieve the original document, a staff member checks the date of the transaction on the computer system and then goes to the file for that date to locate the document.

For example, insurers traditionally maintained individual policyholder files that included copies of all applications, endorsements, policy documents, claim records, and correspondence relating to each policyholder. Staff members obtained required information by referring to a policyholder's file. Now, computers store and retrieve information far more efficiently. As a result, some insurers no longer maintain policyholder files, preferring instead to use **transactional filing** for storing original documents and working with policyholder information exclusively on line. Some insurers have eliminated paper files entirely by relying instead on scanned images of original documents, reports, and photographs that have been stored on the system or by transferring the document management function to their producers.

Gaining Producer and Marketing Efficiency

Technology is evolving at an ever increasing pace and becoming more integrated into people's lives. The percentage of homes with computers and Internet access is increasing rapidly. Automated teller machines (ATMs) and debit cards are replacing bank tellers and cash. Consumers are becoming more comfortable with alternative methods of making purchases and accessing services. Electronic commerce is becoming more secure.

In addition to changing underwriting and support staff roles, technology and expert systems have allowed for the development of alternative insurance distribution systems. Many insurers and independent agents now maintain Web sites to disseminate information and provide quotes. Soon, consumers will be able to shop for coverage, select an insurer, pay premiums, report changes and claims, and receive coverage verification and claim payments electronically perhaps via the Internet or at **touch-screen kiosks**.

Touch-screen kiosks are automated machines at which consumers can get information or make purchases. Consumers make selections by touching words or images on a computer screen, eliminating the need for a keyboard.

Currently, technology helps producers improve their effectiveness in a variety of ways, including the following:

- Automated processes for calculating and comparing insurance quotes free large amounts of producers' time, allowing for more prospecting and follow-up.
- Portable notebook computers allow producers to make professional presentations, collect application data, check policy statuses, and e-mail queries to insurers from any location.
- A personal computer and inexpensive software can allow a producer or support staff member to generate mailing lists to target specific neighborhoods. Word processing software can produce hundreds of prospecting letters in minutes.
- Other software helps producers manage their prospecting and follow-up activities, enhancing sales efficiency.
- Web sites allow producers to provide public relations information and pricing information to a large number of potential customers with a very small investment of time.
- Automated systems in producers' offices allow for quick and easy identification of *monoline accounts* and opportunities for selling additional lines of coverage to current policyholders.

Jargon Alert!

Monoline accounts, also called *orphan policies* or *orphan accounts*, are single policy accounts in which the producer provides only part of a customer's insurance needs, such as a homeowners policy but not the personal automobile policy.

Identifying potential customers and creating new products are two essential marketing functions. Because technology expedites collecting, storing, sorting, and analyzing data, insurers now have significantly more detailed management information than they did in the past. As a result, they are better able to identify the risk characteristics common to their most profitable groups of customers. This in turn allows insurers to tailor existing products and services, to develop new products, and to develop marketing strategies specifically for these groups. Exhibit 8-1 illustrates the effect of technology on policy processing.

Gaining Insurer Management Efficiency

Traditionally, insurance companies have been organized hierarchically. Information was passed upward from workers through supervisors and middle managers to senior managers. Senior managers then made strategic corporate decisions. These were passed down through the organization to the workers in the form of action plans. The process was slow and inefficient, often resulting in miscommunication and lost opportunities. Exhibit 8-2 displays the traditional insurance company organizational chart.

Now, information management systems give senior insurance executives immediate access to current data. Up to date loss ratios, production figures, claim information, and reserve details are always available. This allows managers to closely monitor a company's underwriting performance relative to objectives, identify problems early, and respond quickly.

Exhibit 8-1
Effect of Technology on Policy Processing

Manual Work Flow	Work flow Using Information Systems	Work Flow Using Integrated Systems
1. Producer completes hand-written application 2. Producer mails application to insurer 3. Insurer support staff orders additional information (e.g., MVRs) 4. Underwriting staff reviews application and accepts, rejects, or modifies it 5. Insurer support staff inputs application data into computer for issuance, billing, accounting, and statistics 6. Computer prints declarations page and endorsements 7. Insurer support staff attaches required forms to declarations page 8. Insurer mails copies to producer 9. Producer distributes copies	1. Producer enters application data directly into system 2. Producer transmits application electronically to insurer 3. Insurer's information system screens application; orders reports; and accepts, rejects, or refers application 4. System prints and distributes policy forms for accepted applications, prepares and sends appropriate notice for rejected applications, stores customer information, and creates billing, accounting, and statistical records	1. Individual enters application data on the Internet or at a kiosk 2. Insurer's information system screens application, orders reports, and accepts, rejects, or refers application 3. System prints and distributes policy forms for accepted applications, prepares and sends appropriate notice for rejected applications, stores customer information, and creates billing, accounting, and statistical records

In addition, advances in technology allow insurer staff members to more effectively monitor work flows and production levels, identify bottlenecks, and establish reasonable targets. Insurers can more accurately predict when changes in staffing levels will be required, providing the lead-time necessary to hire and train staff.

Further, technology has developed concurrently with changes in management philosophy, and the integration of computers has allowed for changes in organizational structures and management styles. For example, employees who have access to more information and who can accurately monitor their own performances can be given more authority and responsibility. Information sharing facilitates employee participation and empowerment, strengthening organizations. Finally, technology can provide feedback to help employees improve self-monitoring skills. This in turn allows managers and supervisors to become facilitators and coaches, thereby developing employees rather than controlling them.

Improving Resource Utilization

Improvements in underwriting, support staff, producer marketing, and management efficiency cannot depend solely on advances in technology. This is particularly true given the current pace of change within the insurance industry. People are still an integral part of the business of insurance and an important resource. The creative contribution of every employee can have a significant impact on an organization's overall performance. Successful insurers are those that focus on the development of people as well as of technology. This is reflected in a variety of approaches including the following:

- Empowering employees
- Developing learning organizations
- Instituting knowledge management
- Improving employee relationships

Exhibit 8-2
Traditional Insurance Company Organization

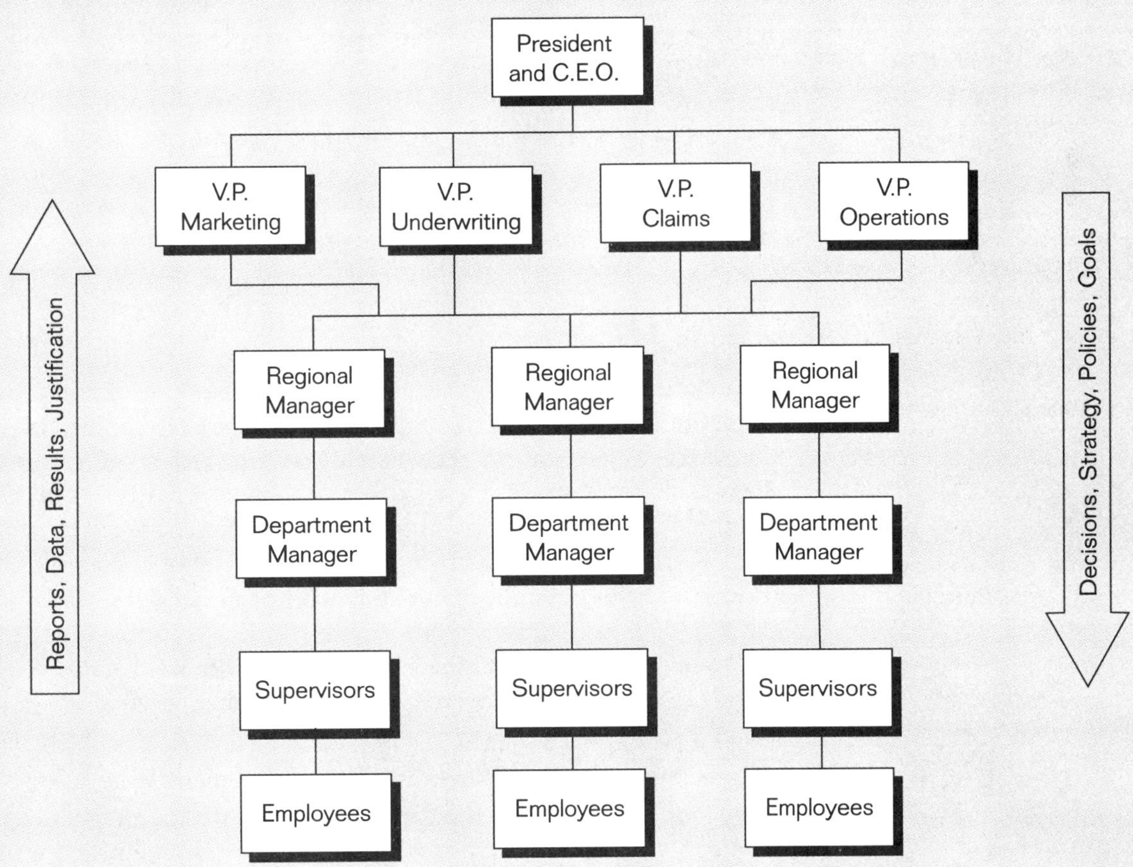

Traditionally, companies were organized hierarchically. Employees passed information up to senior management via several tiers of supervisors or managers. Senior managers made decisions and established goals and passed strategies, policies, and guidelines down through the organization to the employees.

Employee Empowerment

One method of gaining management efficiency is through employee empowerment. Insurers' staff members are involved in management decision making, which improves the use of staff resources and communication. Empowerment is neither simple delegation nor anarchy; it is founded on accountability. Traditional hierarchical management systems are often replaced with self-directed teams and employees who work within specific guidelines and clear frameworks to achieve the organization's business objectives.

Empowerment is the distribution of authority, resources, information, and accountability to employees in an organization in order to make decisions and solve problems.

Effective **empowerment** protects an employee's right to make mistakes and to use those mistakes as learning tools. As a result, the quality of employee decisions, suggestions, and selections improves over time. In addition, empowerment increases employees' sense of ownership within an organization, encouraging them to strive for quality and encouraging risk taking, innovation, and open discussion.

Learning Organizations

Learning organizations are those where people, individually and collectively, continually expand their capacity to produce results and expand their patterns of thinking.

Employee empowerment is far more likely to succeed in **learning organizations**. A learning organization can be described as one that learns and promotes learning among its employees, creating a more knowledgeable work force. Commitment to continuous discovery is an integral part of a learning organization's culture. This commitment enhances organizational flexibility since employees are better able to accept and adapt to new ideas and changes. In turn, this attitude allows the company to anticipate and respond to change, complexity, and uncertainty. These are all elements of the current insurance marketplace. As the pace of change accelerates, the rate at which organizations learn may become their primary source of competitive advantage.[1]

Knowledge Management

Knowledge management is a strategy for capturing and assessing information so that everyone in an organization is able to access the information needed. Knowledge can be explicit or tacit. Explicit knowledge is internal and external information found in documents. Tacit knowledge is the intellectual capital of individuals within the organization. Tacit knowledge is required to apply explicit knowledge.

Knowledge management is often practiced by learning organizations. The term describes a concept in which an organization gathers, organizes, shares, and analyzes the collective knowledge, expertise, and ideas of all its members. Knowledge management involves a synergistic combination of data, information processing technology, and the creative capacity of human beings. This pooling of resources allows an organization to think outside the boundaries of current practices, products, services, and structures and respond more innovatively to the complexities of the business environment. Knowledge management supports competence, adaptation, and hence survival.

Changing Employee Relationships

Employee empowerment changes relationships within an organization. Competitive pressures, advances in technology, and the need for increased operating efficiencies are also changing relationships between employees and their employers in the following ways:

- Rather than reducing the importance of a company's investment in the ongoing development of employees, competition and technology have increased it.
- Technology and automated processing have resulted in reductions in clerical staff and departmental downsizing while creating more opportunities in the systems area.

- Reductions in staffing requirements have created opportunities for part-time work and job sharing in what were traditionally full-time positions.
- Companies that want to control staffing expenses and continue to respond effectively to seasonal changes in work flows depend increasingly on temporary employees or contract staff.
- Advances in technology and communications have created opportunities for employees to work remotely, often from home.

Continuing innovation and evolution within the industry will increase the opportunities and challenges for companies and individuals to work together creatively. Exhibit 8-3 illustrates the evolution of relationships within insurance companies.

Exhibit 8-3
Evolution of Relationships Within Insurance Companies

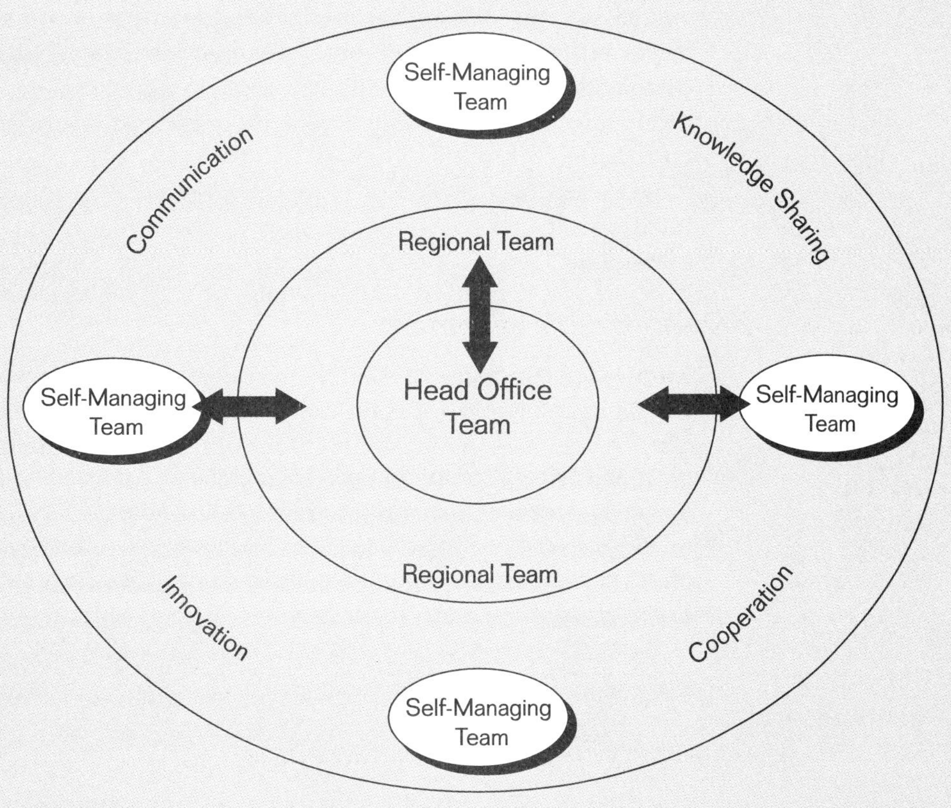

More and more, insurers are reorganizing and rethinking traditional approaches to management. When a company embraces employee empowerment, reorganizes into cross-functional, self-managing teams, implements knowledge management, and becomes a learning organization, the changes in corporate culture that result include increased communication, cooperation, knowledge sharing, and an enhanced ability to innovate.

Educational Objective 2

Given a case study involving an insurer's work flow for personal insurance applications and processing, suggest improvements and justify those suggestions.

Work Flow Case Study

NSW Insurance Company is a midsized, regional insurer offering personal automobile, homeowners, and related lines in a limited geographic region. NSW's 250 producers are independent agents. All producers have sales contracts with other insurers. Although NSW traditionally had very competitive premiums, over the last ten years, the company's competitive advantage has slowly eroded. Sales have slumped and decreasing retention has resulted in a net decrease in policy count. Unfortunately, the company's expense ratio is higher than that of the competition. As a result, NSW is unable to reduce its rates. In addition, producers complain that service from NSW is slow and that policy issuance takes almost twice as long with NSW as with the other insurers they represent.

The company currently uses a computerized policy processing system purchased ten years ago. Because of the limitations of this system, most work is done manually and stored in paper files. While the company does have an internal electronic mail (e-mail) system, it does not communicate electronically outside the organization. Although senior management members have discussed the possibility of upgrading the system, they have been reluctant to proceed due to the significant cost involved and its effect on the company's already high expense ratio. Concerned for the company's future, the president appoints a senior management team to research the causes of NSW's problems and to recommend solutions.

Documenting Current Work Flow

Because of the combination of a high expense ratio and complaints about slow service, the team decides to focus first on NSW's insurance processing work flows. An outside consultant is contracted to complete an analysis and submit a detailed report, including recommendations for improvements, to the team.

The first step is to document current work flows. Exhibit 8-4 illustrates NSW's current new application processing work flow.

Exhibit 8-4
NSW's Work Flow Illustration

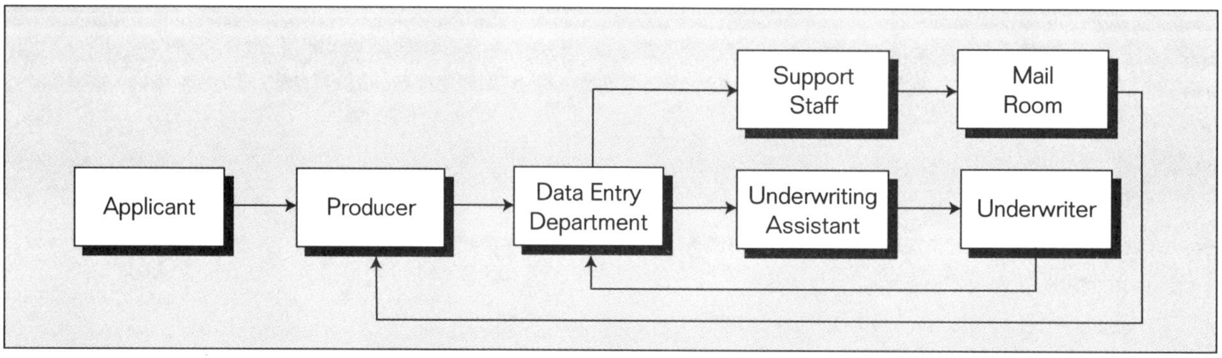

Applications from producers arrive by courier and are sent to the data entry department. Data entry staff members input the information into NSW's computer and route the applications to the underwriting assistants. The underwriting assistants check that all necessary information has been provided by the producer and order any additional information required, such as MVRs or *prior carrier experience letters*. When these underwriting reports are received, the assistants match them with the applications and route them to the underwriters. After an application has been underwritten, the underwriter sends it back to data entry where the data entry staff enters any changes into NSW's computer system. Then, data entry releases approved applications for issuance. Computers batch print all required documents over night. The printing is routed to support staff who attach the appropriate forms and then send the policies to the mailroom for distribution to the producers.

Jargon Alert!

A *prior carrier experience letter* is a letter from an applicant's previous insurer disclosing the loss history of a prior policy or verifying that coverage was provided. Not all insurers provide such letters.

Identifying Work Flow Bottlenecks

The next step in the work flow analysis is to identify any bottlenecks. The consultant reviews production reports and tracks individual applications through the work flow, noting how long each step in the process takes, identifying any factors that affect work flow efficiency, and highlighting any delays. Exhibit 8-5 presents the consultant's results.

Gaining Work Flow Efficiencies

After analyzing the company's current processes and reviewing projections of NSW's growth and expense performance over the next three years, the consultant identifies a variety of ways in which NSW could improve its policy processing efficiency. The consultant's summary table of opportunities for improvement is presented in Exhibit 8-6.

First, the consultant recommends passing the data entry function to NSW's producers. This would eliminate application transit time and data processing time at NSW and reduce data entry errors resulting from illegibility. The consultant suggests that simple changes to NSW's computer system could make all application data fields *required* fields. If producers were unable to transmit applications to NSW until all information was provided, underwriting assistants would no longer need to check applications for completeness.

The consultant also recommends that NSW subscribe to an automated underwriting report service and order prior carrier experience information and MVRs by modem. This would reduce the turnaround time for MVRs from 8 days to 1 day and for prior carrier information from 12 days to 1 day. Programming NSW's computer to connect with the service and order reports automatically would result in additional time savings.

The consultant points out that these simple and relatively inexpensive measures would result in significant increases in processing efficiency as well as allow NSW to reduce operating expenses by reducing data entry and assistant underwriting staff. However, a more significant investment in updated technology could result in even greater efficiencies. Automated underwriting of applications that can be approved without additional information would improve service levels significantly. It would also improve the accuracy and consistency of underwriting for simple risks. A new system would allow underwriters to work from a computer screen rather than from paper applications. As a result, underwriters could make any necessary changes directly on the system and release approved policies themselves. New systems currently on the market are able to select and print all required documents, doing away with the need for manually attaching preprinted forms. This would allow documents to reach the mailroom in time for same-day courier to producers. These changes would result in a significant reduction in average total processing time from thirty-two days to six days. The consultant's proposed new work flow is illustrated in Exhibit 8-7.

Exhibit 8-5
Factors Affecting Work Flow Efficiency

Original Work Flow Steps	Comments	Average Completion Time
Producer completes handwritten application	New business averages 223 applications per week.	1
Producer couriers application to NSW	70 percent arrive next business day; 28 percent arrive within 2 business days; 2 percent arrive within 3 business days	2
Data entry clerk inputs application into computer	Data entry is generally current, completing input within 2 business days of receipt of application. 15 percent of applications cannot be entered because essential fields are illegible or incomplete.	2
Underwriting assistant checks application and manually orders underwriting reports	Turnaround for MVRs is about 8 business days. Turnaround for prior carriers is about 10 business days.	10
Underwriter reviews application and accepts, rejects, or modifies it	Underwriters generally have a backlog of approximately 2 weeks on their desks.	14
Data entry clerk makes any required changes and releases application for billing, accounting, and statistics	Data entry is generally current, releasing 90 percent of applications the next business day after receipt from underwriting.	1
Computer prints declarations page and endorsements	Computer batch prints overnight.	.5
Support staff attach required forms	Support staff are current, matching printing and forms the same day as printing is received.	.5
Mail room couriers copies to producer	Mail room receives policies after cutoff time for courier; documents go out the following day.	1
Total Average Time Required		**32 days**

Exhibit 8-6
Gaining Work Flow Efficiencies

New Efficiencies	Average Completion Time
The producers' inputting application data directly into NSW's computer would result in a saving of 1.3 days courier time plus 2 days in data entry. This would also eliminate the 15 percent of applications that NSW staff cannot enter because essential fields are illegible or incomplete.	2
Ordering MVRs by modem would reduce turnaround time from 8 days to 1 day. Subscribing to an automated prior carrier service and ordering reports by modem would reduce turnaround time from 12 days to 1 day. Programming NSW's computer to order reports automatically would result in additional time savings.	1
Automated underwriting of applications requiring no additional information would improve service levels. Underwriters working from a computer screen rather than from paper applications could make any necessary changes directly on the system and release the policy themselves.	2
NSW's system could print all required documents, doing away with the need for manually attaching forms. This would speed the process and allow documents to reach the mail room in time for same-day courier to producers.	1
Total Average Time Required	**6 days**

Exhibit 8-7
Proposed New Business Work Flow for NSW Insurance Company

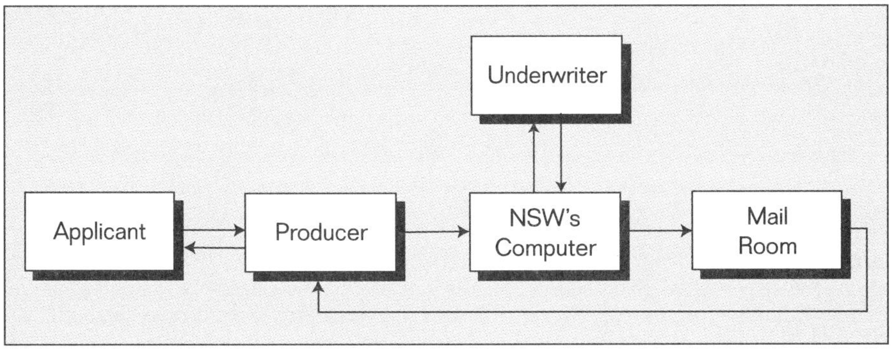

Implementing Efficiencies

The project team reviews the consultant's report and recommendations. Purchasing a new computer system and upgrading NSW's electronic communications ability both involve large investments. However the team estimates that the resulting efficiencies will not only improve the company's service to policyholders and producers, but also allow for reductions in staff. This would generate savings in salaries and benefits that would help to offset the initial large expense for the new system. In addition, the team anticipates further savings from reduced printing costs, reduced long distance telephone charges, and reduced postage costs. Over time, these significant savings are expected to result in a 15 percent reduction in underwriting expenses, allowing NSW to reduce premiums and improve its competitive position. Exhibit 8-8 illustrates the team's projections of costs and savings.

Exhibit 8-8
Cost and Savings Projections—Computer System Upgrade

Expenses	
Purchase new computer system	$1,000,000
Upgraded electronic communications ability	665,000
Total Anticipated Expenses (one-time expense)	**$1,665,000**
Anticipated Savings	
Staff Reductions	
• 15 data entry operators (average salary/benefits: $22,000 each)	$ 330,000
• 12 underwriting assistants (average salary/benefits: $27,500 each)	330,000
• 14 underwriters (average salary/benefits: $38,000 each)	532,000
Printing, long distance telephone, and postage	369,000
Total Anticipated Annual Savings	**$1,561,000**

NSW decides to act on the consultant's recommendations; however, the management team recognizes that the scope of the project is huge. The company will be taking on several large projects simultaneously. These include the following:

- Converting to a new computer system
- Re-engineering internal policies, procedures, and work flows
- Making significant changes to the way the company interacts with its producers
- Reducing current staff by over forty individuals or retraining those individuals for new jobs as vacancies become available when employees leave or retire

To help ensure the success of the project, the management team decides to involve the employees from the beginning. They share information about the company's financial results and sales performance with employees and explain their concerns about the company's future. The consultant makes a detailed, day-long presentation to the entire staff explaining his findings and his final recommendations. The management team openly discusses the costs of the project and its implications in terms of staff reductions or retraining. The team asks the employees to participate in helping their company improve.

The company brings in a change management consultant who recommends, as a first step, intensive employee training in coping with change, team building, teamwork, communication, employee empowerment, and organizational dynamics. Supervisors and managers also receive training in delegation, listening, mentoring, employee empowerment, knowledge management, and communication.

The consultant then breaks the project down into the following four broad areas of focus:

- Human resources
- Technology
- Policies and procedures
- Producer relations

For each area of focus, a project team is formed consisting of employees, supervisors, and managers from all departments within the company. The project teams identify issues, solicit input, make recommendations, and communicate their results both to the employees and to NSW's producers who will also be affected by the proposed changes.

As the project progresses, the culture at NSW begins to change. Employees begin to feel more ownership of the company and personal responsibility for its success. Supervisors and managers learn to value employees' input and suggestions. Within each project team, members share their knowledge and learn from each other. People work together to find new and innovative ways to meet the challenges of the project.

It takes a full two years for NSW to successfully implement the consultant's recommendations; however, the project runs smoothly. By the end of the two years, the corporate culture at NSW has changed significantly and the company has better relationships with both its employees and its producers. It is projecting a 19 percent decrease in underwriting expenses next year. This savings has allowed NSW to apply to regulators for an overall 12 percent decrease in premiums, improving the company's competitive position. In addition, the company has been able to retain, through job-sharing arrangements and training, all employees who would otherwise have been laid off. Exhibit 8-9 illustrates the efficiencies NSW has achieved.

Exhibit 8-9
NSW—Efficiencies Achieved

Old Work Flow	New Work Flow
• Producer completes handwritten application • Producer couriers application to NSW • Data entry inputs application into computer	• Producer enters application data directly into system
• Underwriting assistant checks application and orders underwriting reports manually • Underwriter reviews application and accepts, rejects, or modifies it	• NSW's information system screens application, orders reports, and accepts or rejects application or refers it to an underwriter
• Data entry makes any required changes and releases application for billing, accounting, and statistics • Computer prints declarations page and endorsements • Support staff attach required forms	• NSW's system prints and distributes policy forms or sends appropriate notice for rejected applications, and creates billing, accounting, and statistical records
• Mail room couriers copies to producer	• Mail room couriers documents to producer
Total Average Time Required: 32 days	**Total Average Time Required: 6 days**

Educational Objective 3

Describe the effect that catastrophes have on personal lines insurers and the insurance industry, and give examples of the following:

a. Insurance company response to catastrophes
b. Contingency plans to maintain insurer operations after catastrophes
c. The insurance industry's response to catastrophes

The Effect of Catastrophes on Personal Lines Insurance

The Property Claim Services (PCS) division of the American Insurance Services Group defines a catastrophe as an event that is likely to result in insured losses exceeding $25 million. Although individual insurers may define a catastrophe differently for their own purposes, the PCS definition is widely accepted.

Catastrophes, usually the result of earthquakes or extreme weather events, are devastating not only to their victims and the communities in which they live, but also to insurers. Promptly meeting financial obligations to policyholders after a catastrophe and maintaining business-as-usual service during these times of crisis present significant challenges. An important part of managing insurer operations involves planning for and responding to catastrophes effectively.

Catastrophes and Personal Lines Insurers

Every insurer faces the probability of catastrophe losses; not just those that operate in areas prone to earthquakes, floods, hurricanes, or tornadoes. Natural disasters or other catastrophic events can occur at any time, anywhere. When they do, insurers are called upon not only to promptly fulfill their financial obligations to policyholders but also to provide advice, assistance, and guidance.

The immediate effects of a catastrophe on a personal lines insurer include the following:

- A significant increase in the number of claims reported requiring inspection, investigation, and payments, which create many more claims than regular staffing levels can manage
- Potential disruption to the insurer's operations if its own premises are damaged or must be evacuated
- Difficulty in verifying coverage if records are lost or destroyed or if an insurer's computer system is down
- Inability of employees to report to work due to disruptions in transportation or because they are dealing with damage to their own property

- Potential disruptions in communications hindering claim staff's ability to contact policyholders and settle losses
- Delays in claim settlement due to unavailability of goods and services required to mitigate and settle losses quickly

Catastrophes can have long-term effects on insurers as well. For example, consumer interest in and demand for catastrophe-related coverage increases after the crisis and policyholders may purchase increased limits of coverage. Unfortunately, catastrophes can also result in class action suits against insurers launched by policyholders dissatisfied with the outcome of their settlements.

Catastrophes and the Insurance Industry

Over the past several decades, the population density in catastrophe-prone areas has increased significantly, as have the values of properties located in these areas. As a result, the industry-wide financial impact of catastrophe losses can be staggering. For example, Exhibit 8-10 illustrates the actual cost of several catastrophes in terms of insured property damage.

Exhibit 8-10
Insured Property Damage From Catastrophes

Event	Total Insured Property Damage
Hurricane Andrew (1992)	$16 billion
Northridge Earthquake (1994)	$12.5 billion
Hurricane Opal (1995)	$2.1 billion
Hurricane Fran (1996)	$1.6 billion
Florida Tornadoes (1998)	$100 million

Source: National Oceanic and Atmospheric Administration.

Also, predictions for the future are disturbing. Many researchers suggest that southern California is due for a significant earthquake. A study by Dr. Haresh Shah of Risk Management Solutions and Stanford University estimates that a major quake in San Francisco could result in $100 billion total insured property damage; one in Los Angeles could result in insured losses of $95 billion. In addition, long-term trends in climatic changes suggest that hurricane activity will increase in coming years as will the risk of a major hurricane striking a city in the United States. The financial impact could be devastating. For example, insured losses from a direct hit could be as high as $25 billion in New Orleans or $55 billion in Miami.[2]

Unfortunately, the industry's ability to protect itself from the financial impact of catastrophes is limited. For example, in the 25 years before the Northridge earthquake, insurers in California collected only $3.4 billion in earthquake premiums. That single earthquake cost the industry $12.5 billion in insured losses at a time when the total **capital**

Capital equals total assets minus total liabilities. It is a measurement frequently used to assess the financial strength of the insurance industry.

of the property and liability insurance industry in the United States was calculated at less than $200 billion.[3]

Catastrophe Indexes

To evaluate and manage catastrophe exposure, individual insurers and the insurance industry as a whole need accurate, detailed information. This need has prompted the development of several catastrophe indexes, which are used to estimate and describe the results of catastrophic losses.

Modeling (as it is used in this context) is a system of calculating known outcomes based on current data, and then applying those calculations to new data to predict future outcomes.

The PCS Index estimates the insurance industry's total property losses by region for both personal and commercial insurance based on telephone surveys of insurers, analysis by PCS staff, and results predicted by catastrophe **modeling**.

Risk Management Solutions' (RMS) Catastrophe Index estimates the insured damage from hurricanes and earthquakes by entering specific information, such as the direction, velocity, and pressure of a hurricane, into its own catastrophe modeling software.

The Guy Carpenter Catastrophe Index (GCCI) measures the insured, weather-related damage to homes in over 9,600 individual ZIP code areas throughout the United States by collecting and totaling insurance and loss data from 39 insurance companies.

Exhibit 8-11 describes some of the features of the three major catastrophe indexes.

Using Catastrophe Indexes

Insurers and others use catastrophe indexes in a variety of ways, including the following:

- Quick estimates of potential losses help insurers recognize catastrophes early so that they can mobilize sufficient claim staff and implement any contingency plans immediately.
- By ensuring that catastrophes are recognized early and claims coded appropriately, indexes help insurers and the industry generate detailed, accurate statistical information about catastrophes.
- Detailed information about catastrophes helps insurers make decisions regarding reinsurance arrangements and other ways of managing or transferring catastrophe risk.
- Catastrophe indexes provide a basis for comparing an individual insurer's catastrophe loss experience with that of the industry as a whole.

Personal Insurers' Responses to Catastrophes

Personal insurers respond to catastrophe exposures in the following ways, which are addressed in previous chapters in this text:

- Insurers can assume the risks and attempt to rate appropriately for the exposures through appropriate pricing strategies.
- Insurers can transfer some of their catastrophe risk to others through reinsurance.

Exhibit 8-11
Catastrophe Indexes

Feature	PCS	RMS	GCCI
Geographic Detail	State	ZIP code	ZIP code
Insured Property Perils	All major lines All significant perils	All major lines Earthquake and hurricane	Hurricane, hailstorm, tornado, thunderstorm, winter storm, and freezing conditions
Index Value	Dollars of loss	Dollars of loss	Ratio of losses paid to insured value
Supplemental Information Provided	None	None	Premiums, deductibles, amounts of insurance, claim amounts, paid losses, construction types
Published	3 to 5 days after the event; updated as required	7 days after the event; final value published after 28 days	Quarterly

Source: *Financing Risk and Reinsurance*, International Risk Management Institute, Inc., April 1998.

The next section of the text addresses the following additional methods for insurers to respond to catastrophes:

- Insurers can try to mitigate the impact of catastrophes.
- Insurers can develop contingency plans to deal with catastrophic situations when they occur.

Mitigating the Impact of Catastrophes

Individual personal lines insurers implement a variety of strategies to mitigate the impact of catastrophes. These include the following:

- In an effort to eliminate risk, some insurers withdraw from lines or geographic areas prone to catastrophe.
- Other insurers strictly limit their writings to control their total exposure in catastrophe-prone areas relative to their writings in other areas.
- Many insurers have introduced limitations to coverage or significant deductibles on catastrophe-related coverages. For example, some wordings require policyholders to pay from 2 percent to 10 percent of the insured value of their homes as a deductible on windstorm losses.

Securitization of risk involves an insurer's sale of short-term bonds and other financial instruments to investors in order to generate the cash required to pay potential catastrophe claims during a specific period of time. The investor earns profits if a company's catastrophe losses for the period are less than anticipated. The company's obligation to pay interest, and possibly, to repay the principal on these bonds is suspended in the event of a catastrophe.

- Finally, a financial innovation, **securitization of risk**, can help mitigate insurers' catastrophe exposure. Some large investors, such as corporations and mutual fund companies, have found this an attractive investment option. Catastrophe indexes help insurers, investors, and investment bankers measure the relative risk of the investment and identify appropriate rates of return.

Contingency Plans

After a catastrophe, policyholders and regulators expect an insurer to settle losses quickly, regardless of the volume of claims or any disruptions to the insurer's own facilities or resources. Effective catastrophe response requires careful preparation. Contingency plans, developed before a catastrophe hits, that are detailed and communicated throughout the organization serve the following purposes:

- Contingency plans help identify weaknesses, bottlenecks, and potential difficulties so insurers can prepare to deal with them.
- After a catastrophe, people respond emotionally. If staff clearly understand their roles and responsibilities during a crisis in advance, they can react more productively when the time comes.
- A catastrophe causes significant increases in claim-related work. The organization needs to be free to focus on handling claims without reallocating essential resources to resolve problems for which it was unprepared.

Exhibit 8-12 presents some of the challenges involved in catastrophe response and illustrates how contingency planning can help an organization prepare to meet these challenges.

Managing Operations After a Catastrophe

Catastrophes significantly disrupt the living and working conditions of those affected by them. Insurers can best contribute by settling losses as quickly as possible so that normalcy can be restored. Insurers can initiate some activities to ensure that catastrophe losses are settled promptly, despite the huge volume of claims. These include the following deviations from normal operations:

- Developing and using abbreviated claim settlement procedures to speed the processing
- Temporarily increasing claim settlement authority to producers for the duration of the catastrophe response
- Temporarily transferring claim settlement authority to preselected independent adjusting firms
- Bringing in catastrophe teams of claim representatives from other regions
- Making advance payments to policyholders for expenses such as additional living expenses
- Immediately settling all questions of property valuation in favor of the policyholder

- Suspending all but the most essential record keeping
- Reallocating available employees in critical work areas

Exhibit 8-12
Contingency Planning for Catastrophes

Area	Potential Problems	Possible Responses
Staffing	Insufficient claim staff to handle volume of incoming claims Staff unavailable due to having to deal with their own property damage	Identify and train staff from other areas to help out Establish relationships with independent adjusters to help manage overflow Bring in catastrophe teams of claim representatives from other regions
Premises	The insurer's premises are damaged or must be evacuated	Identify and arrange for the use of alternative premises Secure existing premises
Systems	Records are destroyed or computer systems are down	Maintain current backup at a remote location where information can be accessed
Communication	Communication links are destroyed	Identify public broadcasting services that may be used Arrange for cellular phones
Transportation	Roads and bridges are damaged	Identify alternative routes and resources to move staff and materials into damaged areas
Utilities	Utilities are suspended	Arrange for generator-powered electricity, water tank services, portable toilets, and showers
Material and Labor	Available construction materials and labor are insufficient	Arrange sources of materials and labor from nearby communities
Mass Evacuation	Policyholders are evacuated from an area	Identify temporary housing, including motels, mobile homes, and other temporary buildings
Policyholder Needs	Policyholders are confused, stressed, and anxious	Prepare catastrophe kits, including sources of information and assistance, for distribution to policyholders
Community Needs	Efficient claim settlement depends on restoring resources and community services	Coordinate with other insurers and community disaster relief agencies
Employee Stress	Employee stress levels during catastrophes are high	Train employees in stress management

Insurance Industry Response to Catastrophes

The insurance industry has always been actively involved in promoting loss prevention and control and in lobbying the government for changes in legislation relating to loss. The industry continues to support research and to lobby for improved construction standards and materials that will better withstand the forces of earthquakes and extreme weather events. The industry uses discounts as incentives to policyholders to take preventive measures such as installing hurricane shutters and earthquake bracing to reduce potential losses. Companies participate in risk-sharing pools to protect individual insurers while providing coverage for consumers in catastrophe-prone areas, or they work with regulators to establish state insurance solutions for catastrophe-prone areas. Finally, the industry is working with regulators, reinsurers, and financial service organizations to develop innovative ways of transferring risk and obtaining access to greater sources of capital. This will not only increase the overall capacity of the insurance industry to provide protection but will also improve the financial ability of insurers to respond to catastrophes.

Summary

Policy processing involves gathering information, assessing risk, accepting or rejecting applications, issuing policies, coding and storing information, and generating statistics. The more efficient an insurer's policy processing, the lower the company's underwriting expenses. Advances in technology, the introduction of computers into insurance processing, and changes in management philosophies have resulted in increases in underwriting efficiency, support staff efficiency, producer and marketing efficiency, and insurer management efficiency as well as in improved utilization of insurers' human resources. Knowledge management, the evolution of learning organizations, internal restructuring, and employee empowerment have helped to involve employees in the day-to-day management of insurance companies, thereby strengthening organizations and developing individuals.

Aside from the challenge of maintaining efficient and effective day-to-day operations, insurers face the additional challenge of meeting the needs of policyholders, employees, and communities during times of crisis. Planning for and responding to catastrophes is a significant responsibility of insurer management. Insurers use a variety of strategies to mitigate or transfer their exposure to catastrophes; however, they cannot eliminate it. As a result, contingency planning for effective catastrophe response is crucial. So too is the ongoing, industry-wide commitment to loss prevention and reduction, use of safer construction materials, alternative forms of risk transfer and financing, and working with regulators to ensure that consumers everywhere have access to the protection they need.

Chapter Notes

1. Peter M. Senge, *The Fifth Discipline: The Art & Practice of the Learning Organization* (New York: Currency Doubleday, 1990), pp. 1-14.
2. Ruth Gastel, "Catastrophe Insurance Issues," *Insurance Issues Update*, February 1996, pp. 2-3.
3. Frank Nutter. "Research Is Smart Insurance Policy." *Global Change*, October 15, 1999. World Wide Web: http://www.globalchange.org/editall/95Oct1d.htm (15 October 1999).

Glossary

acceptability Criterion broadly determined by the underwriting guidelines published by an insurer for a type of policy.

account A person, a business, or an organization that has purchased insurance.

account sale The practice of selling two or more insurance policies to the same customer.

account underwriting The process of evaluating all of the policies written by an insurance company for an individual.

accreditation program A certification program for state insurance departments. The purposes of the accreditation program are (1) to provide consistency of solvency regulations among states and (2) to improve the standards of solvency regulation and financial examinations in all states.

ACORD (Agency-Company Operations Research and Development) forms Standardized forms developed to achieve uniformity of data gathering in the insurance industry. They are available in preprinted hard copy or computer software formats.

acquisition The purchase of all or part of one organization by another.

activities Actions required by organizational units or departments for completing a tactic.

actual cash value (ACV) The value of property determined by the cost to replace the property minus an amount that reflects depreciation.

actuaries Individuals skilled in compiling and analyzing statistics and estimating future results.

add-on no-fault laws Laws that require auto owners to buy and insurers to offer coverage for medical expenses and sometimes loss of earnings resulting from an auto accident.

adverse selection The increasing likelihood that customers will purchase insurance when the premium is low relative to the risk. Poor underwriting results might occur if too many of the applicants accepted for insurance are those most likely to incur serious loss.

advisory organizations Organizations that accumulate and analyze insurer premium and loss information and project expected loss costs. Sometimes called rating bureaus.

affinity groups A collection of people who share similar experiences or interests.

agency contract A written agreement between an insurer and an agent that establishes the respective authority and responsibility of the agent and the insurer.

agent A producer who represents one or more insurance companies.

agreed value (or agreed amount) The value of property insured under an agreed value provision is the lesser of the following:

- The cost to restore the property to its condition before the loss
- The amount scheduled

The insured and the insurer agree on the value at the time the policy is written.

agricultural smudging A peril that might occur in the spring in areas near orchards. If a late frost threatens the fruit buds or blossoms, oil-burning smudge pots are burned at night around the fruit trees. A dark oily cloud covers the trees to prevent the frost from killing the buds. If this cloud is blown into a neighborhood of houses, damage can result.

air bags — Automatic restraint systems that require no action on the part of the vehicle occupants. Driver-side air bags are stored in the hub of the steering wheel, and passenger-side air bags are located inside the instrument panel. Air bags are loss-reduction devices designed to inflate in moderate and severe frontal crashes. The bags form a cushion between occupants and the vehicle interior to reduce the force of impact with hard surfaces. Air bags are also called supplemental restraint systems (SRSs).

allegation — A statement by a party regarding the legal action which that party will attempt to prove. This assertion might be unsupported by fact.

"all-risks" — "All-risks" property policies, also called special or open-perils policies, cover any loss unless it is caused by an excluded peril described in the policy. In an "all-risks" policy, the burden of proof is on the insurer. All losses are covered unless the insurance company can prove that the loss was caused by an excluded peril.

all-terrain vehicle (ATV) — A three- or four-wheeled vehicle equipped with balloon tires and designed for off-road use. ATVs can traverse a variety of ground surfaces, including swampy areas, sand, and snow.

annual statements — Formal financial reports presented to state insurance regulators that must be prepared for each state in which the insurer is licensed.

anti-lock braking system (ABS) — In a vehicle with a standard braking system, a driver who brakes suddenly can lock the vehicles' wheels and skid, causing loss of control and extending stopping distances. An ABS pumps the brakes automatically (many times a second) to prevent lockup and to enable a driver to maintain control.

antique auto — A vehicle that is at least twenty-five years old. Vehicles rated as antiques are provided a substantial premium discount, so insurers generally restrict use of an antique vehicle to parades and exhibitions.

antitrust — Legislation that opposes unfair business practices.

application — A written request for insurance coverage containing statements made by the applicant.

arson — The criminal act of burning or attempting to burn property.

at-fault — An insured's responsibility for causing an auto accident. It is not always accurate. An insured might only have contributed to an accident.

attractive nuisance — A dangerous place, condition, or object that is particularly appealing to children.

attrition — The opposite of retention. The percent of policies not renewed at their anniversary date is the attrition rate.

automobile insurance plans — Mechanisms for ensuring that all drivers have access to insurance and for equitably distributing the risks that are not written voluntarily by insurers.

auto physical damage coverage — See *physical damage coverage (auto)*.

auto towing and labor coverage	See *towing and labor coverage (auto)*.
avoidance	A risk management technique that eliminates a loss exposure and reduces the chance of loss to zero.
balanced budget method	A budgeting method that limits the permissible expenditure on advertising to pre-set amounts.
base premium	An amount of money that reflects the basic cost of specific individual insurance policies.
base rate	The price per unit of coverage, such as per $1,000 of Coverage A on a homeowners policy, required to cover the insurer's losses, expenses, and profit.
benchmark rate	A rate established by a regulator, above and below which insurers may set rates within maximum percentages defined by the regulator.
bind, bind coverage, binder	An insurance agent is usually authorized by the insurance company to state that certain specified coverage is in force with a specific insurance company as of a particular date and time (or immediately). An agent's act that obligates an insurer to provide coverage is called binding coverage. A binder is a statement that coverage is in force. Its purpose is to provide temporary coverage until an actual insurance policy can be issued. It is usually, but not necessarily, in writing.
blanket	Blanket coverage or blanket limits apply to classes of property. All items within a class are covered for the total limit of coverage for the class.
book of business	See *portfolio*.
broker	An insurance producer who is similar to an agent except that, in the legal sense, he or she represents the party seeking insurance.
cancel, cancellation	Stopping coverage during the policy period is cancellation. A policyholder can cancel most policies at any time; state laws often prohibit insurers from canceling policies that have been in force for a certain period of time.
capacity	The volume of business (written premiums) that an insurer is able to handle relative to the size of its policyholders' surplus.
capital	Total assets minus total liabilities. It is a measurement frequently used to assess the financial strength of the insurance industry.
captain	The person responsible for the navigation, operation, and safety of a watercraft and crew. Another term for this role is *master*.
catastrophe	Defined by the Property Claims Services Division of the American Insurance Services Group as an event that causes more than $25 million in insured losses (in constant 1982 dollars) and affects a significant number of policyholders. The threshold used to define a catastrophe occurring before January 1, 1997, was $5 million (in constant 1982 dollars).
catastrophe modeling	Using computerized simulations to identify the potential extent of damage from a single catastrophic event such as a hurricane or an earthquake.
catastrophe reinsurance	A special form of reinsurance that protects insurers against the adverse effects of catastrophes and limits the insurer's total loss from a catastrophe to a predetermined amount.

ceding company The insurer that cedes, or transfers, premiums and loss exposures to the reinsurer.

central station alarm A system that contacts a security company that responds to the residence and contacts the police.

certificate of insurance A document that provides information about the liability and workers compensation insurance for a commercial venture.

chartering A boat is chartered if it is rented for use. The insured can act as the boat's captain, or the person renting the boat from the insured can perform that role.

checklist approach A method of screening applications. Only those applications that require underwriting decisions are referred to an underwriter. Obviously acceptable applications are issued as policies, and obviously unacceptable applications are canceled. This is also called *underwriting by exception* and it can be accomplished by a technician who sorts the policies, based on a checklist.

chop shops Garages or lots where stolen vehicles are brought to be stripped of their components.

claim A demand by a person or business seeking to recover for a loss. A claim might be made against an individual or against an insurance company.

claim file A folder or computer record that is created ("opened") when a claim is made.

claim representative The person directly responsible for investigating, evaluating, and settling claims that might be covered by insurance.

claim settlement The process by which an insurer (1) accepts a loss statement from a customer, (2) investigates the details of the claim, (3) evaluates whether the claim is covered, and (4) either makes payment or denies coverage.

claimant Anyone who presents a claim that might be covered by insurance. For a liability insurance loss, the claimant is a person or business that has suffered a loss and seeks to collect for that loss from an insured. For a property insurance loss, the claimant is the insured who wants the insurance company to pay for repairing or replacing his or her damaged property.

claiming behavior The inclination that people have for submitting insurance claims.

classic auto A vehicle that is at least ten years old and has a significantly higher average value than other autos of the same make and model year.

coinsurance A provision found in many insurance policies that requires the insured to carry an insurance limit equal to at least a specified percentage of the value of the property insured. If the amount of insurance carried is equal to or greater than the required percentage, the insurer will pay covered losses in full (minus any deductible) up to the limit of insurance coverage. If the limit of insurance carried is less than the required percentage, the amount the insurer will pay is calculated by the following formula:

Loss payment =

[(Limit of insurance carried / Limit of insurance required) × Loss]
– Deductible

collateral source rule Under the collateral source rule, a defendant cannot introduce evidence showing that the injured party has other sources for compensation for injury.

collision coverage Coverage that applies to the impact of a vehicle with another vehicle or object or the upset (overturn) of the vehicle.

combined ratio The loss ratio plus the expense ratio. It provides a comparison of operating funds that flow into and out of the insurance company. It is the traditional measure of underwriting profitability in the property and liability insurance business.

commission A portion of insurance premiums paid to a producer for his or her sales and service activities.

commodity A mass-produced, unspecialized product. Wheat and cement are examples of commodities.

competition The effort of two or more parties acting independently to secure the business of a third party by offering the most favorable terms.

competitive advantage A significant edge over the competition in dealing with competitive forces.

competitive-party method A budgeting method that maintains a level of advertising spending relative to that spent by certain competitors.

compulsory insurance Insurance mandated by government regulatory groups. Individuals normally encounter compulsory insurance in the form of automobile liability insurance.

consolidated soil Soil made from clay and limestone that has aged for thousands of years to become a solid base for construction.

contractual liability The tort liability of another person (or entity) assumed under contract.

cost/benefit analysis Cost/benefit analysis (sometimes called benefit/cost analysis or C.B.A.) is a study used by insurers when making product development decisions. These studies compare probable costs to develop the new product with the likely benefits, both to the customer (in meeting a need for a product) and to the insurer (in meeting profit and growth objectives).

coverage unit See *unit of coverage*.

crashworthiness The vehicle design engineering that reduces or eliminates injury in an auto accident.

credibility The degree to which loss results are predictable. Credibility increases as the number of homogeneous exposure units increases.

credit report A record of an individual's income, debt, and payment history. Insurance companies use credit reports to identify an applicant's or an insured's financial history.

customer A person, a business, or an organization that has purchased insurance.

daily unoccupancy A term used by underwriters to describe the hazards associated with homes that are unoccupied during the day.

damage Loss or harm resulting from injury to a person, to property, or to someone's reputation.

damage to your auto — See *physical damage coverage (auto)*.

damages — Money that the law requires one party to pay another because of loss or injury suffered by the other party.

daytime running lights — High-beam headlights operating at reduced intensity, or low-beam headlights operating at full or reduced power. These lights increase the contrast between vehicles and their background to make cars more visible to oncoming drivers.

declarations, declarations page — The page or pages of an insurance policy containing information, such as the insured's name and address, that the policyholder declared (stated as facts) on the application for insurance.

declaratory judgment — A court ruling on a coverage point within a policy contract or a judgment on a point of law. This judgment is usually sought only when there is a genuine need to resolve such an issue and the claim is substantial enough to warrant the additional effort.

declination — When an insurer rejects an application before coverage has been bound.

deductible — A portion of a covered loss that is not paid by insurance. The deductible is subtracted from the amount the insurer would otherwise be obligated to pay.

default judgment — When a party against whom a judgment is sought has failed to answer or defend, that party is in default, and a judgment by default may be entered.

defense costs — Expenses associated with defending a liability claim. Such expenses include wages the defendant loses to prepare for a trial, investigation expenses, witness fees, and premiums for bonds.

definitions — In an insurance policy, provisions that define the words and phrases that have a special meaning when they are used elsewhere in that policy. Words defined in some policies are printed in boldface or enclosed by quotation marks.

demand — Buyers' market intentions.

demographic profiles — The common characteristics of a group of people. Demographic profiles can be used to identify market segments.

demographic segmentation — The division of customer markets based on variables such as income, age, sex, education, stages in the family life cycle (child rearing, middle age, and retirement), and lifestyle.

depreciation — Loss in value of property that develops as items age, wear out, or become obsolete. In a sense, depreciation reflects value that has already been used.

diary, diary system — A manual or computer system that calls a file to somebody's attention on a specified date (also called suspense system).

direct marketing system — An insurance marketing system that handles sales by mail or telephone and has no local producers making face-to-face sales.

direct response — Marketing that takes place directly between the customer and the insurer through mail, phone, and the Internet without an agent as an intermediary.

direct writer A producer who sells insurance as an employee of one insurance company. The term "direct writer" is also used to refer to an insurance company that sells insurance directly to insurance buyers through the insurer's employees.

distribution system A system for communicating information between a seller and a buyer (or potential buyers) and distributing the product.

document maintenance Filing, maintaining, storing, and retrieving applications, photographs, inspection reports, policyholder correspondence, and all other underwriting documents.

drive-in claims service A facility for providing repair estimates on damaged cars that are still drivable.

driver training discounts Discounts applied to personal auto policies for youthful drivers who have completed an approved driver training course.

due diligence The level of care, prudence, and activity that is reasonable, depending on the circumstances. Someone required to use due diligence must be able to demonstrate that all reasonable and recognized precautions were taken.

due diligence process Appropriately detailed evaluation of a business opportunity by a business entity before that entity decides to commit resources.

duplication A risk management technique that relies on backups or spares.

earned premium The portion of the premium that the insurer is entitled to keep for the period of coverage that has already been provided.

economy of scale A reduction in the average cost of a product or a process as the size of a company increases.

eligibility Risk eligibility is determined by the rules an insurer adopts and files for use in a state. An eligible risk falls within the broad category of risk that can be written on a policy.

employer groups Collections of customers who have a common employer.

empowerment The distribution of authority, resources, information, and accountability to employees in an organization in order to make decisions and solve problems.

endorsement A document used to amend the coverage in an otherwise complete policy.

environmental scanning The process of (1) identifying factors that are crucial for an organization's success or failure in the marketplace, (2) defining signals or events that affect the factors, and (3) determining the implications of the signals or events.

equivalent property Pieces of property of substantially the same economic value.

ethics An individual's principles of right and wrong. *Moral conduct* is the application of ethical principles.

event marketing Activity aimed at filling a customer's needs at the time of a triggering event.

exclusions Insurance policy provisions that restrict the broad terms of the insuring agreement by stating some exceptions to coverage—certain activities, loss causes, property, persons, and places—for which the insurer does not provide coverage.

exclusive agent A self-employed producer who has a contract to sell insurance exclusively for one insurance company (or several related companies).

expatriates People who choose, for a variety of reasons, to live for a limited period of time in a country other than the country of their citizenship. Also called *foreign nationals*.

expert systems Sets of computer programs that perform tasks at the level of a human expert. Expert systems (also called knowledge-based systems or artificial intelligence systems) are created on the basis of knowledge collected from human experts, and they imitate the reasoning process of a human being.

expirations Lists of a sales agent's current customers whose policies will either expire or be renewed.

exposure analysis A task completed by an underwriter during the review of an application or an existing policy. The task includes the following:

- Identifying loss exposures
- Identifying associated hazards
- Measuring the extent of the loss exposures and hazards

exposure unit Measures of loss potential. Also called *units of exposure*. A house-year, or a house insured for one year, is an example of an exposure unit.

exposures Exposures, or loss exposures, are situations that could lead to an accidental loss.

express warranty A warranty written in a policy.

extracontractual liability An insurer's obligation that goes beyond the terms of a contract.

FAIR plans Fair Access to Insurance Requirements residual market plans provide property insurance for those who cannot obtain coverage in the voluntary market.

felony A crime of a grave or serious nature punishable by death or imprisonment for a term exceeding one year.

fiduciaries Persons or corporations having a duty to act primarily for another's benefit.

fifth wheel A type of trailer hitch designed for pulling heavy trailers. It resembles a flat, metal wheel. The gooseneck hitch from the trailer sits over and connects to the fifth wheel.

file-and-use A filing law that requires the insurer to file rates with the state for a period of time before they are used. If the states do not reject the rates within a stated period, the rates can be used.

filing The process of submitting information to a state insurance department for approval. The term is often used to describe the completed approval.

financial intermediary An entity that obtains money from one source and redirects it to another. Insurance companies and banks are financial intermediaries.

fine arts Works of art and items of rarity or historic value.

first party An individual or entity named in a contract. A named insured is a first party to an insurance contract.

fixed costs Expenses that remain the same, in the short term, regardless of the amount of premium an insurer writes.

focus group A small group of customers or potential customers brought together to provide opinions about a specific product, service, need, or other issue. Focus groups provide qualitative data regarding customers' opinions through open discussion.

foreign nationals See *expatriates*.

form A preprinted document, often several pages long, containing standard wording that makes up the bulk of an insurance policy.

Fortune 500 The 500 largest publicly held industrial and service corporations in the United States in terms of sales dollars. This list is compiled annually by *Fortune* magazine.

fraud Misrepresentation intended to induce another to part with something of value or to surrender a legal right. See also *insurance fraud*.

frequency of loss See *loss frequency*.

geographic segmentation A division of customers by location. This is the most widely used approach to segmentation. Companies target metropolitan or rural markets or regions with different climatic, cultural, and social characteristics.

goals Major planning components that are the target or end result that an organization wishes to achieve.

good student discounts Discounts applied to personal auto policies for youthful drivers who have good scholastic records. Such drivers are expected to have lower loss involvement because they are more responsible in general and perhaps spend more time on school work and less time on the road than other youthful drivers.

graying The overall aging of the population. The "baby boomers," who were born between 1946 and 1964, form a large percentage of the population. As this group ages, the average age of the population increases.

group of homogeneous risks See *homogeneous group*.

guarantee funds A system to pay the claims of insolvent property and liability insurers. Generally, the money in a guarantee fund is provided by charges assessed against all insurers in the state.

guides See *underwriting guidelines*.

hazard Any condition that has the propensity to increase either the frequency or the severity of a potential loss.

health maintenance organization (HMO) Insurance that provides medical services from limited numbers of centrally located facilities to individuals who subscribe to the HMO. Charges to the individual are based on specified fees that are lower than the fees charged by many private medical practitioners.

Highway Loss Data Institute (HLDI) A nonprofit, public service organization. It is closely associated with and funded through the Insurance Institute for Highway Safety. HLDI gathers, compiles, and publishes data regarding insurance loss variations among different makes, models, and kinds of vehicles.

hold harmless agreement — The promise of one party to hold another harmless (blameless) for any liability arising from an activity.

homogeneity — Similar characteristics among insureds in the same rating class. All insureds in rating classifications should have similar exposure characteristics. Homogeneity also describes the similarity among individuals in a market segment.

homogeneous group — Sometimes called a group of homogeneous risks. A collection of risks with similar expected loss frequency and severity. Insurers use characteristics common to members in homogeneous groups to differentiate among different homogeneous groups. For example, a collection of individuals who are single, male, and under the age of nineteen are one homogeneous group. A collection of individuals over age fifty-five who own four-door sedans and live in a particular city are another example of a homogeneous group.

homogeneous products — In a marketing context, products perceived to be the same by consumers. This perception occurs when the market has many undifferentiated suppliers.

housekeeping — A term that underwriters use to describe the general condition, maintenance, and safety of a residence and its land.

hurricane — A storm with winds that exceed speeds of seventy-four miles per hour.

immunity laws — Laws that provide protection to insurance companies for the good-faith exchange of information required to provide information to state insurance departments or law enforcement officials without fear of criminal or civil prosecution.

implied permission — As used in the personal auto policy, liability coverage exists for a person who has reasonable belief of being entitled to use an insured auto. Permission might be explicit (the named insured tells his brother that the brother can borrow the car), or permission might be implied (the insured keeps the car keys on the table by the door with the understanding that a neighbor can take the keys and borrow the car whenever he needs it).

implied warranty — This type of warranty is understood rather than written. For example, for a watercraft to be covered by a yacht policy, a warranty (by the insured) of seaworthiness is implied (the insured watercraft must be in a seaworthy condition).

incurred losses — The total of paid claims, loss expenses, and reserve adjustments that occur during a specified time period.

indemnify — To restore the party that has had a loss to the same financial position it held before the loss.

independent claim adjusters — Independent contractors (usually licensed by the state insurance regulator) who help insurers appraise damage and settle claims, for which the insurer pays a fee.

index system — A computerized database that provides access to a bank of information through search inquiries.

indirect loss — Loss of earnings or extra expenses taking place over a period of days, weeks, or months following a direct loss. Indirect losses increase with the passage of time.

inelastic — The sensitivity of demand in relationship to changes in price. The demand for personal insurance is inelastic because the quantity of product demanded does not fluctuate greatly in response to price changes. In other words, personal insurance customers purchase the same amount of insurance whether prices fall, rise, or stay the same.

inherent expectations Customer anticipations about a business, industry, or product. Customers reasonably assume that certain services are provided by a business or industry because the services are elemental. A customer might have inherent expectations that a policy will be mailed within a reasonable period of time and that a claim representative will contact a claimant within a few days.

injunctions Court orders that prohibit someone from committing a specified act or that command someone to undo a wrong or an injury.

insurance A system by which a risk is transferred from a person, a business, or an organization to an insurance company (insurer), which reimburses the insured for covered losses and provides for sharing the costs of losses among all insureds.

insurance company See *insurer*.

insurance fraud Committed if (1) information in an insurance application is falsified in an attempt to obtain lower premium rates, (2) the amount of the loss in a claim is falsified, or (3) a claim is falsified.

Insurance Institute for Highway Safety (IIHS) An independent, nonprofit, scientific, and educational organization dedicated to reducing losses (deaths, injuries, and property damage) resulting from crashes.

insurance premium A periodic payment by the insured to the insurance company in exchange for insurance coverage. A periodic payment is one that must be made at certain time intervals.

Insurance Regulatory Information System (IRIS) An early warning system for the potential financial failure of an insurance company.

Insurance Services Office (ISO) The largest insurance service office in the United States, ISO performs a variety of services, such as developing statistical classification systems and collecting statistical data on insured claims from a large number of insurance companies, analyzing this information, and using it to develop loss cost data. Insurance companies that subscribe to ISO's services may use this loss cost information in setting their own insurance rates.

insured A person, a business, or an organization that is covered by an insurance policy.

insurer Also known as an insurance company, an organization that sells insurance policies that protect insureds against financial hardship caused by financial loss.

intangible losses Losses that cannot readily be appraised, for example, the sentimental value of some items.

intangible product A product that promises the purchaser uncertain future performance (like an insurance contract) rather than immediate utility (such as a consumer good like a television or a computer).

intrafamily suit A legal action that is initiated by one family member against another member of the same family. For example, a woman sitting in the passenger seat of an auto who sues the driver (her husband) for injuries that she sustained as the result of an accident brings an intrafamily suit.

investment gain — An increase in an investment's value to the investor.

investment income — For an insurer, interest, dividends, and net realized capital gains received by the insurer from its financial assets minus its investment expenses.

investment loss — A decrease in an investment's value to the investor.

investment risk — The possibility that an investment's value will be different from what was expected.

invitee — A person who is on the insured's premises with permission (a guest or customer).

involuntary market — A source of insurance formed by governmental bodies to provide coverage for those who could not obtain it otherwise. See also *residual market*.

knob and tube — An electrical wiring system characterized by glass insulation knobs nailed to roof, ceiling, wall, and floor structural lumber with wire (often fabric-covered or bare) strung between the knobs.

knot — A measurement of speed of watercraft. A knot equals 1.15 miles per hour.

knowledge management — A strategy for capturing and assessing information so that everyone in an organization is able to access the information needed.

law of large numbers — A principle stating that as the number of trials increases, the observed outcome becomes more likely to match the expected outcome of those trials.

learning organizations — Those organizations where people, individually and collectively, continually expand their capacity to produce results and expand their patterns of thinking.

liability — As a legal concept, liability means that a person, an organization, or a group of people is legally responsible, or liable, for the injury or damage suffered by another person, organization, or group of people.

liability insurance — Insurance that covers accidental losses resulting from bodily injury to someone else or damage to someone else's property for which the insured is legally responsible (liable). If the loss is covered by the insurance policy, the payment is made directly to the party that suffered the loss.

licensee — A person (such as a member of a police department, a meter reader, or a surveyor) who is on an insured's premises by mutual consent.

life-tenancy — The legal right to reside in a home for the remainder of an individual's life. Such an individual is referred to as a life-tenant.

litigation — The process of carrying on a lawsuit.

litigious — Prone to engaging in lawsuits. A person who is litigious might seek situations to bring a lawsuit in the hope of a positive financial outcome.

loadings — Additions made to insurance rates to allow for an insurer's administrative expenses.

local alarm — A loud clamor that can be heard only at or near the premises.

loss — The happening or event for which insurance pays.

loss control — A risk management technique that reduces the frequency or severity of a loss.

loss cost — The average incurred loss per exposure unit for a line of business, risk classification, or coverage.

loss development Payment-related changes, such as increases and decreases in reserve amounts, over the life of a claim.

loss expenses The expenses necessitated by the process of investigating and settling insurance claims according to the terms specified in the insurance policy. Also called *loss adjustment expenses (LAE)*.

loss exposures See *exposures*.

loss frequency The average number of covered claims per 100 exposure units over some time period applied for the purpose of ratemaking.

loss prevention A loss control technique that seeks to lower the probable frequency of losses.

loss ratio The percentage of premiums that are used to pay incurred losses (includes paid losses, reserve adjustments, and loss expenses). To calculate a loss ratio, the incurred loss amounts are divided by the earned premium (usually measured for a year). Underwriters (and producers) may be assigned loss ratio goals for the lines of business they underwrite.

loss reduction A loss control technique that seeks to lower the severity of losses that occur.

loss reserves The amounts of money an insurer sets aside to pay losses that are in the process of being identified, evaluated, or settled.

loss severity The average value of a number of claims over some time period. Also, the dollar amount of damage that results or could result from a loss exposure. Also called *severity of loss*.

mail surveys Questionnaires distributed to a target or random audience.

managing general agent (MGA) Performs some of the insurer's underwriting and claim duties in return for higher commissions.

market As it relates to insurance, a market is an environment in which insurers and policyholders interact and trade.

market conduct examination A review of an insurer's underwriting and ratemaking practices conducted by the state insurance market conduct examiners.

market positioning The act of designing a set of meaningful differences to distinguish an insurer's products from the competitors' products so that the insurer's products occupy a distinct and valued place in the market.

market segmentation Grouping customers with similar or related characteristics. These customers might be expected to buy a product or service that satisfies similar needs.

market specialization Targets a specific customer group for product and service development. Multiple lines of insurance products can then be targeted to that customer group.

market tier A term that is used interchangeably with "market plan" or "market level." It describes the groupings of insureds into preferred, standard, and nonstandard categories for marketing purposes.

master See *captain*.

material misrepresentation A fact that has been misstated or omitted if it could reasonably be considered as affecting the insurer's decision to enter into the contract, the insurer's evaluation of the degree of character of the risk, or the calculation of the premium.

maximizing behavior Seeking a solution that offers the optimum or greatest payoff. This behavior is exhibited by an individual who seeks the alternative with the most favorable outcome.

misdemeanor An offense that is lower than a felony and generally punishable by fine, penalty, or imprisonment in a facility other than a penitentiary.

mission An organization's purpose or its fundamental reason for existence.

modeling A method of assisting an underwriter in the decision-making process by identifying hazards that would not be part of an ideal (or model) risk. Modeling is also a term used to describe a system of calculating known outcomes based on current data, and then applying those calculations to new data to predict future outcomes.

moral conduct See *ethics*.

moral hazard A condition that exists when a person might intentionally cause a loss or exaggerate a loss that has occurred.

morale hazard A condition that exists when a person with insurance is not as careful as he or she would be if there were no insurance.

mortgagee A lending institution.

mortgagor The person or entity that owns the property and that is responsible for making the mortgage payments.

motor vehicle reports (MVR) A state's official record of driving information, which usually contains traffic violation and accident information.

named nonowner's endorsement Auto liability coverage for a person who does not own an auto is provided by a named nonowner's endorsement added to a standard personal auto policy. Liability coverage is provided for any vehicle that the insured rents or borrows or for a company car. Liability coverage would apply in excess over any collectible coverage applying to the vehicle.

named perils Coverage provided by an insurance policy that is specified by a list of covered perils. Perils that do not appear on the list are not covered.

National Association of Insurance Commissioners (NAIC) State insurance regulators belong to this organization, which coordinates insurance regulation among the states.

National Flood Insurance Program (NFIP) Flood insurance, which may be sold by any licensed insurance agent, is available through this program, which was developed by the federal government, but is often sold through private insurers.

Nationwide Marine Definition An instrument that describes the kinds of risks and coverages that can be classified under state insurance laws as marine and inland marine insurance.

niche market A group of customers with specialized needs.

no-fault state A state that offers automobile policyholders the right to recover financial losses from their own insurance, regardless of who caused the accident. This recovery is offered in the form of personal injury protection (PIP) coverage.

no-filing laws See *open competition laws*.

nonadmitted insurers — Insurers that conduct business in a state without obtaining a certificate of authority from the insurance department. They are not subject to regulation of their rates and forms, taxes, participation in residual markets, or guaranty fund assessments. State laws limit the kinds of coverage nonadmitted insurers can write and require brokers who sell coverage for nonadmitted insurers to obtain a special license.

nonstandard auto market — This market is used for high-risk drivers whom insurers normally reject in a standard market.

nonstandard market — A term applied to those insurers that provide coverage not available from insurers in the standard market because of exposure exceeding the underwriting or pricing guidelines of those insurers.

nonwaiver agreement — A document designed by counsel that permits the insurer to investigate a claim while preserving the insurer's right to deny coverage later. The form requires the insured's signature. It is stronger than a reservation of rights letter but more difficult to execute.

not excessive — Insurance rates are not excessive if they do not produce an unreasonable insurer profit.

not unfairly discriminatory — Insurance rates are not unfairly discriminatory if rates for each risk classification reflect the proportional difference in exposure to loss compared to other classifications.

numismatic property — This type of personal property includes money and collectible coins.

objective probability — The long-run relative frequency of an event, based on the sum of an infinite number of observations and on the assumption of no change in the underlying conditions. In other words, it describes how often something will theoretically happen.

objective and task method — A budgeting method that develops communication budgets by defining specific objectives, determining the tasks to be performed, and estimating the costs of performing those tasks.

open competition laws — These laws, also called no-filing laws, permit insurers to use rates without regulators' approval.

operating profit — The total of underwriting profit and investment income.

operating ratio — The operating profit plus incurred losses and underwriting expenses, compared to earned premium, for a specified time period. The operating ratio is like a combined ratio that includes investment income.

other than collision (OTC) — Sometimes called "comprehensive," this coverage is found in personal auto policies. It covers physical damage perils that are not otherwise excluded. The following list of perils is presented in the policy to clarify those perils not considered to be collision: missiles or falling objects; fire, explosion, or earthquake; theft, larceny, vandalism, malicious mischief, riot, or civil commotion; windstorm, hail, water, or flood; contact with a bird or animal; breakage of glass.

owner give-up — A term used to describe a vehicle owner who conspires with others to commit fraud.

pairs, sets, or parts — Items that increase in value because they are part of a group. The loss of part of the group greatly reduces the value of the items that remain. Consequently, losses are adjusted to take into consideration the economic loss of the whole group.

penetrating storm — A storm that enters a coastline at a right angle to the land, causing less damage than a raking storm.

percentage-of-sales method — A budgeting method that assumes that a certain amount of advertising creates a certain amount of sales. It limits communication expenses to a percentage of sales volume over a period of time (usually a year).

peril — A cause of property losses. Fire is one example of a peril.

permissive use — As used in the personal auto policy, permissive use describes permission granted to an individual to use an automobile. Permission might be either explicit (such as verbal or written permission) or implied (such as an understanding or a reasonable belief).

persistency — A measurement of retained policies over a long period of time.

personal articles floater (PAF) — Provides broad coverage for specified items such as jewelry, furs, silverware, and fine arts.

personal auto policy (PAP) — A specific standard auto policy designed to meet the auto insurance needs of a typical person or family.

personal auto voluntary markets — Insurers that willingly offer personal auto coverage for sale to customers who can meet the insurer's underwriting guidelines are called the voluntary market. Prices differ, based on the customer qualifications and degree of loss exposure each insurer is willing to accept. Prices tend to fall into categories of preferred (lowest price), standard, or nonstandard (highest price). Categories are sometimes called "programs" and can differ greatly among insurers.

personal autos — Vehicles that are structurally created for individual and family use; personal autos include private passenger autos, vans, and light-duty trucks (generally described by the manufacturer as capable of carrying loads of less than one ton).

personal injury — A group of offenses specified within the umbrella policy language that includes bodily injury as well as many other offenses.

personal injury protection (PIP) — No-fault coverage that applies to auto-related injuries.

personal interview — A group of individual responses to a series of questions. This method is used to test customer receptivity to a new or modified product or service.

personal liability — The general (nonauto-related) liability exposures that accompany a person's nonbusiness activities.

personal property — Property other than real property.

philatelic property — Collectible stamps, post marks, etc.

physical damage coverage (auto) — Auto physical damage coverage, also known as damage to your auto coverage, insures against loss resulting from damage to an auto owned or operated by the insured, and it also provides coverage if the car is stolen.

pilot test — A trial of an advertisement or a product to a limited group or a limited geographic area in order to determine whether the desired results can be achieved.

planned urban development (PUD) — A preplanned community consisting usually of single and multifamily housing surrounding shops, restaurants, and offices. Motor vehicle use is restricted within a PUD; to travel within such a development, people normally walk or ride golf carts.

policy — A contract that states the rights and duties of the insurance company and the insured.

policyholders' surplus — An amount equal to an insurer's total admitted assets minus its total liabilities.

policy limits — Limits, also called limits of insurance or limits of liability, that indicate how much insurance is provided. The limits in the policy set the maximum dollar amount the insurance company will pay.

policy provision — Any statement in an insurance policy.

policy term — The period during which a policy provides coverage.

portfolio — A group of policies with a common characteristic (such as type of coverage or territory). As a group, policies are analyzed for losses, change in size of the group, and trends. A portfolio is also called a portfolio of policies, a book of business, or a portfolio of risks.

portfolio management — The activity involved in developing new insurance products, establishing profitability goals, pricing products, managing profitability, and managing operations associated with a portfolio of insurance policies.

portfolio profile — The set of risk characteristics common to all risks in a portfolio.

portfolio of risks — See *portfolio*.

predictive models — Statistical maps of the relationships among data elements for a specific purpose. The resulting statistics can be used to predict outcomes, which can help to guide decisions.

preferred auto market — The typical preferred program has lower rates than the other programs, coupled with stricter underwriting standards. Most insurers allow only one conviction for a moving traffic violation (and no accidents) for such a program. Other requirements might involve the type of car (such as no sports cars) or the age of the drivers (for example, all over twenty-five).

preferred provider organization (PPO) — An example of a managed care provider. A PPO agrees with an insurer (or group of insurers) to voluntarily limit medical procedures to those that are deemed necessary and to adhere to a schedule of fees for services.

primary policies — Liability policies that provide the first level of coverage for a liability loss. The umbrella policy specifies the type and amount of coverage that must be provided by primary policies. Also called *underlying policies*.

primary data — In the marketing research process, primary data are data collected to answer specific questions about a current or future product.

primary insurance — As the term is used with personal umbrella insurance, primary insurance refers to the coverage provided by underlying policies. The umbrella policy stipulates the limits that must be provided by those policies.

primary rating factors Many auto rating systems use these factors to differentiate the premium according to major classifications of driver characteristics. Secondary rating factors refine the premium for selected driver and use characteristics.

prior approval A filing law that requires an insurer to file rates with the state insurance department and receive approval before the rates can be used.

private passenger autos Vehicles that are individually or family owned and used primarily for the transportation of people.

probable cost The combination of the potential loss frequency and severity. It is an estimate of how often a loss is likely to occur and how severe the economic loss might be as a result.

producer A common term used to refer to individuals who sell property and liability insurance. The term encompasses agents, brokers, solicitors, and customer service representatives who work directly with the customers.

product development Product development is a three-step process:

- Developing the insurance contracts (and their endorsements)
- Identifying the services to be provided by the product delivery team
- Packaging the products and services

product specialization When used in insurance, this term refers to tailoring an otherwise standard policy to meet the needs of a market segment.

profit cycle A recurring rise and fall in profits, usually profits in just one industry.

proof set A group of coins that are uncirculated (they have never been used as money). All coins in a proof set reflect the same mint year. The coins are valuable because they are in mint condition and because they are part of a set.

proposal A report that identifies a customer need, suggests how to meet that need, evaluates costs and benefits, and defines steps to be taken.

proprietary alarm In the event of a break-in, a proprietary alarm notifies a security guard on the premises, who responds.

protection class (public protection class or PPC) A number from 1 to 10 assigned to property that signifies the level of protective services in an area. A 10 represents little or no fire protection or public service. A 1 represents the highest level of service.

protection and indemnity (P&I) An old marine insurance term. It includes bodily injury and property damage liability.

proximate cause That which in a natural and continuous sequence, unbroken by any intervening cause, produces injury or damage. Without proximate cause, an event or loss would not have occurred.

psychographic segmentation The division of customers according to their lifestyles so that buyer behavior can be identified. It focuses on individual consumption patterns, according to the theory that people project a lifestyle through the products they consume.

purchasing group A group of insurance buyers who purchase liability insurance together.

pure premium The average amount of money an insurer must charge per exposure unit in order to cover the total anticipated losses for that line of business.

"R" value The degree of resistance to heat transfer. The higher the value, the better the resistance and insulation.

radiation shield A device that protects combustible surfaces from the heat generated by a wood stove. The shield can be made of metal or a composite stoveboard material.

raking storm A storm that "rakes" the coastline by alternately covering land and water. This type of storm is usually more intense than and may cause more damage than a penetrating storm.

rate The price of insurance for each unit of exposure coverage (such as per $1,000 of homeowners Coverage A). The rate is multiplied by the desired number of coverage units in order to arrive at a premium.

rate class A group formed when there is not sufficient information to estimate a rate for an individual risk. To derive a rate, individuals who are expected to have the same loss experience are grouped together.

rate factor A number used to compare the rate for one classification of risks with the rate of another classification of risks.

rate filing document A collection of information submitted to a regulator that explains why an insurer wants to change its rates, rules, or forms.

rate filings Documents submitted (or filed) with a state insurance department that contain the proposed rates and also, when necessary, the statistics on which the rates are based. Rate filings explain why an insurer wants to change its rates.

ratemaking The process of determining the appropriate premium that should be charged to a given group based on the expected expenses and losses for that group.

rate regulation The control by state insurance regulators over the rates, classification, and rating systems used by insurers.

rate relativity factor A number by which a base rate may be multiplied to reflect the relatively higher or lower loss exposure of one homogeneous group compared to that of another.

rate rules Describe the ways in which rates are applied and modified.

rating bureaus See *advisory organizations*.

real property Land, buildings, and other structures permanently attached to the land.

realized capital gain The profit earned by an insurer when an asset, such as a bond or stock, is sold for more than its cost.

redlining A practice underwriters once used of drawing a red line around an area on a map. Applicants within that area would be rejected solely on the basis of geographic location. This term has been extended to mean an exclusionary practice that judges an applicant on criteria that cannot be statistically substantiated. Redlining is a prohibited practice.

regulations Federal, state, and local governments develop laws, but the details and enforcement of the laws are carried out in the form of regulations. These regulations are developed, altered, and enforced by regulatory agencies, such as a state's insurance commission.

reinsurance (treaty) See *treaty reinsurance*.

reinsurance recoverables Amounts that are to be paid to insurers by reinsurers on losses and loss expenses that have already been paid to claimants by insurers.

relationship building A method for delivering services that approaches the customer as an associate rather than as a source for sales.

remainderman The person who will assume possession of the property at the death of the life-tenant.

representation The customer's statement giving information that is relied on by the insurer as factual.

renewals Lists of a sales agent's current customers, whose policies will either expire or be renewed, are referred to as expirations or renewals.

reservation of rights A general notice sent to an insured advising that the insurer is proceeding with a claim investigation. The notice advises the insured that this action does not create an admission of liability.

reserve adjustments Changes to individual reserves that affect the total of all claim reserves.

residual market An applicant rejected by underwriters in the voluntary market might find insurance available through residual market programs such as auto insurance plans and FAIR plans. Governmental bodies sometimes create residual market programs to provide insurance for those who could not otherwise obtain it. See also *involuntary market*.

retention This term has several meanings:

1. When used in reference to risk management, retention means self-insurance. An individual retains the loss exposure and pays for any losses from the individual's own funds.
2. This term can be synonymous with deductible. The insured will retain the first $100 to $1,000 of any loss, depending on the size of the deductible. Deductibles in personal insurance are almost always flat dollar amounts that apply to every loss.
3. This term can also mean the percentage of policies that are renewed at an anniversary. The opposite of retention is attrition. An insurer might have a 90 percent retention rate for homeowners policies. This would mean that the attrition rate is 10 percent.
4. Under an umbrella policy, this term acts like a deductible for any loss not covered by an underlying policy. The insured is responsible for the retention amount (usually $250 to $1,000). The umbrella policy insurer then stacks the coverage limit on top of the retention limit.

reunderwriting The process of analyzing the characteristics of policies within a portfolio and the trends of those characteristics. Through this analysis, insurers identify common loss exposures that generate losses that were not anticipated at the time rates were established for the exposure units. Possible activities for correction are then identified and one or a combination of activities is selected for implementation. The portfolio is monitored to determine the effectiveness of the reunderwriting activity.

risk This term has many meanings. In the API program, two applications of the word are used:

1. The possibility of financial loss.
2. The subject matter insured or being considered for insurance.

risk analysis The process of identifying loss exposures and estimating the potential financial consequences of those losses.

risk averse People uncomfortable in assuming the uncertainty and consequences of unknown outcomes.

risk-based capital A model for developing the amount of capital an insurer must have available. It takes into consideration the insurer's assets (and their strength), the insurer's credit (including receivables and reinsurance recoverables), and the underwriting risks assumed by the insurer.

risk classification The formation of different premiums for the same coverage based on a homogeneous group's characteristics. The group formed for this purpose is also referred to as a risk classification or a rate class.

risk management The application of techniques to eliminate, control, reduce, or finance loss exposures.

risk profile The set of characteristics common to all risks in a portfolio.

risk purchasing group A group of insurance buyers who purchase liability insurance together.

risk retention group A special type of group captive insurer that provides limited insurance coverage to business organizations that would otherwise have difficulty obtaining such insurance.

risk selection The process of defining and adhering to underwriting guidelines that specify the risk characteristics of customers that should be accepted for coverage at a given price.

risk takers People who have a higher degree of comfort with the unknown than those who are risk averse.

roll bar A device to protect vehicle occupants from being crushed if a vehicle overturns. Often made of a heavy metal tube, it is attached to the vehicle frame and passes over the passenger compartment.

salvage title The vehicle title applicable when a vehicle has sustained damage that exceeds its value.

satisfactory service The value that an individual customer seeks from a provider. The definition of satisfactory service varies by customer and situation.

schedule A list of property items insured. Each item must be fully described in the policy and have an applicable limit of coverage per item.

scoring A method of screening applications. Scoring is performed by a computer program that assigns a number grade to an application, based on the information in the application.

screening A process of categorizing applications to allow underwriters to concentrate only on those applicants that require a decision. It involves comparing the customer's risk characteristics with the insurer's underwriting guidelines to identify customers who match the characteristics specified as desirable by the guidelines. See also *checklist approach.*

secondary data In the marketing research process, secondary data is information that has already been collected for another purpose. Secondary data might be collected inside an insurance company (financial reports, loss histories, or policy records) or outside the organization (government reports, business or trade reports, or published reports).

securitization of risk An insurer's sale of short-term bonds and other financial instruments to investors in order to generate the cash required to pay potential catastrophe claims during a specific period of time. The investor earns profits if a company's catastrophe losses for the period are less than anticipated. The company's obligation to pay interest and, possibly, to repay the principal on these bonds is suspended in the event of a catastrophe.

semicompulsory insurance Insurance required by an organization other than a government regulatory group. For example, insurance required by a lending institution is semi-compulsory.

separation A risk management technique through which resources are divided to minimize the effect of a single event.

severity of loss See *loss severity.*

shared market See *involuntary market* and *residual market.*

smudging See *agricultural smudging.*

social equity A comparable level of social benefits provided to all citizens regardless of their ability to pay for it.

special investigative unit (SIU) A unit within an insurance company dedicated to investigating suspicious claims and other possible frauds. SIUs also exist within the insurance departments in some states.

spontaneous expectations Customer expectations that occur during a transaction with a customer as a result of the situation or circumstance.

spread-of-risk The disbursion of loss exposures in a portfolio of policies. An adequate disbursement is achieved when single losses cannot create claims for a significant number of individuals or properties insured within the portfolio.

SR-22 The form number of a document that an auto insurer can provide confirming the existence of auto liability insurance for a specific driver. A state motor vehicle department might require a driver to furnish an SR-22 form to confirm that required coverage is in force, particularly if a driver had previously been an uninsured operator in a motor vehicle accident.

stacked limits The option given customers in some states to add the limits of auto liability coverage for each car insured by the same person to increase the available per accident limit of protection.

stakeholders Those who will gain or lose, depending on how a business performs.

standard market The market that comprises insurers that provide coverage satisfying the insurance needs of the majority of customers with expected losses at or near the group's average.

state-made rates Calculated by the state under the direction of the insurance commissioner.

stated amount A loss settlement option that might be applied to a personal auto policy for physical damage coverages. A vehicle appraisal serves as the basis for rating. However, the maximum loss settlement is based on the lowest of (1) the stated amount, (2) the actual cash value (ACV), or (3) the amount to repair or replace.

stated-value policy In personal lines, this is a nonstandard or specialty physical damage policy that might be written for vehicles that have unusual values (such as antique autos, classic autos, or all-terrain vehicles). Because such policies are nonstandard, the provisions vary among insurers. Loss settlement is usually based on a stated amount, but some insurers offer an agreed-value loss settlement provision. If agreed value settlement is offered by the insurer, the amount of payment in the event of a total loss is the agreed value.

stoveboard A shield made of twenty-four gauge or thicker steel plate that should be placed between the woodstove and a wall or floor.

strategic business unit (SBU) A division within an organization that is defined for the purpose of measuring that division's productivity. These units are called profit centers or silos by some insurers. (Note that the term "silo" can have negative connotations when it indicates divisions that have isolated objectives.)

strategy Large-scale action plan for interacting with the business environment in order to achieve long-term goals.

subjective probability An individual's personal estimate of a chance of loss.

subrogate, subrogation When an insurer pays an insured for a loss that is caused by a third party, the insurer takes over (is subrogated to) the insured's right to collect damages from the responsible party. An insurance company pursues (subrogates against) the responsible party (or his or her insurer) to collect damages in a legal process called subrogation.

subsidization A redistribution of one group's costs among the members of another group.

sue and labor charges Expenses incurred by the insured to take reasonable measures to prevent damage or injury.

supplemental application A form requesting additional, specific information used in the underwriting process (such as driver-training certification or verification of safe woodstove installation) and to document customer coverage selection (for example, choice of limits, rejection of uninsured motorists, or other regulated coverage).

supply Sellers' market intentions.

surge protectors Electrical circuit breakers that are plugged into an outlet into which computers, stereos, and other electronic devices can be plugged to reduce the possibility of damage from uneven electrical flow.

surplus lines Insurance offered by an insurer that is not licensed within a state as an admitted insurer. Such insurance covers loss exposures not typically available from standard insurers. States regulate the sale of surplus lines policies by requiring agents and brokers to meet certain licensing requirements.

suspense system See *diary*, *diary system*.

SWOT analysis A method of analyzing an organization's competitive situation that involves assessing organizational strengths (S), weaknesses (W), opportunities (O), and threats (T).

tactics The specific actions required by the organization to implement its strategy.

tangible product A product that can be seen, touched, and tested. In insurance, the tangible product is a legal contract represented by words on paper.

target marketing A market segmentation approach that focuses marketing efforts on specific customer groups.

tasks Defined limited assignments with target completion dates.

team approach The use of temporary or ongoing task groups whose members are charged with working together to identify problems, to form a consensus about what should be done, and to implement necessary action in relation to a particular task or organizational area.

telephone checks (or verification) A method used by insurers of verifying application information, typically by phone contact. Insurer employees, or independent contractors of the insurer, ask applicants to verify statements made on the application. Questions might be worded differently to discover potentially conflicting information.

telephone interviews A popular way of collecting primary research data, especially when research involves random population samples, when questions are few, and when face-to-face contact is unnecessary or impractical.

term (or policy term) Policy period; the period during which a policy provides coverage.

termination A policy cancellation during its term or a nonrenewal at the end of its term. Losses occurring after the time of termination are not covered.

thimble A double-walled pipe that allows a chimney pipe to pass through a combustible wall without heat contact.

third party An individual or entity, not a party to the insurance contract, to whom an insurer might become obligated as a result of an insured's covered negligent acts.

third-party liability A term used in many countries for bodily injury and property damage liability.

tort A wrongful act other than a crime or a breach of contract for which relief may be obtained in the form of damages or an injunction.

tort reform Any legislative action intended to restrict lawsuits for negligence.

tort state A state that provides for compensation to a victim of an auto accident through legal remedies.

tort-feasor An individual who performs a wrongful act that might form the basis for legal action.

touch-screen kiosks Automated machines at which consumers can get information or make purchases. Consumers make selections by touching words or images on a computer screen, eliminating the need for a keyboard.

towing and labor coverage (auto) Pays for road service or towing, up to some specified amount.

transactional filing A filing system in which all paper documents for all clients are filed by the date on which they were processed. To retrieve the original document, a staff member checks the date of the transaction on the computer system and then goes to the file for that date to locate the document.

transfer A risk management technique through which the financial responsibility for loss exposures is shifted from one party to another.

treaty reinsurance An arrangement whereby a reinsurer agrees to automatically reinsure a portion of all the eligible insurance of the primary insurer.

trespasser A person who is on an insured's premises without permission.

umbrella policy A liability insurance policy that provides coverage limits in excess of those provided by basic liability policies. Personal umbrella policies typically provide $1 million or more worth of coverage in addition to auto or homeowners policies. An umbrella policy might also provide some coverage not provided by basic liability policies, subject to some retention amount.

unconsolidated soil Soil that is made up of gravel and sand used to fill in low or wet land to create building sites.

underlying policies See *primary policies*.

Underwriters Laboratories (UL) An organization that tests and certifies electronic devices, alarm systems, and many other items for conformity to standards of safety and accuracy of operation.

underwriting cycle A commonly used term for a recurring rise and fall in profits and prices in the property and liability insurance industry. Underwriting cycles are the property and liability insurance industry's profit cycles.

underwriting by exception See *checklist approach* and *screening*.

underwriting expenses An insurer's costs for acquiring new policies, general expenses for operation, taxes, and fees.

underwriting file A record of the available information about a customer and the customer's exposure to loss.

underwriting guidelines Also called guides or underwriting policies, these are a set of parameters or limitations for the type of risks to be written. Guidelines are established by each insurance company for each line of business written. Underwriting guidelines define the characteristics of those customers who will have the numbers and types of claims for which the insurer's products and rates were designed.

underwriting income The difference between the premium income for a specific time period and the incurred losses and underwriting expenses for that period. The difference can be an underwriting profit (gain) or an underwriting loss.

underwriting loss See *underwriting income*.

underwriting policies See *underwriting guidelines.*

underwriting profit (or gain) See *underwriting income.*

unfair discrimination Applying different standards or methods of treatment for risks that have the same basic characteristics and loss potential. Insurers establish rates and underwriting guidelines based on "fair discrimination," which is the use of loss statistics to group individuals with similar loss exposure characteristics. Members of groups are then charged the same statistically supportable rate or are treated by the same underwriting guidelines.

unfiled Policies, coverage, or risk classifications for which states do not require forms or rates to be filed.

unibody A method of automobile construction. Unlike the construction of some large passenger cars and trucks in which the engine, transmission, and body are attached to a heavy steel frame, unibody construction uses no frame but achieves strength by attaching components to interlocking vehicle body sheet metal.

uninsured motorists coverage A coverage in personal or commercial auto policies that provides protection against bodily injury loss (also property damage in some states) when the insured is injured in an accident with a hit-and-run motorist or a negligent motorist who has no insurance.

unit of coverage A standard block of insurance protection used in rating a line of business. Also called *coverage unit*. For example, each $1,000 of Coverage A insurance is a unit of coverage used to rate a homeowners policy.

unit of exposure See *exposure unit.*

unity classification A rate class selected as a baseline, to which all other rate classes are compared.

unrealized capital gain When the market price of an asset exceeds its cost and the insurer continues to hold the asset. It is a profit that is not yet earned.

use-and-file A filing law that allows an insurer to use rates before they are filed with the state.

variable costs Expenses that change relative to premium volume increases or decreases.

vehicle identification number (VIN) A unique serial number assigned to each vehicle. The seventeen-digit number identifies the make, model, year, body style, factory, and engine size of a vehicle. The VIN can also be used to identify the symbol used in rating physical damage coverages.

vicarious liability When one party is held liable for the actions of another. If an employee acts on the instructions of an employer, the employer might be held vicariously responsible for the employee's actions.

virtual team A group of insurance company employees or employees of associate organizations that might not work at the same location, but they share information through a database and converse through electronic media.

voluntary market Those coverages that insurers willingly provide at a standard price to applicants who meet their underwriting guidelines.

warranty A representation by an insured that some condition exists on which the insurer relies in deciding to offer coverage. In marine insurance, an insured warrants to the insurer that a vessel is seaworthy. If the insured's statement is later proved false, coverage could be denied. Warranties also appear in insurance policies to require insureds to maintain certain conditions during the policy term. If the insured fails to maintain the condition, coverage might be denied.

work flow The collective actions that must be completed, in sequence, to accomplish a complex task.

work-in-progress Any activities, customary to the organization's normal business activities, that have been begun but are not yet completed.

wreck removal A coverage that provides funds to remove the remains of watercraft from the waterways after total loss.

written premium The amount the insured would pay if coverage remains in effect for a year.

zero-based budgeting An internal budgeting process in which each business unit begins with no debt or credit. Each unit begins every fiscal year new with a zero balance in the budget.

Appendix 2-A

Insurance Fraud: Key State Legislation

Key State Legislation on Insurance Fraud and Auto Theft as of August 1998

	AL	AK	AZ	AR	CA	CO	CT	DE	DC	FL	GA	HI	ID	IL	IN	IA	KS	KY	LA	ME
Classified as a Specific Crime:																				
• Insurance Fraud 1. Felony		X	X	X	X	X	X	X		X		X	X	X	X	X		X		
2. Misdemeanor		X								X	X			X		X				
• Attempted Ins. Fraud 1. Felony					X	X	(b)							X		X				
2. Misdemeanor							(b)							X						
Immunity Statutes		X	X	X	X	X	X	X		X	X	X	X	X	X	X	X	X	X	X
Fraud Bureau		X	X	X	X		X	X		X	X	X	X			X		X	X	
Mandatory Insurer Fraud Plan					X	X				X								X		
Mandatory Photo Inspection					X*					X(a)										
The Coalition to Reduce Auto Theft and Fraud (CRAFT) Model Laws:																				
• Vehicle Chop Shop, Stolen and Altered Property Act							X		X					X						
• Salvage Certificate Junk Vehicle Act					X		X		X	X			X	X					X	
• Vehicle Owner Fraud Act									X					X						
• The False Police Report Act					X				X					X						

Key State Legislation on Insurance Fraud and Auto Theft as of August 1998

	MD	MA	MI	MN	MS	MO	MT	NE	NV	NH	NJ	NM	NY	NC	ND	OH	OK	OR	PA
Classified as a Specific Crime:																			
• Insurance Fraud 1. Felony	X	X	X	X	X(b)	X(b)		X	X	X	X	X	X	X		X			X
2. Misdemeanor				X			X	X							X	X	X		X
• Attempted Ins. Fraud 1. Felony			X	X			X	X											X
2. Misdemeanor				X			X	X											X
Immunity Statutes	X	X	X	X		X	X	X	X	X	X	X	X	X	X	X		X	X
Fraud Bureau	X	X		X(b)	X	X	X(b)	X	X	X	X	X	X	X	X(b)	X	X(b)		X
Mandatory Insurer Fraud Plan	X			X						X	X	X	X(d)			X			X
Mandatory Photo Inspection		X									X		X						
CRAFT Model Laws:																			
• Vehicle Chop Shop, Stolen and Altered Property Act	X		X													X			
• Salvage Certificate Junk Vehicle Act	X	X	X	X					X		X		X			X			X
• Vehicle Owner Fraud Act	X	X									X					X			X
• The False Police Report Act	X	X	X						X		X								

Key State Legislation on Insurance Fraud and Auto Theft as of August 1998

	RI	SC	SD	TN	TX	UT	VT	VA	WA	WV	WI	WY
Classified as a Specific Crime:												
• Insurance Fraud 1. Felony	X	X	X	X(b)	X	X			X		X	
2. Misdemeanor			X			X			X		X	
• Attempted Ins. Fraud 1. Felony												
2. Misdemeanor	X											
Immunity Statutes		X	X	(1)	X	X		X	X	X	X	
Fraud Bureau		X		X(b), (c)	X	X		X(e)	X(b)			
Mandatory Insurer Fraud Plan				X(b)					X			
Mandatory Photo Inspection	X											
CRAFT Model Laws:												
• Vehicle Chop Shop, Stolen and Altered Property Act		X										
• Salvage Certificate Junk Vehicle Act						X						
• Vehicle Owner Fraud Act												
• The False Police Report Act		X										

(a) Limited to selected counties.
(b) Workers compensation insurance only.
(c) Tennessee's fraud bureau has the authority to investigate fraud at agencies and companies only.
(d) For insurers writing more than 3,000 policies.
(e) Fraud bureau within the state policy.
*Repealed effective January 1, 1999.

Information adapted from the Coalition Against Insurance Fraud, the Insurance Information Institute, and state insurance departments, as compiled by Ruth Gastel, "Insurance Fraud," *Insurance Issues Update*, August 1998.

Index

Bold page numbers refer to definitions of key words or phrases. Italic page numbers refer to exhibits.

A

B

C

G

H

I

J

K

L

P

Q

R

S

Y

Z